3-5-79

BASIC
BUSINESS
AND
PROFESSIONAL
SPEECH
COMMUNICATION

BASIC BUSINESS AND PROFESSIONAL SPEECH COMMUNICATION

Ted Frank

University of Arkansas at Monticello

David Ray

University of Arkansas at Monticello

PRENTICE-HALL, INC., Englewood Cliffs, New Jersey 07632

Library of Congress Cataloging in Publication Data

FRANK, TED (date)
Basic business and professional speech communication.

(The Prentice-Hall series in speech communication)
Bibliography: p.
Includes index.
1. Oral communication. 2. Public speaking.
3. Communication in management. I. Ray, David
(date) joint author. II. Title.
P95.F7   808.5   78–19122
ISBN 0–13–057273–X

THE PRENTICE-HALL SERIES IN SPEECH COMMUNICATION

Larry L. Barker and Robert J. Kibler
Consulting Editors

Printed in the United States of America

10 9 8 7 6 5 4 3 2 1

Editorial/production supervision by Joan L. Lee
Interior design by Allyson Everngam
Cover design by Peter Ross
Manufacturing buyer: Harry P. Baisley

PRENTICE-HALL INTERNATIONAL, INC., London
PRENTICE-HALL OF AUSTRALIA PTY. LIMITED, Sydney
PRENTICE-HALL OF CANADA, LTD., Toronto
PRENTICE-HALL OF INDIA PRIVATE LIMITED, New Delhi
PRENTICE-HALL OF JAPAN, INC., Tokyo
PRENTICE-HALL OF SOUTHEAST ASIA PTE. LTD., Singapore
WHITEHALL BOOKS LIMITED, Wellington, New Zealand

To
P.K. and John
Loyce, Erik, and Heather

CONTENTS

PART 2

PERSON-TO-GROUP
SPEAKING IN BUSINESS
AND THE PROFESSIONS

PART 3

OTHER FORMS
OF BUSINESS
AND PROFESSIONAL SPEECH
COMMUNICATION

PREFACE

This book is written to serve as an active participant in the development of professional communicators. The authors realize that people work out guidelines for themselves to help in everyday exchanges, and so our aim is to provide a wide variety of tasks and encounters as tests for these self-found principles.

This is a basic business and professional speech book. It adheres to a view fundamental to professional growth: that professional communicators try to stimulate effectiveness in others; when they do this for their associates, they end up doing it for themselves. As a basic approach to interpersonal communicating, we offer materials and examples that attempt to help the reader/participants develop skills they need to become more effective communicators in both formal and informal settings. The text orientation is both perceptual and behavioral, in that how communicators perceive themselves, others, and their circumstances affects their communicative behavior.

The presentation is divided into three main parts: the first defines the how and why of communication, the second deals with person-to-group communication in business, and the third covers other forms of business and professional speech. The reader/participant is introduced to three prime areas of concern to the business/professional communicator: small group communication, interviewing, and person-to-group speaking. Students are challenged to go from their initial self-diagnosis of communication skills and of their grasp of basic theory toward the actual practice of 26 "enactments" of business and professional encounters. Checkpoints on principles are given in 45 projective exercises called "tasks"; these offer a flexible way to test for comprehension as well as insight.

Each of the ten chapters suggests specific behavioral objectives in the "chapter challenges" at the beginning of the chapter, and a "chapter chart" at the end of each outlines the key ideas discussed in the text. Short lists of pertinent readings are supplied for each chapter as well. Finally, the case studies in the appendix may be used as starting points for the study of complex communication settings.

We are indebted to our many friends, students, and colleagues in both the business and education communities for their encouragement and support during the development and writing of this text. Our special thanks to the following reviewers who offered helpful, constructive suggestions: Theodore G. Grove, Portland State University; Don Marine; George W. Ziegelmueller, Wayne State University; Roy M. Berko, Lorain County Community College; L. David Schuelke, University of Minnesota; and R. Wayne Pace, University of New Mexico.

Also, special thanks to our P-H editors who have demonstrated the true meaning of professionalism.

We hope that practitioners and students of business and professional communication will find this "thinking about and doing" text an effective way to enhance communication skills.

BASIC
BUSINESS
AND
PROFESSIONAL
SPEECH
COMMUNICATION

PART 1

COMMUNICATION – WHAT IS IT? WHY IS IT?

chapter 1

chapter challenge

Inventory your communication skills
Explain the communication process
Practice supportive feedback
Enact the idea behind COM-together
Describe the SMCR components
Use examples of digital and analogic coding
Prove that communication is inescapable
Predict why interface is crucial to a professional career

THE BUSINESS AND PROFESSIONAL COMMUNICATOR

COM-together   COM-together   COM-together
COM-together   COM-together

Basic professional and business speaking encounters ask of you what the basic business of living asks: that you come together with friends, colleagues, and the public you will serve. As a college student immersed in preparing for a career, you may forget that long before you planned your business or professional life you were working hard to grow and develop as a professional *person*. As a participant in the vast social process, you gradually assemble a sense of self and begin to suspect that coexistence with people and things is the essence of living.

What is communication? A partial answer might be that it is a condition of coexistence between and among entities. People often think of communication as a relationship composed of actions and energies that are sent and received. Considered this broad way, the experience you call communication is sharing. It could be said, for example, that subatomic particles share a language of electrical discharges that attract or repel; plants coexist with and share a chemical and physical relationship with earth and air. People move continuously within the process of coexisting and sharing, discovering the uses of languages and the ways of coming together. This is what communication is mostly about—the various languages of give–take, ask–answer, send–receive.

In the pages that follow, you will examine many of the communication situations encountered in the specialized area of business and professional coexistence. To prepare for your participation in the

3

explorations of this book, ask yourself: "What do I already know? What do I already do to coexist as a 'professional' communicator?"

task 1 INVENTORY OF SKILLS AND EXPERIENCE

The diagram in Figure 1–1 may be familiar to you as the DNA molecule model. The sketch has been used in several areas of study to illustrate relationships and to stimulate new routes of thinking. In the communication field Robert Goyer employed this "coil of life"[1] to help explain communication systems and their study. As an aid in helping you become more aware of yourself as a professional communicator, this diagram can suggest ways of coming together and sharing.

contact points with others

Like the two spirals shown, you have already developed and are developing contact points with others. You may be able to cite hundreds of ways and occasions in which you cross paths with friends or your life intersects the lives of others. Perhaps you have been highly mobile, living in many places, attending many schools. Each encounter was a contact point. Maybe you have moved across cultures as well as

[1]Robert Goyer, "Communication, Communicative Process, Meaning: Toward a Unified Theory," *Journal of Communication*, 20, no. 1 (March 1970), 4–16.

figure 1-1 The Double Helix

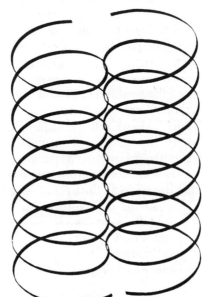

across land. Your exposure to varying ethnic systems with individual styles, customs, likes, and goals was part of your preparation for this course.

You may have made contact points across a wide range of age groups. When you were a child everyone was "old," but now you probably have a number of techniques for meeting and exchanging thoughts and feelings with those younger and older than yourself.

patterned similarities with others

Up to this point—in fact, even as you read these words—you have been expending energy searching for and being directed toward similarities between yourself and other people. The spirals in Figure 1–1 are shown in a reverse relationship: one mirrors the other. It seems fairly certain that one of the coils is trying to "copy" the other. Your communication experience has likely been filled with people trying to tell you what to do, what to be, how to behave, how to talk, how to "get along"— the list of rules for surviving and coexisting.

You can find models of coexistence in religious teaching, family life, schools, and the media. "Professional" interpersonal exchanges require you to model yourself on or accommodate yourself to the person with whom you are sharing your thoughts. It helps to be able to fit in, while still retaining your individuality.

growth in a chosen direction with others

Your choice of a career is pictured in the double helix as a gradual, spiraling ascent toward a goal. Whether you see the spirals in the diagram as going up or down, they head in a specific direction. Similarly, your life so far has had purpose and motive pushing you along. All your communication exchanges, even those that seemed pointless or accidental, contained growth patterns in a chosen direction. They happened for a reason that led you somewhere.

Your development, like the rings of the helix, might appear to be going in the "wrong" direction, taking its time, or getting there in a roundabout way. Growth is sometimes hard to detect. It may show up only if you can take a kind of time-lapse film view of yourself.

exchanges with others

Your growth in a chosen direction has been nourished and helped by the exchanges you have had with others. The inner column in each spiral might be said to represent a sphere of influence—a core of the person you are, who melds and shares with others. A communication exchange is a transaction of give and take. The exchange creates a bond, enriching each participant. The idea of exchange applies to all sectors of professional activity—the stock exchanges and cultural exchanges, for example.

In taking an inventory of your personal knowledge and skills as a professional communicator, you should also appraise your ability to exchange trust, esteem, and respect. What are you willing to take in exchange for risking your judgment—perhaps your reputation and job—during a communication transaction? As a life-long communicator, have you developed a sensitivity to situations and words that invite a response?

task 2   SHARING INVITATIONS TO COMMUNICATE

As you assess your personal experiences over the years in agreeing and disagreeing, in making bargains and questioning, you may feel that your contact points with others were not accidental. Your patterns of similarities with friends and relatives, your growth in a chosen direction, and your many exchanges with people and things may seem to have occurred because of certain "forces" that placed you in those situations. You may have had the feeling that people's words and looks somehow invited you to participate in an exchange.

How good are you at inviting others to talk? How many times have you entered into a communication exchange by accepting a person's invitation and then offering your own? It might help you in Task 2 to think of the twin spirals as inviting each other to share communications. In business situations it might also help you to think of these communication "lures" as intentional vacuums that you create in the hope that the silence or "space" will be filled by someone else.

Invitations to communication are at the very heart of business transactions. Bartering in all its many forms, negotiating, collective bargaining, and the many types of bidding for contracts are a few of the occasions in which your invitation might lure an exchange. To what extent have you developed a belief that giving up something will benefit both you and your associates? To what degree do you work to allow others to succeed? How often do you invite a response by enhancing the other person's self-esteem? How quick are you to defer or sacrifice or "let things go by." when talking? Perhaps you have known people who tend to send out negative invitations, who may "give the silent treatment." This is taking, not giving.

The sharing attitude that you are building will strengthen your future sender–receiver exchanges. Whatever loss of face or advantage you may think you suffer by giving something away is regained by cementing a solid communication bond. Your invitation to excel tends to stimulate a similar response in other people.

task 3 YOUR SENSITIVITY TO INVITATIONS

The final task in checking where you stand as a communicator is to review how sensitive you are to opportunities for giving and sharing. This is essential as the basis for communicating in the professions. Look at the double helix again. Try to think of it as a picture of yourself as you speak with a friend. Try to see the following characteristics of the professional communicator in the diagram and in yourself:

1. Each "side" seems to know when to advance and when to retreat. Each seems to sense when to dominate and when to submit, when to support and when to challenge. Do you observe and evaluate proof of actions that attract or repel? Do you recognize thresholds of tolerance, "flashpoints," delicate and sensitive topics?
2. Each "side" enhances or gives something to its counterpart. Do you accept the possibility that you can overcome deficiencies and learn from your friend?
3. Each "side" momentarily detaches itself from its neighbor as if to reach out for a new encounter. Do you remain yourself, independent and separate from your friend, so that you can also seek new relationships and enlarge the number of encounters?
4. Each "side" is open-ended. There are no limitations placed on the potential, development, and reach of either. Do your communication invitations encompass a variety of growth areas and reference points? Does your basis for exchange span many subjects and viewpoints? Do you relate at several levels of shared experience?
5. Each "side"—taken at any segment of its spiral—is satisfied, coherent, complete, and symmetrical. Both are in balance and in harmony. Do you strive to come together with associates?

The double helix can also help you look ahead. How effective can you expect to be in your chosen business or profession? Let the sketch represent you as you might project yourself in some professional transaction. Now, ask yourself why you can or cannot find reasonable clues to these questions:

1. Who is superior, who is inferior?
2. Who is the supervisor, who is the staff member?
3. Who is the client, who is the broker?
4. Who is the salesperson, who is the customer?
5. Who is profiting, who is losing?
6. Who is manipulating, who is being manipulated?
7. Who is participating, who is observing?
8. Who maintains his or her identity, who is losing it?
9. Who is more sensitive to invitations to communicate?

10. Who is more open, revealing of self, and giving?
11. Who is working harder to communicate?

Gaining a kind of personal communication skills inventory—past, present, future—serves to introduce to you the larger communication theories and their concepts. Use the inventory you have made as a referent or checkpoint, because it is now part of your professional person and contributes to what will later be called your *competence factor.*

COMMUNICATION COMPONENTS

Communication in its broadest sense cannot be adequately defined and can be only partially described. Frank E. X. Dance, an authority in business and professional speech, once noted 95 attempts to define communication.[2] Even that number is easily surpassed, if you consider people's pet definitions. For purposes of study, four components might serve as a basic framework: (1) sources, (2) messages, (3) channels, and (4) receivers. David Berlo constructed this SMCR[3] model as a means of studying the communication process.

This schematic list is meant to freeze the communication act. Most of us know, however, that communication events are rapid, quickly shifting relationships that are never as cut-and-dried as a diagram. Sources, messages, channels, and receivers take turns being any or all the basic functions in a real transaction. If you were to add merely the few categories listed beneath each component in the discussions below,

[2]Frank E. X. Dance, "The Concept of Communication," *Journal of Communication,* 20, no. 2 (June 1970), 201–10.

[3]David K. Berlo, *The Process of Communication: An Introduction to Theory and Practice* (New York: Holt, Rinehart and Winston, 1960), p. 72.

figure 1-2   Berlo's SMCR Model with Feedback Loop. From *The Process of Communication* by David K. Berlo. Copyright © by Holt, Rinehart and Winston. Adapted by permission of Holt, Rinehart and Winston.

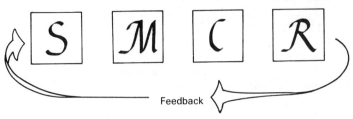

the different combinations would exceed 3,000 possibilities. Let us examine just the four.

Source.   The source is the initiator. For our purposes it is the person who first speaks, signals, or emits directed energy toward another person. In professional encounters you can think of the initiator as the person who *needs* to interact the most, whose sense of sharing is strongest and most urgent. It may be the partner who is most skilled, at ease, or best prepared—perhaps the one who is most professional in his or her approach to exchanges.

Message.   The message is the *thing* you are sending or giving. It is made up of what you put in, what you leave out, by choice or accident, and your selected mode of *encoding* or packaging. Since receivers are unable (as yet) to get inside your mind, you select a kind of "language of lure," which you hope will be understood and shared. Messages are symbolic representations of what you have on your mind and wish to share. They are not the real thing but rather your best attempt to express what you want to pass along. Word language, made up of sounds or phonemes, is perhaps the most commonly used code, but even within that one code there are numerous possibilities for variation. Any word may be individually interpreted and imprinted with special characteristics. In-jokes, jargon, dialects, and technical vocabularies are a few of the endless choices available as languages of lure.

Channel.   The channel of communication is the vehicle that carries the message. As the Berlo model suggests, a channel is the means through which you get the message—through your eyes, ears, skin. There may be other channels through which thought is transmitted. Professional people have been known to get "hunches," to have an intuitive sense of timing and flashes of insight. These originate someplace. There is also the collective sensory power of the "grapevine," through which employees get a sense of premonition. *Interface* is the term used here to mean all the links by which people come together.

Receiver.   The fourth indispensable component is the receiver—the designated target. The receiver encounters the message, scans or reads its symbols, decodes it into mental pictures and word-thoughts, and *reacts* to its stimulus. This *reaction*, in turn, becomes a message *feeding back* through some channel to the initiator, and the communication loop has completed one entire cycle.

Feedback.   The idea of feedback might be included as the fifth ingredient in the event. Actually feedback means the echo or rebound reaction that released energy stimulates and sets resonating. The words *answer, reply, response,* and *effect* are commonly used to mean types of feedback. Early work in cybernetics by Norbert Wiener dealt with machines that could "serve" themselves—check or monitor, stop and start, and regulate their own functions. The term *feedback* represents the response to the question "How am I doing?" In professional situations phrases such as take a poll, check your barometer, test the water, send up trial balloons, and take the pulse, are indications that a person wants to monitor the effects of statements, policies, or actions.

Feedback tests the sender's choice (or accidental use) of a message element: Did you say the right thing, at the right time, to the right person, in the right way? Feedback also provides a channel effectiveness rating: Did you use the right setting, timing, vehicle (such as telephone, memorandum, intermediary/messenger/middleman)? Did you use only speech, speech and physical display, perhaps physical display only? Feedback helps determine whether the right person got the word; you may have been talking to a wrong number.

Understanding and using *positive* or supportive feedback are essential traits of professional communicators. When you signal support or show receptiveness (not necessarily approval) of a message and its sender, you help cement the *interfaces* that make further exchange easier. Stated in the form of a testable rule to ponder . . .

axiom 1: SUPPORTIVE FEEDBACK INCREASES THE BASIS FOR SHARING

ROLES/ENACTMENTS/ENCOUNTERS

Before continuing in the discussion of the communication process, you may want to test what you know by enacting a simulated communication encounter. The encounters suggested throughout this text are aids for involving students and instructor in sample business/professional situations. Any or all of the following restrictions, plans, or methods might be incorporated into an enactment to suit individual class needs:

1. Division of the class into:
   a. Participants playing a specified role.
   b. Observers recording and evaluating the enactment proceedings.
   c. Intruders playing people who "accidentally" drop in or walk by.
   d. Critique team members monitoring and reporting on communication standards.
2. Taping for later diagnosis of strengths and weaknesses and for compiling libraries of "classic" encounters.
3. Placement of enactments in real locales, such as hallways, stairwells, and parking lots.

4. Use of simultaneous enactments for comparing "control" variables—time, distance, locale, age, gender, and ethnic factors.
5. Use of guest participants—faculty, friends, school personnel, and community business/professional people.

participants

As a participant assigned a role, you need only assume the basic *attitude* of the *name* in the enactment, not someone else's personality. Try to grasp the problem and assert that basic attitude, as if you were filling in for that person. Of course, be yourself.

observers

As an observer, you note or record the enactment and make a professional report on what happened from your vantage point.

intruders

As an intruder, you can be used to enter the communication field and test the spontaneity and resourcefulness of the participants.

critique team

As a student chosen to critique, you are the "audience" and more. Your task is to troubleshoot ineffective or undesirable behavior in the enactment by showing how it could be done or said better. You are also responsible for giving your colleagues a written score on specific objectives. You may be assigned to one or more participants or grouped into a critique team.

encounters

The encounters provided are scenarios for exchanges and contain the following kinds of information: *names* for participants to adopt, *relationships* between sender and receiver, *problem* or *need-to-speak* descriptions, and *time/locale*. Encounters may easily be altered to meet specific needs, but they have been designed to demonstrate your understanding of interpersonal communication and of the concepts that immediately precede each enactment project.

enactment 1   KEN AND PROFESSOR COLEMAN

Demonstrate these terms by enacting them in . . . .

enactment 1: KEN AND PROFESSOR COLEMAN

invitations—positive and negative
positive feedback
channel
encoding

participants

Ken, a college freshman, single, on athletic scholarship in a work-study program, a psychology major, living away from home; *Professor Coleman*, age 50, female, married, childless, chairperson of the psychology department.

relationship

Professor Coleman is Ken's advisor. Ken is enrolled in Professor Coleman's introductory psychology class which meets at 8:00 A.M., twice a week.

problem

Ken's job is to mop the floors in the psychology building. Regardless of how he plans his task, students and other traffic invariably slog the length of the wet floors. Students also allow animals used in their experiments to leave deposits in unexpected places and at unexpected times.

need to talk

Students complain about feet slipping, teachers complain about "odors affecting their experiments," and Ken gets complaints from everybody including his work-station supervisor.

time/locale

Ken and Professor Coleman meet on a Friday morning at 7:40—on a wet floor—just before their class meets.

critique 1   TROUBLESHOOTING

1. Which parts of the problem were shared?
2. Who was the first to show he or she wanted to help?
3. Who expressed the problem better?
4. How would you score each participant on the use of invitations to communicate?
5. Who took blame or responsibility?
6. Were ultimatums or threats used, perhaps in a disguised way?
7. Who was the more apologetic?
8. Was a contract or agreement made?
9. Did either forget to show satisfaction or fulfillment?

DEMONSTRATE HOW YOU MIGHT IMPROVE IT

COMMUNICATION PROCESS

When does communication begin? When do encounters begin? You see things in your unique way. You read and get from words something different from what others who read or even who wrote those words get. This text reflects the belief that professional encounters are *personal* and that so-called communication and credibility gaps are essentially unfulfilled opportunities for exchange. Communication might be said to begin when you realize that opportunities exist and will continue to exist, that communication is an *alternating* condition, a process of ask–answer, give–take, send–receive.

Years ago, people made jokes about the genius trying to perfect a "perpetual motion machine." *Process* is perpetual motion, endless interaction. It never really breaks down or develops gaps. You simply tend to "read," interpret, and decode stimuli in your own way. You get the word, but you get the word you want. Businesses and professions strive to give you the words, products, and services they believe you want.

The communication process involving Ken and Professor Coleman is perpetual and will continue, if only in the memories and subsequent experiences of students who enacted it. You may never have the same classroom opportunity to improve your exchange, but you will unquestionably have the chance to try again in countless future exchanges, and that enactment will be a part of your future *present*. In this sense communication is a process, and every process is ongoing.

axiom 2:   PROFESSIONAL COMMUNICATION PROVIDES SECOND, THIRD, AND FOURTH ATTEMPTS TO COM-TOGETHER

Since the enactment was part of a process, you can assume that its component parts—the SMCR—occurred simultaneously. At some point in the exchange, you alternated as each of the other components. Sometimes you were the channel, sometimes the message. You "took turns" being various components, and sometimes you were all four at once—*you talked to yourself*, and parts of you (memory, muscles, nerves) talked back. This reciprocal or alternating pattern is central to the idea of process.

One difficulty you may have had as Ken or Professor Coleman was that you and your partner were never quite sure which of the four components you were supposed to be at a given moment. Maybe both of you waited for the other person to be the sender; did you both send at the same moment? Had this encounter been a real one, you might have felt that the hallway was not an appropriate environment for pouring out your life history. Maybe the sticky, reeking hallway floor was not the best place to meet, because your message would have to compete with *its* message. Perhaps Professor Coleman's lab coat facing you across her desk in her office was not very inviting or represented an "unfair advantage."

A possible conclusion to be drawn from this is: *Relationships* between components are more important than the components themselves. Think through another communication definition: "Communication is a social function . . . , a *sharing* of elements of behavior, or modes of life, by the existence of sets of rules. . . . Communication is not the response itself but . . . the relationship set up by the transmission of stimuli and the evocation of responses."[4] In Colin Cherry's definition the *sharing* of information and the relationships are bound up with "sets of rules." Are the sets in process? Do they reciprocate? Where do they come from?

The diagram in Figure 1–3 is derived from Raymond Ross's Transactional Model,[5] and it shows again the SMCR at the center, but with several other "influences" surrounding the event. Using the persons in the model to represent your enactment, the "star" in the head might signify a thought you needed to say—maybe, "Help me." The blob around the thought is all the experiences you have stored. During your encounter you had only a moment or less to rummage around for answers to questions like: "What do I have filed under *help*? Under *professors*? *Students*? What does my partner have filed under *me*?"

The SMCR components and their *relationships* emerge a little more clearly in the Ross model and may help you to know what happened during your enactment that was different from what you perceived to have happened. Examine five relationships and compare them with the feedback you received from critiques. Look at *set, coding, signs/symbols, nonverbal codes,* and *propositionality.*

set

Your critique sheets might have revealed behavior you were not aware of because of habitual, set ways of seeing. Your set ways affect your assessment and judgment. If you rely on prejudging, you may set your attention toward only evidence confirming your prejudgment; new perceptions get screened out. Sets can impair your aptitude for new encounters and new combinations of experience. The three triangles in

---

[4]Colin Cherry, *On Human Communication* (Cambridge, Mass.: The M.I.T. Press, 1966), pp. 6–7.

[5]Raymond S. Ross, *Speech Communication: Fundamentals and Practice,* 3rd ed. (Englewood Cliffs, N.J.: Prentice-Hall, Inc., 1974), p. 15.

figure 1-3 Ross's Transactional Communication Model. Adapted from Raymond S. Ross, *Speech Communication: Fundamentals and Practice,* 3rd ed. (Englewood Cliffs, N.J.: Prentice-Hall, Inc., © 1974), p. 15, by permission.

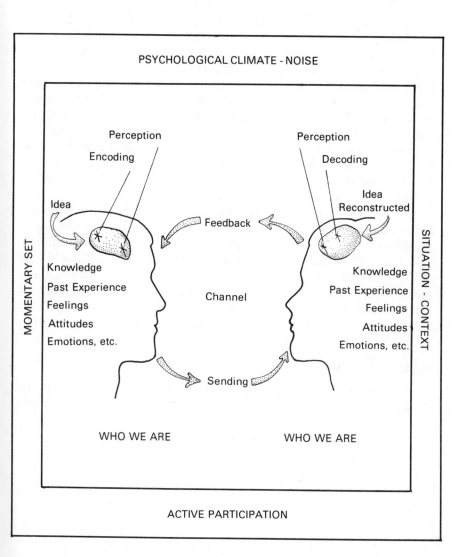

Figure 1–4 are sample ways in which people conform to set methods of perception. If you scan the words quickly, you may fail to notice the extra words in each phrase.

coding

A code is a collection of rules for assigning significance to symbols. Ken's statement, "Professor Coleman, I need help," was an elaborate language code whose ordering of vocalized sounds, Ken hoped, would be received, decoded, and sympathetically fed back. The two basic methods of coding messages are digital and analogic. Digital coding contains a fixed number of elements, such as an alphabet, arabic numbers, or a binary number system. Messages formed using a digital code have no resemblance to the actual objects or actions intended. They are totally abstract, statistical, straightforward. Coded digitally, "I need help," is a straightforward statement of felt need. Coded analogically, the same message might contain moments of high drama, emotionality, pathos—elements that are or are very close to the actual condition.

As long as everyone learns the same digital code, this method is the more precise of the two, but precision in communication is an ideal state not a real one. Ken's digital request might receive the answer, "Oh, okay. Which part of that chapter is giving you trouble?" His "I need help," accompanied by a flailing gesture toward his feet, the hall, and the classroom would have added the analogic coding necessary for clarity and perhaps sympathy. Professor Coleman's reaction might then be something like "Yes, I know. We both need help." Was coding a problem in your enactment?

signs and symbols

There is some parallel between the terms sign/symbol and digital/analogic. Signs direct us to act. Motions that mean "stop," "come

figure 1-4 Perception Triangles

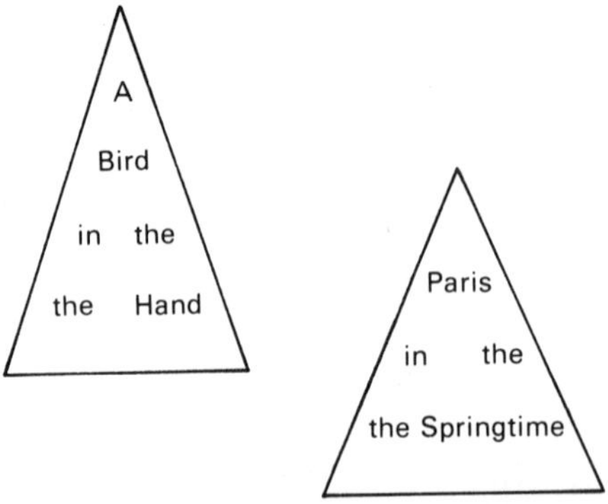

in," or "have a seat" are signs that we learn to follow. *Symbols*, like analogic coding, are open to multiple uses, references, and interpretations. Signs have a one-thing-meaning-one-thing relationship; symbols possess a one-thing-meaning-many-things relationship. Chapter 2 explores this area in greater detail and includes enactments of nonword (nonverbal) encounters.

nonverbal codes

So far, the discussion of process has centered on sharing verbal or word codes that are received by ear, eye, or skin—spoken, written, or "drawn" through gesture. Nonverbal codes are not restricted to these three ways of encoding. They can be used singly or in combination with other basic body expressions. Nonverbal codes do not always refer back to words; verbal codes do. Whether nonverbal codes can be expressed digitally as well as analogically is a problem that researchers have still not solved. Chapter 2 treats this area in the business/professional interaction.

propositionality

Propositionality (momentary set) is really another word for the sender's *intent*. Ken's coding, as we noted, could have caused confusion if interpreted the "wrong" way. He knows what he intended, but clarity required that he be aware of his intent, so that he might check and carefully select his coding, languages, and channels. Ken's intent might have been to recite a well-rehearsed statement, and his intent could have been decoded as a call for lesson-help not job-help. He could, however, have combined complex symbols—verbal and nonverbal—into a spontaneous plea that proposed exchange and feedback.

The satisfaction of controlling effective professional transactions rests on understanding these relationships. Your flexibility, sensitivity, and willingness to accept new relationships strengthens your personal *competence factor*.

axiom 3: SECOND, THIRD, AND FOURTH ENCOUNTERS COMPOUND RELATIONSHIPS

COMMUNICATION CHARACTERISTICS

Communication, like religion and politics, is nice to know about; it is nice to know a little of what others have thought and done. You are probably better off for knowing something about human desires and needs, however you learn it. Speech communication in the professions is also a process of information-gathering—allowing data to register. Most of your energy will be expended actively not passively in professional communication. You will be participating, and knowing about communication and doing it are not the same.

Despite all we said about the inadequacy of definitions of communication, we offer six characteristics that might serve as observable limits to the communication process.

communication is intrinsic

First, communication is a sensibility—what the French mathematician Poincaré called the *heuristic* character. It is everywhere, noticeable, and influential, but it defies satisfactory measurement. You use it, you are immersed in it, and you are it, but you fall short of pinning down its essential nature. Communication is said to be *intrinsic* to nature, because it is fundamental to life itself. The coexistence of various kinds of matter and the interaction of life systems are states of communication. You are equipped at birth with the built-in ability to perceive the world, process its data while you are awake or asleep, and find and use symbols for transmitting messages about those data.

In a social framework—as people collect into organizations—speech communication is one of the intrinsic binders, cementing shared thoughts, feelings, needs. As you seek uniqueness and your personal signature, trademark, logo, and character, your style of communicating sets you apart. What you bring to encounters reveals your differentness, while proving to you that alikeness exists. The patterns of similarity you see help you develop the patterns you will become. These exchanges are intrinsic to all coexistence.

communication is behavioral

Businesses and professions deal with goods, products, and services in a controlled economic system. The communication process is also a controlled system. The characteristic of communication that people set about learning to control very early is its outward or visible and audible dimension—behavior. Through countless repetitions of muscular movement, as a child you exercised your memory and neural pathways, so that sending messages might be willed, controlled, and coordinated. Although your copying of behavior was not always intentional, it served to improve these skills and prepared you for intentional interaction.

Psychiatrist Eric Berne has coined the term *transaction* to name this exchange event. According to Berne:

When two people meet . . . sooner or later one of them will speak, or give some indication of acknowledging the presence of the other. This is called the

transactional stimulus. Another person will then say or do something which is
. . . related to the stimulus, and that is called the transactional response.[6]

Communication has this characteristic exchange behavior—
your partner gives you something, and you give your partner something
in return. As a behavior, communication has this rhythm of stimulus–response–stimulus; it invites a reaction.

Another way of understanding the behavioral aspect of transaction is to say that it is performance-centered. People sometimes pay
money to watch a great athlete work out or an accomplished artist
rehearse, but the fame and livelihood of these celebrities depend on their
behavior during performances, not during their rehearsals and warm-ups. Your training in basic business and professional speech is, likewise, a warm-up for professional communication behavior.

communication is dynamic

Communication behavior implies action—mental, emotional, "psychic," or muscular movement. The speech transaction is partly
an attempt to move and be moved. Its purpose is to effect changes in
others and in yourself. Your effectiveness and satisfaction rely, to a
degree, on the "physics" of communication, though the physics of this
field is not measured in terms of electromotive force or pounds per
square inch. Certain terms are frequently borrowed and literally applied
to speaking: *leverage*, *posture*, and *interface* are three examples. Five
dynamics of communication, derived from physics, may be introduced
here: communication is directional, refractive, channeled, shaped, and
temporal.

Your glances, stares, and expletives are aimed directly or
obliquely at an object, a person, a group, perhaps yourself. Focusing is
the term most often used to denote *direction*. Like anything directional,
messages are *refractive*. Their two central properties, light and sound,
bounce and rebound from person to object to person and back to you.

The *channeling* or "clothing" of messages was introduced
and shown in the models earlier in this chapter. You surround expression with complex forms of imagery, sound, and circumstance, creating
pathways for thought that may grow to expressway capacity. They may
remain busy with traffic or become empty and unused. Similar to this is
the characteristic of *shape*. The pressure and size of behavior—the
glance or the expletive—has a controllable contour; this is its shape.

What you say reveals your respect for duration, the *temporal*

---

[6]Eric Berne, *Games People Play* (New York: Grove Press, Inc., 1964), p. 29. Reprinted by
permission of Grove Press Inc. Copyright © 1964 by Eric Berne.

feature. The speech act may be elongated, constricted, or perhaps interrupted for a short or long term; it may never be completed. In organizational communication others may attempt to restart, complete, and repeat a message transmission, because the time factor is critical.

communication is contagious

The act of reaching out is contagious. Its infectiousness touches that intrinsic need for attention—for what Berne calls "stroking." Some people are aware that a very enriched form of nourishment is obtained from relating well with others. Certain entertainers, for example, feel compelled to receive this kind of attention and may go to extreme lengths to get it.

Communication is a positive contagion, because it tends to amplify itself like acoustical feedback. Success tends to breed success. Your successful encounter becomes your partner's successful encounter; shared energy grows. The effectiveness does not get multiplied by two, it becomes squared—a logarithm of two.

Effective communication is catching because people tend to emulate success. Your school, operating with relatively fixed policies, is testimony that people hope what seemed to work before will work again. Contagion might also be seen as the instrument of process; the process of communication keeps on because of its contagiousness and because of its infinite market and lack of competition.

The concept of an invitation embodies the contagion principle. The intrinsic human need to communicate represents a vacuum to be filled. The fact that you are needed to solve problems and map plans provides an added incentive for you to communicate well.

communication is harmonious

Participants in a transaction seek a shared alikeness. You search for kinships and affinities with others so that encounters may be built on commonalities, shared experiences, mutually acknowledged symbols and languages. The person who blurts "Now you're talking my language!" is conveying this recognition of alikeness. A common interface has been found, and that person is telling you: "I agree. I have similar thoughts and feelings. You have tried hard to find a bond with me, and I appreciate it. Now I will try harder to be a little like you."

Many exercises and enactments suggested here have the underlying objective of keeping the participants "in phase" with each other. Real professional encounters frequently aim toward a compact of some type. When speakers "click" with their audiences and when business exchanges result in contracts, sales, or policy decisions, the communication relationships were harmonious.

You have no doubt known misfits. You probably have felt like one yourself in certain awkward or strange situations. Perhaps through experience you discovered that meeting people on equal terms helped reduce your tension and sense of difference. The pressures of family, peer, and organizational expectations limit your choices of behavior, but even these expand and grow through shared reference points and values.

communication is aesthetic

Communication can be said to be aesthetic in that it transforms seemingly opposite, disparate, and sometimes pointless factors into a coherent, harmonious, and new experience. Was there a feeling of "rightness" and satisfaction in your first enactment? Did you get a sense of accomplishment?

The aesthetic character of effective communication is in the symmetry of links developed and distances shortened between one motive, one mind, one person and another. It can be seen in patterns discovered for the first time—insights into your job and how it relates to other jobs, other organizational structures.

The exchange process has the aesthetic feature of creative problem-solving. Groups of workers pool experiences and skills. Designs are formulated and expressed using novel combinations by communicators who can see the wholeness of the process. They grasp unities of purpose and need, offering fresh approaches and modifying old ones.

Communication is a building process, too; its edifices are complexes of associations—*interfaces* of person–person, person–people, and people–people. Efficiency and productivity may be transaction goals—company goals—but they are balanced by self-revelation and spontaneity, which are products of a professional attitude toward human interface and encounter.

task 4   UNDERSTANDING INTERFACE

Interface is a term used by engineers to describe the relations between machines, machine systems, and people. As adopted by management specialists such as Paul Mott and Randall Harrison, interface means about the same as the older term *channel*. In our opinion, the term *interface* better conveys communication characteristics by including the concept of *surface sensitivity*. The Frank Interface Model in Figure 1–5 depicts this *single* viewpoint made possible by an interlocking of surfaces directed at a given task. The eight interfaces—experience, perception, coding, intent, set, feedback, invitation, and need—are shown as paths or vectors of alikeness. These paths not only converge on the

figure 1-5 Frank Interface Model

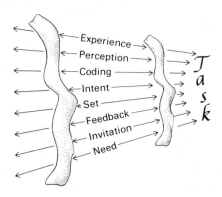

task but also continue toward an infinite number of other matches and tasks.

The energy built by sharing and focusing on the task suggest the control that good communication can exert over the human condition. And to COM-together is the basic *task* of the communication process.

enactment 2   TABLE GREEN

Demonstrate these terms by enacting them in............

enactment 2: TABLE GREEN

interface
harmonious behavior
transaction
propositionality

participants

Ms. *Adams,* single, with a two-year-old daughter, a public relations consultant for a strip-mining company; Mr. *Baker,* married, six children, ages two to nine, chairperson of the Rotary Club Beautification Project, owner and operator of a small bulldozing and bush-hog business; Mr. *Clay,* married, with two sons, twins, age twelve, a farmer; Ms. *Diggs,* married, no children, director of the forestry department at the state university.

relationship

The four participants are guests of the graduate school curriculum symposium—a special review program for the study of each graduate and professional school at the state university. They have not met each other before, but they have been assigned the same table for their introductory coffee meeting—Table Green, Graduate School of Forestry.

problem

The task of these four is to make a list of the "Top Ten Problems Facing Forestry Graduates."

need to talk

Each has been charged to represent his or her sponsor's own priority list. Mr. Clay represents the independent farmers' group.

time/locale

The meeting is held at a cafeteria table in the middle of 30 other coffee meetings in a large dining hall. The time is 9:30 A.M., Saturday.

critique 2   TROUBLESHOOTING

1. What transactions occurred because of age, gender, amount of formal education, community prestige?
2. Who were most "clear" in communicating propositionality?
3. Cite any invitations to communicate that were not accepted.
4. Were interfaces revealed? Did some exist that might surface at the next encounter?
5. How many shared codes were revealed?
6. Which codes were unshared, because they were unknown, strange, confusing, or inefficient?
7. What evidence did you detect of attempted harmonious behavior?

DEMONSTRATE HOW YOU WOULD IMPROVE IT

COMMUNICATION IN BUSINESS AND THE PROFESSIONS . . . TOWARD THE TWENTY-FIRST CENTURY

Communication is not really something that can be produced, and no single course or textbook can be expected to "turn out" communicators. Communication in the broadest sense, however, is an inescapable process that plays a major role in determining the smoothness and efficiency with which product-makers and problem-solvers will span this century and the next.

The basic problems you will face as a professional communicator go back as far as humanity's efforts to farm, manufacture, trade, lend, govern, and travel. Those problems existed in the past. For today and tomorrow, however, the numbers and quantities defining the problems are changing to billions, trillions, and parsecs. Then, as now, usable space translates into real wealth, and energy and its sources are increasingly seen as precious commodities, but the factor of time is perhaps the most precious and crucial.

Space, energy, and time—their storage, use, distribution, and communication—are the vital tasks facing businesses and professions as the new century approaches. An overview of these major communication tasks is presented here for students concerned with their contribution to and role in the process. Your awareness of communication problem-solving might be said to be the desired "product" of this book.

space

Space for living is shrinking and is forcing business and government agencies into new ways of dealing with community planning, building, and mass transit practices. Worldwide rethinking of humanity's inner space as well as near, outer space use will probably mean new message symbols and codifications. Communicators in business will have to include more orientations and reference points into their dealings with each other and the public. A diminished personal space will change how you see yourself and others, and the tendency to group more people in less space will affect how well you communicate.

As you know, special technologies are required to support the general principle of miniaturization. It is likely, too, that living in the reduced space of your private self may tend to compress your ideas and viewpoints. You may even have to redefine your notion of what a group or a family or a couple really is. It may well be that the social impact of this collapsed space will force businesspeople toward a greater self-understanding, so that they can become adept at understanding and using interfaces to focus their energy and communication skill on a given task.

As the professional approaches the next century, legal questions pertaining to use of vertical space will affect family exchanges, use of leisure time, and perhaps the allocation and even definition of privacy. The business questions of ownership, leasing, and property rights of the space above you may fashion new regulatory or monitoring systems that will have to interlock and work closely with investment and speculative enterprises.

energy

Transforming the potentials for power into real disposable power is one of the key reasons for organizations to exist. The ongoing questions of political power—sovereignty, group and individual rights and responsibilities, the will of the people, and the common good—are issues that demand increased input and greater feedback. Thus, in the post-Watergate and post-Vietnam eras, business and professional organizations will be constantly reassessing "who gets in," and "who gets heard."

The scarcity of physical energy affects more than your mobility; it may dictate the mobility of your messages. When energy is scarce, you are forced to use a substitute or surrogate force, just as you vicariously share an event by reading about it or seeing it on film or television.

Human energy will continue to be carefully used, particularly when machines are so much more efficient and easily replaceable. Specialized data-processing skills such as analysis, tabulation, sorting, recording, and storage will continue to be relegated to nonhuman systems. The husbanding of energy will be reflected in switches from inefficient units of weights and measures to metric and binary systems of coding. These tendencies may remove professionals of the future even further from the "real thing itself," so that they deal with digests and abstracts of people and events. Professionals in banking and currency are already seeking ways to eliminate money and other communication channels of exchange that waste time, real money, and energy.

Small groups will continue to need professional "social technicians" who can be total communicators with a professional outlook and a high degree of communication skill. What might be termed associations of associations in business—interelated crossovers and exchange networks—will require professionals to grasp the differences between machine talk and people talk and to effectively separate the biases of each.

time

Instant information through instant research relieves the time drain for some but makes added demands on others who must assimilate digests of digests. *Long-term, short-term, workday, hour, minute, second,* and *millisecond* will find new meanings. Lengthened life spans will give new real significance to duration for people.

Prospects for multiple careers in life already exist. People "retire" in order to try something else. It is commonplace for grandparents to sit next to grandchildren in educational programs. Successive generations see an expansion of childhood, adolescence, young adulthood, middle age, and old age. Communication demands that professionals match this elongation of traditional life structuring. Market and investment forecasting will realign to meet the breadth of new conceptions of age.

Changes in your body clock affect the rhythms of your language systems. Daytime, night, work shifts, breaks, vacations change their real implications. Division of labor and management, and definitions and formulas for seniority and advancement may become further dependent on your total communication ability, as you adapt to different organizations of the calendar and timetable.

If time equals distance-in-space, as dance theorists insist, then the idea of time is both shrinking and expanding. Print media took people lots of time to encode and decode. Electronic media now shrink "the time it takes." People have learned to scan as well as read in the usual sense. The next chapter will examine differences of perception and how they are influenced by prejudices of up, down, left-to-right, and dimensionality (seeing things as flat or in three dimensions). Dimensionality is a time perspective. Organizations will seek to shorten "the time it takes" by using various caucus groups that exchange views like those in the Table Green encounter. "The time it takes" for special interest groups, such as consumers, students, or senior citizens, to reach consensus and implement policy will be affected by instant media exchanges and by plural encodings.

The "organization man" of the 1960s becomes the "media person" of the '80s and '90s. Your expectations in business and the professions may rest, largely, on your willingness to COM-together.

task 5   ASK YOURSELF . . .

1. If communication is "built into" people, why do so many encounters get messed up?
2. What kinds of transactions have you had with the person who sits behind you in class?
3. How do you describe a "professional" student, person, and consumer?
4. What do you feel will be the most important communication skills needed for proficiency in your chosen business or profession?
5. How do you measure a sincere invitation to communicate?

READ FOR YOURSELF

BERNE, ERIC, Games People Play. New York: Grove Press, Inc., 1964.

MORTENSEN, C. DAVID, Communication: The Study of Human Interaction. New York: McGraw-Hill Book Company, 1972.

PETERSON, BRENT D., and others, Communication Probes (2nd ed.). Palo Alto, Calif.: Science Research Associates, Inc., 1977.

ROSS, RAYMOND S., Speech Communication: Fundamentals and Practice (3rd ed.). Englewood Cliffs, N.J.: Prentice-Hall, Inc., 1974.

CHAPTER CHART

Inventory of Skills and Experience
Contact points with others
Patterned similarities with others
Growth in a chosen direction with others
Exchanges with others

Sensitivity to Invitations to Communicate
Observe and evaluate proof of actions that attract or repel
Learn from others
Be yourself
Share several levels of experience
Strive to come together

Basic Communication Components
Sender
Message
Channel
Receiver

Five Communication Relationships
Set
Coding
Signs and symbols
Nonverbal codes
Propositionality

Communication Characteristics
Communication is intrinsic
Communication is behavioral
Communication is dynamic
Communication is contagious
Communication is harmonious
Communication is aesthetic

Interface: Paths of Alikeness
Experience
Perception
Coding
Intent
Set
Feedback
Need

Future Tasks
Distribution of space, energy, and time
Use of space, energy, and time
Storage of space, energy, and time
Communication of space, energy, and time

chapter 2

PERCEPTION, COGNITION, VERBAL AND NONVERBAL LANGUAGES

In this next series of warm-up probes, the larger view of communication is narrowed down to the question, "How and why do you perceive?" The material offers some suggestions on the concept of perception and transactions—how you receive and process stimuli—and examines a few of the major obstacles you may encounter in using languages. Taken together perception and use of languages are termed *cognition*—how you think and feel about your thoughts and feelings. Cognition of messages deals with how-you-think-you-think-and-feel-about-what-others-think-and-feel-you-are-thinking. What are the nonverbal and verbal signs, symbols, and sympathy you send and receive while you . . .

double-think   double-think   double-think   double-think?
qonpʃǝ-ʇʃuiʞ   qonpʃǝ-ʇʃuiʞ   qonpʃǝ-ʇʃuiʞ   qonpʃǝ-ʇʃuiʞ¿

PERCEPTION

Checking back to the inventory you have made, perhaps you have begun to suspect that a great deal depends on relationships in the communication event. How you perceive the light and dark patterns in Figure 2–1 depends on how your mind relates the light to the dark. If, for example, your mind "allows" the darker pattern to dominate, you will probably register the idea of *bird* or *dove*; if the lighter portion dominates, you will see an entirely different type of bird. And if your seeing alternates between the two, perhaps a whole new *concept* will emerge

figure 2-1 Dominance

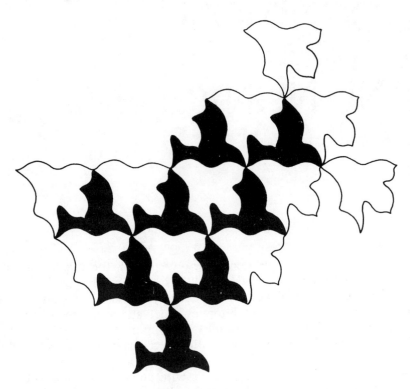

from the two perceptions, such as hawk–dove or bird-of-prey–bird-of-peace. Perhaps nothing specific—no definite relationship—will pop into your mind.

Suppose you are among ten vice-presidents at a conference chaired or dominated by the board president. When the president enters and asks, "Ladies and gentlemen, shall we begin?" the relationships are adjusted and fixed. Nine of you direct your attention toward the president. One of you says, "No." How do you perceive that stimulus?

1. You identify *what* it is from other stimuli—sights, sounds, smells, tastes, skin sensations—and where or who it came from.
2. You *select* to hear it or not; you check your senses, wonder about verifying the "No." You discriminate the stimulus from others arriving at the same time.
3. You *organize* "No" into a relationship that makes sense to you.

Your judgment/conclusion might be: "All our relationships are changed. All bets are off, because somebody else is temporarily dominating." The president's judgment might be: "Someone has stolen

my scene. Either I didn't hear that right, or that fool's got to be kidding."
By processing their individual perceptions, the members of your group
arrive at independent judgments, each selecting an arrangement that is
personally desired and reasonable. Relationships will be determined by
the stimuli they think are *dominating*.

selecting stimuli

When you are hired, you are paid to apply specialized skills.
A surgeon is expected to have a high degree of hand/finger dexterity,
lower-arm strength, and visual acuity, which are necessary for this work.
He or she may possess other skills in only small amounts. Like everyone,
surgeons are hired for what they can do and not for what they cannot do.
Perception involves a selective seeing of stimuli that can do something
for you—sensations of pressure on your retina, eardrum, tastebuds,
olfactory membranes, and skin surfaces. You tend to select just those
sensations that are needed, that fit in with your requirements at the
moment. Your board president may not have needed to hear a "No" to
his or her question; if the president laughed and released a little nervous
tension, maybe that is just what he or she needed.

Preparation for a stimulus frequently leads you to *expect* to
perceive something, making selection and organization easier. The
double-think habit of verifying and endlessly monitoring is a classic
symptom of the message bind—misinterpreting intent by "doing what is
expected." An organization that *expects* garbled messages within its
routine will get them.

Some people are *suggestible* to experience. If you are told,
"That's the greatest show on earth," you may do your best to experience
it that way. If all the clues suggest that the president is about to call the
meeting to order, you expect and work to perceive the signals that
confirm that expectation. Likewise, if you expect to see evidence that
this is a dog-eat-dog, highly competitive world, you may have constructed a picture of that in your mind when you examined the birds in
Figure 2–1.

Effective business communication may also be plagued by
selective *exposure* to data. These phrases are typical of people who
refuse to allow stimuli to touch their sensors:

1. Would you get to the point?
2. You're in the wrong department. Try somebody else.
3. I don't want to hear about it.
4. I'm not in!

Selective exposure is also seen in the needs of self-insulating
persons, those who employ human "shields" made up of yes-men and

figure 2-2   Perception Test

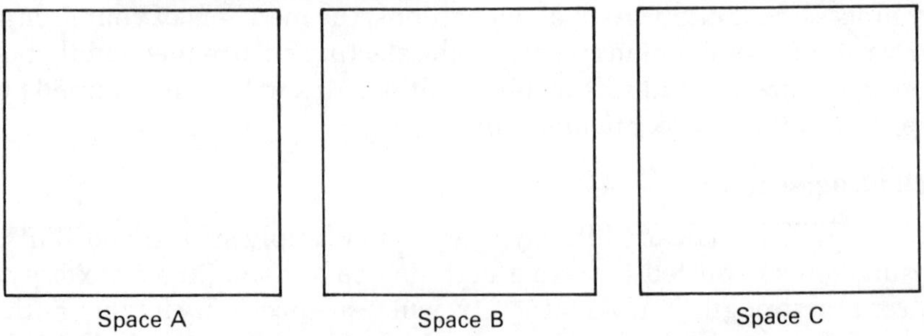

Space A   Space B   Space C

coteries. Certain people in organizations seem to create power centers, cult followers, claques, flunkies, and goons, forming a kind of protective coloration around themselves to avoid unwanted stimuli.

task 1   A PERCEPTION TEST

Look into Space A of Figure 2–2. List in the order of occurrence the first four things you see in that space. Give yourself 30 seconds.

I saw:

1. _____

2. _____

3. _____

4. _____

Look into Space B. List in the order of occurrence the first three things you see in that space. Give yourself 20 seconds.

I saw:

1. _____

2. _____

3. _____

Look into Space C. List in the order of occurrence the first two things you see in that space. Give yourself 10 seconds.

I saw:

1. _____

2. _____

Read the nine words you have written and seen in the spaces. On the basis of all clues, *what would you expect to see* in a fourth space, if there was one? What single word would you write to convey what you saw?

1. _____

organizing stimuli

Task 1 combined a number of steps in organizing perceptions into conceptions. You organized what you felt were the dominant *figures* in a descending order. Stimuli tuned out were relegated to the background and became subordinate *ground* for your figures. Another basic step involved the tendency to fill in white space. Filling in lines where you find gaps and supplying bits of conversation you do not really hear are common ways of filling white space or *closing*. Your mind may have closed the broken lines in Figure 2–2; maybe you mentally "sanded down" any rough edges you saw. Since not much information was given, you probably filled it in for yourself. Would you have any trouble closing the message: "And furthermore, I don't give a . . . !"? Anybody who has seen a burned-out electric sign would quickly and accurately complete:

MONTICELLO

BU N SS C L   GE

A third characteristic of organizing perception is to simplify. The law of efficiency operates, so that you follow a "least resistance rule" or adopt *Ockham's Razor* as a guide: Whatever explanation requires the fewest assumptions is preferred. Faced with floods of reports and bulletins, personnel may prefer simple questions, answers, and solutions.

interpreting stimuli

The patterns you organize and the significance you attach to them are unique to you. If even a semblance of agreement about the world existed, this course would be without purpose, but the harmonious ideal continues to be elusive or rare.

A tendency to simplify also occurs in interpreting data. You may form sets of habitual shortcuts. For example, some decision-makers look or listen first to the "bottom line": "hire," "fire," "buy," "sell," "initial-and-return," "go," "launch," etc. Past decisions and the total context in which you witness events determine how you interpret them, and sometimes you apply what you are learning while interpreting.

Your projection of something into the missing "fourth space" in Task 1 was partially based on what you "learned" from the first three experiences. Trying to make sense from the flow of words and their personal significance, you mapped out whatever relationships you found or made up in your sequence. The result, of course, was your version of a four-part concept—you "made" a four-part movie with four major roles (the top word in each list) and six supporting ones (the other words). You may call what you did a book outline or speech outline or whatever, but your perception of limited stimuli was translated into words that could relate to other words. Your final word pulled together the whole interpretation into a "title"—a single word that symbolized the whole.

What do you *think* about the test? How you think leads to a consideration of what you do while you are selecting, organizing, and interpreting experience. You think about it.

COGNITION

The functioning of the human brain—the inclination to scan, identify, select, verify, store, and respond to stimuli—is often referred to, collectively, as information-processing. *Cognition* is an older and shorter term. *Thinking* is what most people call it. Your thinking derives from lifelong, on-the-job training and from practice in testing things for yourself. You try to acquire a judgment edge in searching for comfort, self-gratification, and general enhancement of your condition.

learning

How much of this skill is *learned*? How much is provided by nature? The DNA molecule in Figure 2–3 represents a chemical explanation of how genetic information is passed from generation to generation, from cell to cell. This molecule is able to manufacture *messenger* and *transfer* RNA (ribonucleic acid), which alerts protein centers of needs and helps obtain supplies. At birth, you started out with a full complement of wiring; each sensory system had complexes of relays, storage units, and so on. Structural systems for communicating within yourself and beyond fed connections to the cerebral center or cortex in your brain. The trillions of neurons, zapping across one another at points of contact or *synapse* require an enzyme (ACh) to control this chemical reaction. When a contact ended, another chemical (AChE) destroyed the igniter ACh so that the impulse would stop.

The pioneer studies of David Krech and Mark Rosenzweig at

figure 2-3   DNA Molecule

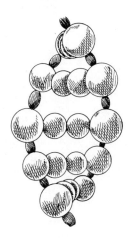

Berkeley[1] suggest that learning is related to the body's ratio of ACh to AChE, since a proportional balance seems to ensure that an efficient, properly timed charge will take place.

Your acquisition of thinking capacity and efficiency is also related to your body's manufacture of RNA. One problem in defining learning is that whatever is "learned" is not necessarily apparent in a bodily change. You can see what a salesperson has learned about a product line by observing his or her behavior and results, but has a change taken place in his or her nervous system? Where in the body does learning take place? No answer is yet conclusive, but a likely explanation might be: throughout the entire cortical system, its assemblies and subassemblies. Perhaps clusters of neurons "grow" with use, as muscles do. A high-protein diet certainly is necessary during the developmental stages of the brain and for general alertness.

So-called conditioned learning occurs over a prolonged period of exposure to a stimulus. Your acquisition of perceptual and motor skills depends on practice—whether they are worked on in part or as a totality. As your skills begin to layer one another, a total or *global* skill—such as playing a piano—emerges, with various parts (fingers, hands, wrists) combining their functions into a unified ability.

Reward, success, and proficiency aid learning: these are explored further in Chapter 5. General agreement exists about the effect of an "enriched environment" on learning. Many and varied kinds of

[1]D. Krech and others, "Enzyme Concentrations in the Brain and Adjustive Behavior Patterns," *Science,* 120 (1954), 994–96.

stimulation and interesting, engaging surroundings help develop a "stronger" neural system, which helps to make learning easier.

memory

The "old pro" in the factory is often apt to say to an apprentice: "Kid, I've forgotten more about that machinery than you'll ever learn." In this special way, the pro is saying that his or her "short-term" memory is as large as the "long-term" memory.

You can generally manage to remember certain details over relatively short periods. This is your short-term memory. Phone numbers, street names, and the like can be summoned from it at will, but you quickly forget them if they are not used. The short-term memory may also serve as a standby storage tank, protecting your main memory banks from overloading. Your ability to retrieve experience is unique to you.

This quick review of sensing and thinking about experience points a little more specifically toward the overall topic of human *motivation*—the *why* of basic business and professional speaking. What you do to send your thinking on to others and how you encode verbal and nonverbal languages are still closer to that topic. The following enactment situation can test the human tendency to complicate exchange. Enactment 3 asks: "Do you see what I see in the way I see it?" This is a *reversed* enactment where participants attempt the opposite of good interpersonal exchange: They try to be "difficult" by using deliberate misconception and misperception.

enactment 3   "GOOD MORNING, CUSTOMER SERVICE!"

Enact these problem-making mental quirks in................

errors of identification of stimuli
errors of selecting stimuli
errors in organizing relation-
    ships
errors of figure and ground
errors of closing
errors of simplifying

enactment 3: "GOOD MORNING, CUSTOMER SERVICE!"

participants

Receptionist, male or female, new on the job, young and eager to help; *supervisor*, male or female, any age, eager to help trainees learn the ropes—this person serves as the *second stage* problem-solver after the receptionist fails to solve a customer's problem; *customers*, persons fitting any description.

relationship

The receptionist and supervisor are briefly acquainted only through their job assignment. Customers seek answers to the basic consumer questions: who, what, where, when, why, how much, and how many?

need to talk

The receptionist is approached by customers needing assistance.

time/locale

Monday morning; a very large retail store, dealing with a wide variety of services and hard and soft goods, from car rentals and insurance to expensive jewelry and antiques. Customer Service is an office without walls.

critique 3   TROUBLESHOOTING

1. List the major instances of misunderstanding.
2. Can this trainee look forward to a brilliant career in retailing?
3. How did the supervisor and the trainee get in each other's way?
4. What was needed more in this exchange, a good long-term or short-term memory?
5. What do you think the customer will remember most about this experience?
6. Can you cite examples of misunderstandings hurting the encounter?

HOW WOULD YOU CORRECT THE PROBLEM?

LANGUAGES

Enactment 3 should point out confusions in which participants are wondering: "Are you thinking what I think you are thinking?" The business world enlists and uses coding symbols, hoping that what is intended will pass accurately and swiftly from sender to receiver. This enactment might also have raised the question of a "single reality," whether your reality and another's are the same. Which of you is right—neither? Both? Symbols help to bridge the differences between your separate realities and make synchronization of different views possible.

symbols

Symbol codes are designed to serve as intermediaries between minds. If you cannot move your entire reality into your partner's mind, you can offer a small rendering of it in the form of a substitute—a symbol. Nobody "owns" a true symbol. There is an infinite supply, and if someone destroys a print or sound symbol, its referent—the thing, person, or organization it stands for—is not impaired, because a symbol is not the thing itself. As we have stressed, the tokens and trappings of our existence are not the existence itself. This important communication axiom was stated interestingly by Alfred Korzybski, who wrote: "A map is not the territory."[2] Professional communicators, aware of the possibility of confusing symbol and referent, might consider . . .

axiom 4:   AN OBJECT IS MERELY AN OBJECT, BUT A PERSON IS A HUMAN BEING

A serious communication error is the tendency, sometimes, to perceive people as objects. The temptation to think of persons as you think of numbers, reports, quantities, or symbols may lead you to pervert the valuable service of symbols: They remove ideas from entanglement in all those neurons and help objectify and define messages by placing your intentions on the table, away from personal complications. Symbolizing may be a kind of public gesture for your audience that helps reduce circular double-thinking. Inasmuch as symbols express your personal reality, the coding itself can distort the messages; misleading cues can somehow creep into your statements or writings.

written language

Written language symbols are usually intended to be read, silently. Sometimes they are read aloud and may even be "translated" into illustrations, a film, or television program, but the rules governing the original expression were in the language of its creator. In this way even rules of writing are at least partially unique to the writer. Strictly interpreted, a word symbol for a person—I, he, she, you, they, we— would require a dictionary that listed all the Is and theys who ever lived, just so readers would know who was who.

A word means only what its user intends it to mean. Your use of I at the beginning of an important job interview will not have the same

[2]Alfred Korzybski, Science and Sanity (Lakeville, Conn.: Institute of General Semantics, 1st ed., 1933, 4th ed. 1958).

meaning as at the conclusion. You are not the same person. Your neurons have imprinted changes, and so have those in your interviewer's nervous system. If hired, you are the *I* with a new job; if not, you are the *I* who is still out of work.

The field of language study is called *linguistics* and concerns itself with letter symbols and groupings, word clusters, and vocalization of words. *Semanticists* focus their attention on *meaning*, a word's *denotation* or the thing referred to, and a word's *connotation* or the thing evoked and brought to mind by it. Connotations are all the varied associations that crowd in along with a word's specific referent; a connotation is a word's overtone of pun, triple pun, or multiple meaning. What connotations did you attach to *bird, hawk, dove?* The magnificent word-play in Shakespeare's *Romeo and Juliet* still illustrates the disasters that can result from mislabeling and misnaming families and organizations. Poor Juliet knows that a rose would still smell as sweet if it were called scrap iron, and she agonizes over her boyfriend's name, Romeo Montague—a name connoting hatred to her family.

task 2   CALL IT THE WAY YOU SEE IT

Discuss what is denoted and connoted in these names and phrases:

Mr. Hu	One Wall Street	INTERFLUB, Inc.
the United States of England		*Norway v. Drew County*
Victor Frankenstein IV		"I will always love you, but I can never become Mrs. Schlemiel"

Three suggested cautions by semanticists can help transactions:

1. Cautious use of the verb *to be—is*. Axiom 4 uses the word *is* twice. Taken literally, the proposition dares to be all-inclusive.
2. Cautious use of generalizations and a tone of finality. Memos, directives, and pronouncements that presume to be the "final word"—*like Axiom 4*—must fall short of all-inclusiveness.
3. Cautious use of bipolar (either/or) judgments—*like Axiom 4*—to avoid oversimplifying complex issues.

spoken languages

How you speak and how you perceive speaking follow similar patterns, but knowing the words of a language is not the same as knowing the language. *Morphemes* are the smallest language units of sound, and their serial order and relationships give clues to the sense of speech. Generally, spoken and written systems share similar syntactic or structural rules. You say as well as write "the job" and not "job the."

Your *coding* of speech uses both verbal and nonverbal signs and symbols. It is a true synthesis of your thinking and feeling capacities. Psychologist Jean Piaget noted that children encode speech *egocentrically* or from their own point of view. Later, his subjects seemed to acquire a more socialized pattern, indicating consideration of what others do.

Basil Bernstein's research in England led him to identify what he calls a restricted code and an elaborated code. The *restricted code*, stressing "we" rather than "I," is "created by a community-based culture." Its messages are simple and assume the receiver knows all the words and referents, so that long explanations are not needed. The *elaborated* code, however, emphasizes the speaker's experience and takes great pains to explain in detail. Bernstein found greater use of restricted coding among the working classes and more of the elaborated coding in middle- and upper-income groups. An interesting point for communicators is that "richer" experience and word exposure helped people to be good at using both codes, and at "talking their language" with whomever "they" might be.[3]

What languages do people use other than written and spoken? The interface concept suggested a spectrum of surfaces that link participants and their language systems. All this theorizing perhaps became more immediate to your real-life experience during the enactments. Language possibilities that were not explained might have been revealed: Did your partner's way of speaking tell you something? Did the distance between the two of you tell you something? Motive, intent, character, and personality are often conveyed in languages without words—nonverbal languages.

NONVERBAL LANGUAGES

Trying to use word symbols effectively is difficult and frustrating. Talking, as you have seen, is a cheap way to substitute for the real thing. It is also, perhaps, the most sublime attribute of man; but people get sick of word games, sometimes they demand: "Don't talk! Show me!" You have seen movies where characters say things like: "I let my gun/hands/feet do the talking." People sometimes fall back on the action side of communication by talking shop, talking guns, talking cars, or in

[3]Basil Bernstein, "A Sociolinguistic Approach to Socialization: With Some Reference to Educability," in *Language and Poverty*, ed. Frederick Williams (Chicago: Markham Publishing Company, 1970), p. 37.

business transactions by insisting that you put "your money where your mouth is." Partly to offset the demands of word symbols, people accompany one language system with one or more nonlinguistic or nonverbal languages such as *paralanguage*.

paralanguage

The board president's shock at hearing a vice-president answer with a single "No" could have been softened by certain cues accompanying that word. The knack of "doing" other people's voice colorations is the goal of professional mimics or impersonators. Finding the right combination of vocal characteristics or cues means "getting the voice" of someone.

task 3   GETTING THE VOICE

Match colorations or vocal characteristics to the personalities in the lists.

Vocal Characteristics   **Personalities**

silky	musty	aching	ringing	your mother
smoky	jerky	billowy	sticky	• coach
cooing	gravelly	stringy	zippy	• minister
leaky	bumpy	lilting	squawky	• best friend
raspy	gurgling	droopy	nagging	• worst enemy
looping	flying	flitting	picky	• speech teacher
rolling	sagging	tripping	thundering	• pet

George L. Trager uses a more precise breakdown for paralanguage cues. His three categories are *characterizers, qualifiers,* and *segregates*. Characterizers set a mood, show crisis, secretiveness, or an emotional state. They include yelling, crying, sniffing, whispering, voice-clearing, sobbing, and moaning. Qualifiers refer to pitch, rate, and volume colorations that indicate new points of attack, new topics, or a new relationship, such as when someone enters the communication field. A vocal segregate is a sound or voiceless energy (silence) stuck between statements to break up patterns, show deliberation, or restart thinking. *Ahs, hmmmms,* and *erruhs* do this.[4]

Your professional role may or may not depend on what kind of voice you have and what you can do with it, but your vocal quality will certainly affect the way in which you are perceived. One application of this information is to make you aware of the vocal cues you give and of how people organize pictures of what you are like from hearing and

[4]George L. Trager, "Paralanguage: A First Approximation," *Studies in Linguistics*, 13 (1958), 1–12.

seeing you. D. W. Addington's studies indicated some evidence that people assign labels such as lazy or energetic, honest or dishonest, and healthy or ill on the basis of vocal coloration.[5] Task 4 checks your set of vocal preconceptions for job titles.

task 4   SOUNDING LIKE A PROFESSIONAL

In your opinion, what should these jobholders sound like?

Job-Title	Ideal Vocal Characteristics
pediatrician	---
auctioneer	---
university president	---
florist	---
marriage counselor	---
mortician	---
hairdresser	---
warden	---
park guide	---
special duty nurse	---

Much will be said later about personal image, integrity, credibility, and persuasiveness. Obviously, your opinion of yourself is reflected in how you speak, in the habits you develop, and in the models you follow. Changing your voice during an encounter is, according to Erving Goffman's analysis of ritual, one way to change "face." Depending on your message, the event context, and your audience relationship, your vocal changes may undermine or increase your acceptance as a speaker and as a professional person.

enactment 4   DAYDREAMS

In this enactment you are asked to speak freely about your daydreams and to swap ideas and opinions of your version of the "perfect life." Try to be aware of the several languages you are using and which ones you feel are most effective for you.

Be aware of these concepts in doing . . . .

enactment 4: DAYDREAMS

connotations
paralinguistic cues
qualifiers
segregates
characterizers

[5]D. W. Addington, "The Relationship of Selected Vocal Characteristics to Personality Perception," *Speech Monographs*, 35, no. 4 (November 1968), 492–503.

participants

Student 1, any description; student 2, any description.

relationship

A shared friendship.

need to talk

Each needs to examine his or her own vision of the good life.

locale

The back of your speech classroom, before the class starts.

critique 4   TROUBLESHOOTING

1. Did vocal coloration help or hinder understanding?
2. Which words misled, because of connotations?
3. Was either participant "expecting" what the other said?
4. Did "hesitancy segregates" affect the trust between friends?
5. Which topics seemed to be out-of-bounds?
6. Was anything solved by the exchange?
7. Were channels left open for further communication?

HOW WOULD YOU IMPROVE DEFICIENCIES?

face language

"A good face is a letter of recommendation." The seventeenth-century essayist/journalist Joseph Addison found that a good face helped the professional when traveling. Considering the number of people who suffered rotting jaws, scrofulous and pockmarked faces, early baldness, and malformations of all kinds, a good face in that era was pretty hard to find. You could redo Tasks 3 and 4 substituting *face* for *voice* to obtain more insights into nonverbal talk, but it might be even more valuable to think of the voice as coming from the face—two languages. Which dominates?

The classic symbols for tragedy and comedy in Figure 2–4 do not require a lot of explanation. Usually there is immediate recognition of their meaning, but how do you know what ideas are behind the masks you see others wear? Startling techniques in cosmetic surgery make it hard to be certain of a good face when you see one. People can be shortened, lengthened, made wider, flabbier, skinnier, or hairier. Cosmetic manufacturing is one of the world's largest industries; faces are fortunes and bankruptcies.

figure 2-4 Faces of Comedy and Tragedy

Job applicants are frequently asked: "How many jobs have you had, and why did you leave them?" In your encounters you also tend to search for cues about the faces people have and why they leave one for another. Aside from the painting and plastering you do, your faces reveal information about who you are and who you would like to be. If your face is not quite a letter of recommendation, it is frequently a letter of intent.

Researchers are not certain whether facial muscles react before or during, in concert with or in response to, emotional states. The old James-Lange theory held that an emotional state like "sorrow" caused weeping, and the weeping, in turn, caused more feelings of sorrow. Some people can induce certain emotional states by "priming the pump" in this way. Silvan Tomkins suggests that people generally recognize basic facial arrangements such as anger, shame, surprise, enjoyment, excitement, fear, and contempt.[6] Some people are so adept at muscle control that their emotional states are displayed in the subtlest of degrees—only glimmers, flickers, or hints of emotion.

In professional transactions forcing or "putting on" faces is part of asserting a competence; set faces are cultivated to match specific contexts. Many cultural studies, tracing myth and ritual, have pointed out how people construct scenarios to enhance their ability to cope, excel, dominate. Joseph Campbell's *The Hero with a Thousand Faces*

[6]Silvan S. Tomkins, *Affect, Imagery, Consciousness*, 2 vols. (New York: Springer Publishing Co., Inc., 1962–63).

suggests, for example, that the professional medicine man's task was to make symbolic systems "visible and public."[7] If shark's teeth, for example, were powerful medicine, then a medicine man made certain that the shark motif was heavily used in tribal face makeup.

The modern business and professional sector has many arbiters of symbolic systems. Commercial enterprises themselves hope to influence standards of appearance—personal hygiene, grooming, hair styles, and face decoration or adornment. They grasp face languages, capitalizing on the common belief that if your face looks good, you will feel good; if you look competent, you will feel and communicate competence.

hand language

The legal profession is a "word" profession. Like teaching, selling, and promoting, the practice of law stretches words as far as they will go and then looks back to the fixed word printed in the statute for comparison. Figure 2–5 shows how hands *stretch* spoken words. From the sound originating in the throat, to its shaping by the tongue and teeth, the word travels from *mouth* and *face* the length of the arm to the *hand*—three distinct languages. Which dominates?

The stretching of the speech impulse from brain to hand is a way of further externalizing or showing intent, another instance of "putting your cards on the table," so others can *see* what you mean. The old drawings in Figure 2–5 are from John Bulwer's *Chirologia* and *Chironomia*, two of many attempts to catalog hand movements that have a meaning or give a sign. After reading the meanings freely translated from the Latin, you might think that nobody talks that way anymore, but some variations can still be found. These hand symbols were used by rhetoricians of the time—doctors, lawyers, clergy, statesmen—who debated and decided great issues.

Hand gestures like these frequently help speaker and listener to punctuate messages by illustrating separations of ideas, marking divisions of viewpoint, and providing a rhythm accompaniment to speech. In Task 5 try to *feel* the intent or impulse-to-speak in your arms and hands. See if the gesture helps the speaking and the speaking the gesture.

task 5   A WORD IN THE HAND

1. Practice the 25 gestures of Figure 2–5 in front of a full-length mirror. Adapt them to your own natural motions.

The Hero with A Thousand Faces by Joseph Campbell, Bollingen Series XVII (Copyright 1949 by Bollingen Foundation), reprinted by permission of Princeton University Press: short quote from p. 101.

figure 2-5 Hand Gestures

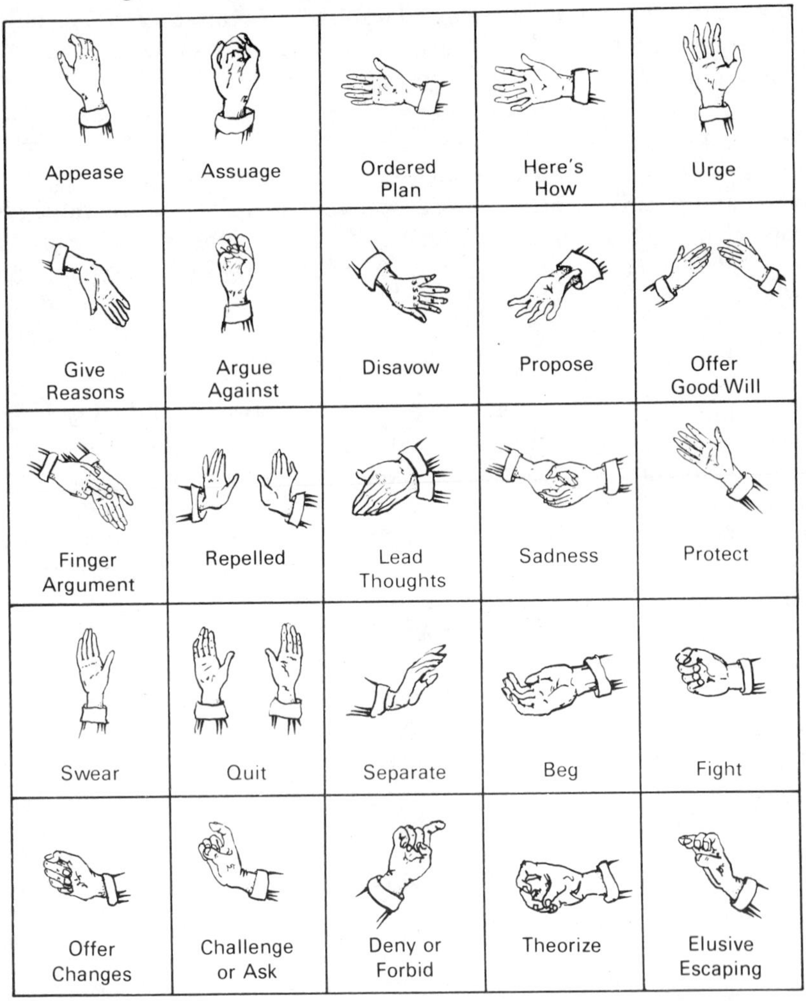

Appease	Assuage	Ordered Plan	Here's How	Urge
Give Reasons	Argue Against	Disavow	Propose	Offer Good Will
Finger Argument	Repelled	Lead Thoughts	Sadness	Protect
Swear	Quit	Separate	Beg	Fight
Offer Changes	Challenge or Ask	Deny or Forbid	Theorize	Elusive Escaping

2. Read each of the statements under 3, below, and *write in* a gesture where you think it would help illustrate a point.

3. Read or memorize one of these statements and accompany yourself with appropriate gestures.

    a. "I don't agree. If we accept that proposal, we'll get one of three things: more people with less income, fewer people with more income, or everyone with the same income."

    b. "You've got to listen! We're your friends. Let's forget about all that pessimistic ranting. I promise you, we can help."

    c. "Okay, look at what you've just said. The key point is that our competition wouldn't touch that candidate with a ten-foot pole, which means we've got a real fight on our hands."

d. "Those figures are just too elusive. We can't really come to grips with their real significance, until we've stopped or slowed the flow of products that keep dribbling away, a little here . . . a little there."

Today's investigators generally divide the types of gestures into five categories: *illustrators, regulators, affect displays, adaptors, and emblems.* Our hands illustrate by pointing and by showing size, shape, space. They draw rough pictures and outlines and illustrate emphasis through repetition. Regulators are gestures of stop, start, give, take, or interruption of proceedings. They include use of all parts of the communicating surfaces. For example, students learn when permission is given to speak through nods, eye area movements, posture changes, and so on. Affect display is the psychologist's term for "state of mind" or emotional state. Gestures of great energy or rigidity, aimless flutterings and ambiguous, out-of-control movements are well-known samples. Adaptors are gestures that include physical bodies—objects, other people, yourself—into the *stretched* word impulse. Adaptors touch things and handle them like props. Emblems are hand signs and symbols. "Okay" signs, victory gestures, and hand signals where sound will not carry or where silence is imposed are emblematic. Faces and hands move in space, the space *between.*

space language

The first space you know is the womb, closed, snug, encircling. You learn to *stretch* your sense of space, like your sense of words, as you relate to objects, people, territory, domain. The counterpart to hand language is your sensitivity to pressures of distance between things. The power of words is extended to hands, and from hands to objects and people. The significance of space between things is the study of *proxemics,* and it has useful applications to professional communication.

Your analysis of space language should begin with a reexamination of the gestures you made in Task 5:

1. Did your hands ever *touch* anything? How close did they come to touching?
2. What does it *mean* to you/what does it feel like to touch and to *almost* touch an object or another person?
3. What does it feel like *to be* touched or almost touched?
4. Why do you sometimes take the shortest route and sometimes take the longest to get some place?
5. Why do buildings have offices with walls, rather than one big chunk of space?
6. What do the following phrases have to do with space language: a con artist; people on the other side of the world see everything upside down; claustrophobia; lining up for Disney World; picture windows; escalator clauses; big-screen TV; seats on the 50-yard line; French perfume; wall-to-wall carpeting?

These and thousands of other considerations affect messages sent with space between. For example, animals and plants are spaced to balance interdependent needs; animals know just how much space can be given up before running away; your body knows how much ventilation space it needs before it works to reduce your temperature. As a prelude to enactment of business/professional encounters, the impact of these questions might become clearer if you study four commonly held notions about space. Each of the concepts determines how you transact with others, how you conduct yourself in groups, and how you stretch your mental yardstick to include *valuation* of human transactions.

Space suggests the idea of what is *distal* or away from us. You may say a person is tall, fat, chunky, and so on—comparing him or her with some personal standard. In other words, you use space as a measurement. Now, think about these four propositions:

Bigger means better
First is better
Highest is best
Apart means away

task 6   JUDGING PEOPLE SPATIALLY

Each of the four propositions deals with space, but space problems are also *time* problems—the time it takes to find, reach, climb, grow, or move from place to place. List some of the communication problems that arise when you judge people spatially:

Judgment	Communication Problem
"You're biggest, you must be the leader."	---
"Look at all those big presents!"	---
"Let's make this the biggest party ever!"	---
"Those are mighty big words for such a little squirt."	---
"They live in a big house and drive a big car."	---
"Did you see the size of that ring?"	---
"We're number one in sales."	---

"I had it first!"   --

"Who would like to be the first to show

    us how it's done?"   --

"We sat in the first row, of course."   --

"She was last in her class at medical

    school."   --

"Well, that's the first thing that came to

    mind."   --

"Last one in is a rotten egg!"   --

"Last, but not least . . ."   --

"Everything that goes up must come

    down."   --

"The lowest rung of the ladder . . ."   --

"The top of the heap . . ."   --

"They live on a hill."   --

"I can't seem to get close to her."   --

"Well, they're just beside themselves

    with . . ."   --

"He was listed as a runaway."   --

"That person's really gone the route."   --

"The cream always rises to the top."   --

"The Lone Ranger . . ."   --

"Did you ever see anyone so uppity?"   --

"The world's richest recluse . . ."   --

"They live in an ivory tower."   --

"It's a nice place to visit, but I wouldn't

    want to live there."   --

    In applying these measurement judgments to people, you may commit errors of valuation—placing a price on morals and ethics. This task reveals how people order their exchanges using spatial references. In speaking the language of space, you often presume *terri-toriality*—who "owns" that space, that building, parking space, restroom? This designation of home turf or stomping grounds reflects your sense of territory; a sign reading "Home of the Untouchables" above a child's treehouse warns that a nest or homestead has been declared, a stake has been claimed.

The space language you speak is also colored by how you orient or place yourself in relation to people and things. Turning your face or back to persons, "fronting" or crowding, giving a cold shoulder, or looking askance and turning your head as far as it will go without turning your body are ways of lining up with others through spatial coding. Some people slouch to be on the same level, others stretch or tilt their heads back to gain an illusion of height.

Seating arrangements communicate and effect communication. Dinner tables, conference tables, gaming tables, head tables, side tables, and reserved tables affect the flow of information. Just as you would not reach across a table to help yourself to food, your exchanges are inhibited by the natural obstruction of persons to your right and left. Do you feel comfortable talking to someone through a cage or a little hole in a glass window? Does a witness box seem somewhat like a prison cell cut in half? The interface diagram in Figure 2–6 depicts a "wedding" of persons focusing on a task; it shows receptivity. The professional communicator's posture "lets you in." It uses the languages of space, time, face, and hand to receive messages and people.

figure 2-6 Physical Space Barrier

enactment 5   THE OVAL OFFICE

Test your nonverbal skills. An "oval office" is pretty close to a circle, and a true circle enforces arrangements and positions with a particular weight and pull. It is rather like a circular bed, which "pulls" your idea of right and left into a different orientation. The "weight" of a circular room—its greatest tension—is at the center, the middle, the "spotlight." The audience for this enactment should be seated as if along the walls of a circular room.

Participants may use any language except a *verbal* one. Use of the digits *1–10* or *a-b-c-d* is suggested as a replacement for vocal word language. Thus, instead of saying, "Please, sit down," the participant may substitute, "a, bc."

Demonstrate nonverbal skill in.............................

enactment 5: **THE OVAL OFFICE**

participants

The chief executive, any description; a student, any description.

relationship

The chief executive works for the student by virtue of his or her election to office.

need to talk

The student has suggestions for legislation and seeks assurance that he or she is being represented.

locale

The oval office of the chief executive.

critique 5   TROUBLESHOOTING

1. How did the nonverbal language force either participant to listen more carefully?
2. How did the nonverbal language force you to watch and listen more carefully?
3. What differences might you expect if the exchange had taken place: (a) with no furniture between participants? (b) in a square-shaped office? (c) in a long, narrow one? (d) on a sofa?

DEMONSTRATE HOW YOU MIGHT HAVE IMPROVED COMMUNICATION

4. Which participant was dominant?
5. Were gestures helpful in understanding messages?
6. Could you tell which political party each belonged to by their use of nonverbal language?

afterthought DOMINANCE

The question "Which is dominant?" is central to speaking as a professional. As a summary to this chapter, the dominance issue converges on each of the major concepts presented: perception, cognition, and languages. Ideally, there is a blend—an orchestration of interfaces, each adding an extra nuance to expression, so that the whole person communicates in a total way.

The dominance of a thought or an impression dissolves and reasserts itself in a reciprocal manner—like talking and listening. There never is, of course, a perfectly separate half-cycle of talking or of listening. Rather there is an attitude that will be introduced in the next chapter—the *competence factor*. This modulating attitude provides professional communicators with a motive and an aim whose energy controls their partners' perceptions of figure–ground, superior–inferior, and professional–layperson. Chapter 5 examines these crucial attitudes and your professional competence factor.

READ FOR YOURSELF

BIRDWHISTELL, RAY L., *Kinesics and Context: Essays on Body Motion Communication.* Conduct and Communication Series, ed. Erving Goffmann and Dell Hymes. Philadelphia: University of Pennsylvania Press, 1970.

EISENBERG, ABNE M., *Living Communication.* Englewood Cliffs, N.J.: Prentice-Hall, Inc., 1975.

HALL, EDWARD T., *The Silent Language.* New York: Fawcett World Library, 1959.

HARRISON, RANDALL P., *Beyond Words: An Introduction to Nonverbal Communication.* Englewood Cliffs, N.J.: Prentice-Hall, Inc., 1974.

HOCHBERG, JULIAN E., *Perception.* Englewood Cliffs, N.J.: Prentice-Hall, Inc., 1964.

KNAPP, MARK L., *Nonverbal Communication in Human Interaction* (2nd ed.). New York: Holt, Rinehart and Winston, 1978.

CHAPTER CHART

Perception
   Identify the stimuli
   Select significant or dominant stimuli
   Organize the relationships of the stimuli
   Key idea: People perceive what they want to perceive

Cognition
   Practice to learn, learn to practice
   Learning is helped by exposure to an enriched environment
   Key idea: Achievement breeds achievement

Languages
   A symbol is an intermediary between minds
   Languages are systems of symbol-making
   Word symbols denote specifics and connote generalities
   Key Idea: The professional communicator tries to send and receive in the
      other person's denotative and connotative language

Nonverbal Languages
   Paralanguage consists of all the nonword cues people send and receive
      through vocalization
   Voice coloration is sometimes associated with job title
   Key idea: Paralinguistic cues reveal a great deal about you
   "A good face is a letter of recommendation"
   People notice when the words do not match the face
   Voices carry further than faces
   Key idea: Composing facial expressions helps to generate a matching state
      of mind
   Hand gestures help the sender and the receiver draw the picture and agree on
      dominance
   Proxemics analyzes the degree of intimacy in the communication process
   Judging people and things from a spatial viewpoint hurts communication
   Key idea: All factors in a transaction possess a spatial relationship to the
      participants and affect the outcome of the exchange

chapter 3

chapter challenge

Understand the difference between hearing and listening

Assess your personal ability to hear

Assess your personal ability to listen

Identify the conditions that make listening difficult for you

Demonstrate common, nonverbal cues that tell people you are
   listening

Recognize the basic reasons why you need to listen

Illustrate touch-by-talking examples

LISTENING

listen-respond   listen-respond   listen-respond

Communicating in business and professional situations is risky; you give something away, you reveal something about yourself in the process of sharing. You have to respond. Listening is also risky, because you must invest part of yourself, which means that you run the risk of learning something and of being changed. In your task and encounter work in perception (Chapter 2), you recognized how people select experience. They find wonderfully ingenious ways to ignore stimuli or to not respond. If you have looked ahead to Chapter 8, you will know that simple, self-revealing measurements such as the Johari Window reemphasize how people hide, use camouflage, and even "change their spots" in order to present the right face. People in business and the professions are acutely aware of the impressions they give and receive. Lacking precise terms to describe these impressions, they often fall back on phrases such as "put on a happy face," "put your best foot forward," or "show your good side." These clichés strike at the essential difference between *hearing* and *listening*.

Hearing is the physiological process of receiving sound. You hear sound accurately or inaccurately for a variety of reasons—they all deal with physics:

your hearing range (20–11,000 cycles
   per second)
the decibel level   your mechanical links
your head cavity patterns   your bone structure
                                          your sinus drainage

your neural wiring	the acoustical environment
your line of sight to the source	the duration
interference from multiple sources	the amount of repetition

Listening is the intentional reception of stimuli. You listen because you *need* to—for any of the needs that are reviewed in Chapter 4. You can listen better, however, if you work at it. Consider the occasions when the buzzing and chattering of groups of people filled your ears and then suddenly dropped to zero—absolutely quiet. Do you remember why they needed to be quiet? Check the *need* to listen in Task 1.

task 1   SCREAMS OF SILENCE

Cite the basic needs that you might be satisfying in these situations:

1. You would listen to the "last words" of a wealthy relative, because ———

————————————————————————.

2. You would need to listen to a fireman who has broken down your door, because

————————————————————————.

3. You would need to listen to a phone call from your boss at 3:00 A.M., because

————————————————————————.

4. You would listen to the tape recording you found buried at Stonehenge, because ———————————————————

————————————————————————.

5. You would need to listen to a jury foreperson read a verdict, because ——

————————————————————————.

6. You would need to listen to your best friend who is crying, because ———

————————————————————————.

7. You would need to listen to someone telling you that a rabid animal is in the house, because ———————————————————

————————————————————————.

8. You would need to listen to your enemy's "farewell speech," because ——

————————————————————————.

9. You would need to listen to the first words spoken by a new professor, because

_____.

10. You would need to listen during a job interview, because _____

_____.

Filtering. Selective listening is a kind of filtering out of sounds you feel are not important to you. Leon Festinger coined the term *cognitive dissonance* to describe the concept that, for example, you do not listen to messages that run counter to or collide with what you deeply believe. This filtering may even cause you to tune out different cues and signals that follow the dissonant messages. Unfortunately, you may often filter on the basis of immediate sensory impressions; if the aesthetics of looks, voice, fluency, articulation, or delivery are unpleasant or boring or offensive, you may not listen.

On the other hand, you may tune in to just those sounds that have strong appeal or that you have conditioned yourself to listen to—you usually hear your own name when it is said anywhere, anytime, in a crowd, over the noise of train wheels, even in the wind. Some people listen to only the "good news," such as optimistic forecasts, praise, flattery. Some thrive on the failure of others, relishing juicy rumors, bad news about other people's troubles, the details of their flaws—anything that might be construed as weakness, as inferior, as below standard.

Listening Contact. You may now have become more alert to nonverbal ways of listening and nonlistening. Hearing contact is *physical*—the sound waves striking the eardrum. Listening contact is totally *personal*—physical, psychological, mental, and psychic contact. The most important contact point for listening, however, is eyeball-to-eyeball. What kind of listening is characterized by:

Your partner's eyes shifting from your eyes to your forehead, back and forth?
Your partner's eyes looking at the floor or ground?
Your partner's eye winking at you?
Your partner's eyes closing tightly and then looking away?

Listening contacts are greatly influenced by the arrangement of people and furniture. The proxemics of small group interaction induces relationships and confirms or solidifies bias. Look at the sketch in Figure 3–1. A and B are both loan officers in a bank. If several other people were invited to attend this luncheon conference, where do you think they would want to sit? Why?

figure 3-1 "Intimate Business Lunch"

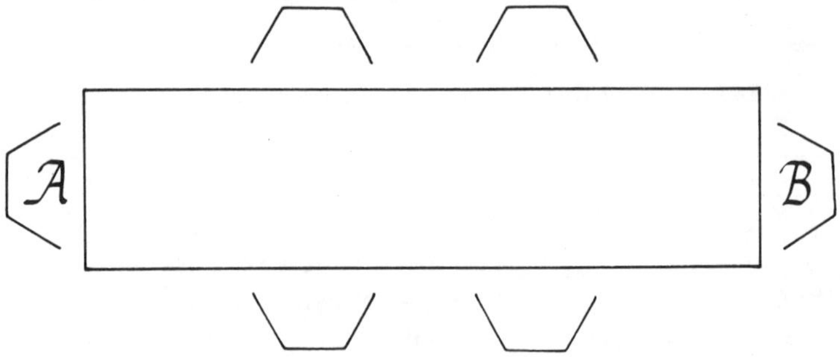

task 2 GET A GOOD SEAT

Using Figure 3–1 as a beginning arrangement, sketch in where you think the following members of this small group would sit:

C is president of the bank
D is president of another bank
E is the majority stockholder of a large foreign bank
F is director of the regional federal reserve bank

Looking at your arrangement, A would have good visual contact with ___, because

_____ .

B could help ___ listen, because _____

_____ .

___ would be better able to filter, because _____

_____ .

The greatest amount of self-disclosure might occur between ___ and ___, because

_____ .

Touching. People who touch during an encounter are saying to their partners, "Now, listen; let me explain; get this important point," or "Let's reduce tension—we're both flesh and blood." Certain types of nudging and guiding touch may indicate taking charge or separating from others. You can probably envision many of the touching gestures condoned and permitted within the various cultural groups you belong to. There is no way to learn accepted codes of touching in your profession, your region, your specific sphere except by observation. High-salaried directors of athletics may slap their students on the buttocks; professors of English may not, but they may lightly slap or pat their students' backs, for example. Verbal intimacies such as "Mr. President, sweetheart!" or "Okay, booby-baby!" are hackneyed attempts at touch-by-talking and seek an intimacy conducive to listening.

Listening is helped by physical arrangement and proximity. The classic circular table deemphasizes rank, lets people sit side-by-side, provides more line-of-sight contact. Circular groupings are also whole-making. They serve as a sort of *mandala*, the ancient Indian design signifying wholeness, integration. Circular seating helps cohesion and to some degree enforces it; and cohesive groups are listeners.

IMPROVING LISTENING SKILLS

Listening is an improvable skill. Many companies invest large sums of money to train personnel in listening. Job interviewers are increasingly alert to evidence of good listening attitudes in their applicants. Think about the suggestions for better listening below.

Use Energy. Communication requires expenditure of energy, and energy burns calories. You may sometimes consider listening as passive, because it is *thwarted* energy—the impulse to shake all over and perhaps snarl and gnaw at words is contained, but it is not locked in. Skin surfaces, eyes, face, hands, feet, body, and handled objects drain off and project this listening energy outward to your partner. In some business transactions, the "best talkers are the best listeners."

Do not Judge. Avoid wasting your energy by using it to judge appearances, sounds, correctness, attractiveness, and all the sensory impressions you receive. *Accept the good and the bad*, but concentrate on helping people feel like successful communicators, while you work to receive useful, enlightening messages. Listening to someone does not mean agreeing with that person. If somehow the speaker gets that impression, you will have plenty of opportunity to set the record straight when your turn comes to talk.

Give Something. Cultivate small signals conveyed by head, hand, and so on, that give listening energy to the talker. Your contribution of feedback is needed and used; it is real. Merely leaning forward is an indication of giving yourself in the form of reducing distance. It does not mean like or dislike, agreement or disagreement, but it communicates a willingness to consider the talker as a person with something to say that you can listen to.

Separate Words and Concepts from the Speaker. Do not blame bad news on the speaker. By the same token, try to keep your feelings about negative information, pessimistic views and opinions, and supportive data apart from your feelings about the person uttering them. The words are not necessarily the person. People often *transfer* reactions or make false associations. The people on television who say bad things are not necessarily bad; nor are the networks that produce the bad words; nor are you and others who listen to the bad words. The prophet of doom in a small group provides an extremely important ingredient for effective interaction—plurality—something to react to, another facet, another variable.

Need to Listen.   Locate your need to listen. If you cannot see any possible satisfaction directly, create one. It is difficult to conceive of information that is not at least indirectly valuable, instructive, enriching in some way. As a last resort, when you are confronted with talk that is painfully useless and beneath your dignity as a professional, assume that active listening is needed by the speaker. Another need attitude that will help your listening is to assume that what is being said will become important to you later in the meeting or at the next session.

Do not Switch the Channel.   Avoid the temptation to "see what is on another channel." If you are having real difficulty concentrating, you may switch to something else—your notes, your fingernails, unopened mail, or the friend sitting next to you. You and your friend may commiserate over the vapidness of the presentation, and even strike up quick exchanges as an escape from the hard work of listening. You probably did this when you were in grade school and while you were growing up with the multiple choices of television viewing, but it will hurt sustained communication in your professional life.

Do not Expect Fireworks.   You may sometimes confuse everyday communicating with the frantic, hyperactive crisis exchanges heard on playgrounds, where everything is taken as a matter of life and death. If you assume your teachers, parents, ministers, and business associates are in the entertainment business for your benefit, and if you listen with this expectation, you are bound to have trouble getting useful information. Likewise, if you filter out everything from an address or summation because you are waiting for verbal fireworks—the spellbinding phrase, the flashing rhetoric—you will miss the simple phrasings of honest, down-to-earth talk.

Fill in Gaps.   Your listening will improve if you make an effort to fill in what speakers leave out. Checking back to the perception test of Task 1 in Chapter 2, you probably remember filling in gaps by labeling the boxes with words to form a structure or sequence of your thoughts. Each of the critique sections presented here requires the critique teams to fill in their observations and responses to complete the enactment experience. No one, obviously, can say all there is to say; all speakers abstract their thoughts and hope they are not leaving out essential points that listeners may fail to fill in for themselves.

Participate. Filling in gaps is a kind of active participation. This "sing along" listening attitude suggests that you try to project or "throw" your thinking into the stream of thoughts coming from the speaker. One way to do this is to find the speaker's thought cadences— the phrase lengths, the indicators of stress and emphasis, and the "throwaway lines" of lesser importance that give everyone a break, a rest.

Involve Your Muscles. Listening is helped by kinetic involvement. Doodling is the most common practice and is sometimes a relief or escape. Note-taking can help listening as long as you do not expect your outline to make sense to anyone but you. Some people feel comfortable and release tension by swinging their feet, tapping their fingers, crossing and uncrossing their knees and legs. Some prefer hand toys—rings, watches, beads, ballpoint pens. These kinetic maneuvers can be harnessed to help you listen, if you match them to the impulses of energy released by the speaker.

Think Ahead. According to Ralph Nichols of the University of Minnesota, you can improve your listening by using your ability to think your own words about four times faster than the average speaker can talk them.[1] Try to anticipate or guess what is coming; use the time you have to make summaries, check the speaker's facts against your facts, and watch for nonverbal indicators that may be the *real* or most important message.

creative listening

Your ability to shift from one speaker to another while fitting in your own talk/self-listening turn is a remarkable achievement. The professional communicator has an advantage in accomplishing this, because the professional outlook juggles all the considerations of the group, the topic, and responsibility, rather than focusing on selfish considerations. You have probably known people who work at getting the "feel" of a house, a game, a boat, etc. Perhaps you have had that happy revelation of knowing something really well that way and have experienced the difficulty of describing your feeling to someone else. Finding the range, getting the rhythm, empathizing, having rapport are all phrases used to express the idea of creative listening. Task 3 examines your sensitivity to sound and your ability to "get the feel of" your situation or environment.

[1]Ralph G. Nichols, "Listening Is a 10-Part Skill," *Nation's Business*, 45, no. 7 (July 1957), 56–60.

task 3 A TEST OF CREATIVE LISTENING

1 Name the Source	2 Name the Sound	3 Name What Comes to Mind
---- Cindy's shoe ---------	----- squeaking -----------	-- oil, gas, shortage ----
-----------------------------	-----------------------------	-----------------------------
+ ----------------------	+ ----------------------	+ ----------------------
1	+ 1 = 2	× 3 = 6

In a 60-second, timed period, list all the sounds you hear, as you hear them, in column 1; simply write the source, such as "Cindy's shoe." In column 2 of your paper, try to write a one-word name for the sound, such as "squeaking." In column 3 write whatever words/ideas/associations come into your mind, such as "oil, gas, shortage."

Scoring: Add up the sources in column 1; add up the names in column 2; add the column 1 total to the column 2 total. Multiply the combined total by the number of word associations. A score above 50 indicates that you can write pretty quickly, you understood the instructions, and you probably can listen creatively when you work at it.

Enactment 6 is also a type of listening test; it gives you a chance to add the listening dimension consciously to your fund of communication experiences.

enactment 6   NEW CITY

Group discussion in this enactment is restrained by two rules: (1) All participants must have done "their homework"; and (2) in order to express an opinion, a speaker must listen closely so that he or she can continue what the previous speaker was saying in midsentence.

Try to assert these professional traits in..............:

enactment 6: NEW CITY

effective use of face and hand
    language
listening skills
cohesiveness

participants

Each group of five to eleven students is given the tasks of selecting its own speaker/leader/manager/gatekeeper, and arranging its own seating and distance patterns.

problem

Each small group is given a specified period of time to meet and demonstrate ways of planning New City. In order to participate, members must listen to their colleagues in such a way that they are able to carry the discussion/demonstration on at any point in the proceedings, incorporating what has already been said as they inject their own planning concepts and demonstration. Each group has access to and full use of ten types of "city structures": (1) utilities, (2) vehicle traffic paths, (3) foot traffic paths, (4) shopping facilities, (5) educational buildings, (6) government buildings, (7) residential areas, (8) recreational areas, (9) industrial areas, and (10) agricultural areas. These model structures can be marked by flags, cans, boxes, books, etc.—anything handy that can help demonstrate planning for New City.

need to talk

Each member should plan beforehand (as "homework") how to place the ten functioning areas in the city and why. Each member lives in what will be New City and has a stake in its arrangement.

critique 6   TROUBLESHOOTING

1. How did the use of muscles for demonstrating help or get in the way of participants?
2. How did use of objects drain off tensions, lessen concern with self, and help listening?
3. How would a stranger walking in get the feeling that this group was professional and cohesive?
4. How did members' plans reveal "where they stood" and "who they were"?
5. If this had been a large group meeting—a large audience with an expert symposium presentation—which plan do you think the large group would have voted for?
6. On the basis of how it "carried the problem," would you hire this group to plan your city? Why or why not?
7. Cite four or five points in the meeting when you had trouble listening. What did you do to overcome your inclination to "switch channels"?

HOW WOULD YOU HAVE IMPROVED IT?

8. What feeling did you get about the audience's listening ability? Did you notice anyone having difficulty listening? What were the symptoms?
9. What language did the audience obviously react to?
10. Name some aspects of professional communicating that helped the audience to listen.

afterthought   LISTENING–RESPONDING

The skill of listening well goes back to the basic idea expressed in the double helix of Chapter 1. All communication implies coming together to share, giving and receiving. When you listen well, you are giving speakers that all-important chance to succeed in asserting themselves. You are providing a clear view of the respect and esteem you are giving, which is so necessary for long-term sharing of viewpoints and needs.

READ FOR YOURSELF

BARKER, LARRY L., Listening Behavior. Englewood Cliffs, N.J.: Prentice-Hall, Inc., 1971.

WEAVER, CARL H., Human Listening: Processes and Behavior. Indianapolis: The Bobbs-Merrill Co., Inc., 1972.

CHAPTER CHART

Listening skills
Avoid filtering
Make strong physical contact through use of space—get close
Avoid prior judgment
Give something—feedback
Avoid confusing words and concepts with the speaker
Locate your need to listen
Avoid switching channels
Do not expect fireworks
Key idea: Actively participate and think ahead

chapter 4

BARRIERS TO COMMUNICATING EFFECTIVELY

problem-THROW FORWARD   problem-THROW FORWARD
problem-THROW FORWARD

A great deal of your work in a business or a profession will be communicating, and much of what you will send and receive will center around the often-used and often-misunderstood term *problem*. Communication problems have been described variously in this text as barriers, obstacles, or lacks of some kind. You probably recognize that problems are like words; they are anything you say they are. A family that does not consider itself poor may not admit or recognize poverty to be a problem. On the other hand the wealthy businessperson may need to seek a little poverty through philanthropy or tax-exempt projects to enhance his or her overall income potential. The "poverty problem" for one may not be a problem for somebody else.

This chapter explores ways of approaching problems and begins to look at the way professional groups identify, examine, and express methods of creative problem-solving. You will be asked to examine for the first time the whole idea of audiences—where they come from and why they assemble to hear a problem discussed. Let us start with the old problem of language.

The languages you must use in business are treacherous; one of the basic difficulties facing group work is the precise determination of problems the group thinks it has and the words to convey their description. A problem that brings individuals together might be defined as a felt imbalance or disequilibrium; a state or condition where something is "thrown forward," creating an imbalance. Common, single-word problems are frequently used, because they have the built-in denotation of disequilibrium; these include the use of certain prefixes such as . . .

A-	Dis-	In-	Mis-
*a*morphous	*dis*harmony	*in*humanity	*mis*apprehension
*a*morality	*dis*unity	*in*justice	*mis*management
*a*sexuality	*dis*enfranchisement	*in*tolerance	*mis*judgment
*a*sociality	*dis*content	*in*competence	*mis*trust

Other prefixes of this type are: *anti-*, *non-*, *over-*, *un-*, and *under-*. As starting points for consideration of problems, these expressions of imbalance suggest the first barrier to effective group communication—the problem of language.

LANGUAGE BARRIERS

definitions

In order to have something to talk about in business meetings, forums, and other large group exchanges, "house rules" for linguistic or word codes must be uniform and uniformly used. *Sociolinguistic theories of word usage, such as that offered by Dell Hymes and Basil Bernstein's work with restricted and elaborated codes, give the businessperson one usable guide: "When in Rome, . . ."* This view simply means that you talk and define your words to suit the receiver and the occasion. Your vocabulary, sentence structure, amount of description and elaboration, terminology, phrasing, and word length will differ with the social occasion or transaction. How would you say "I'm tired" when speaking to the following persons in the following contexts:

One of your professors, following an important examination?
Your supervisor, after you have completed his or her work?
A 90-year-old whose hearing cannot detect *t*s or *d*s?

Some guidelines for defining words are:

1. A definition should apply to all situations, all people, all times that are included in the term defined. What is a *nice* person? What was a *nice* person ten years ago? What was a *nice* raise ten years ago? What is a *nice* raise for a career journalist? What is a *nice* raise for a career short-order cook?
2. A definition leaves out situations, times, and people that you are not including in the term. What does your family, your area of town, or your subculture

consider *nice* people to be? What is a *nice* raise for a career short-order cook who owns a fast-food service in Tanzania?

3. A definition must not include the word you are trying to define. Can you define a *nice* person as "someone who is nice"? Can you define a "nice" raise as "an increase in pay that is really nice"?

4. A definition must not connote. What are the connotations of "nice guy," "nice girl," "nice setup," "nice letter"? Connotations are determined by the way you perceive the word in its context on the occasion of use. Large, diversified groups multiply the likelihood that current and outmoded connotations will distort your intended meanings.

5. A definition should be as simple as possible.

task 1   DEFINING "NICE" WORDS

Write a brief definition that fits the five guidelines above for these terms:

1. An unfair grader _____

_____.

2. An unresponsive employer _____

_____.

3. An unjust law _____

_____.

4. A chronic loser _____

_____.

5. Group friction _____

_____.

6. Self-serving _____

_____.

7. Professionalism _____

_____.

8. Work _____

_____.

Definitions of terms are also constructed through less rigid application of formal rules. A frequently used rule of thumb is to define something by explaining what it is not. This method eliminates charac teristics or factors until a *residue* is left. Sometimes called the *process of elimination*, it is also used to narrow choices and options. This is somewhat like going through all the keys on a key ring until you find the one that unlocks the door. Another technique for defining terms is to demonstrate how they work, how they are experienced or lived through; this is sometimes referred to as an *operational definition*.

Words symbolize things and have histories of use. Terms also become associated with people, so that you sometimes can clarify by saying: "in the executive sense," "in the Kantian sense," "in the Aristotelian sense," "in the Keynesian sense," etc. Quoting a term as it is used by an authority tends to extend that authority to your definition.

Group work, as you know, is an evolutionary process. Because of this, the terms and concepts employed and discussed in groups are susceptible to change, refinement, and abandonment. Words, things, people that do not work out tend to be thrown out, or changed.

syntax

Dealing with words *as words* is difficult. The sequencing of words into groups is very, very difficult. Pioneer linguist Benjamin Lee Whorf believes that the language structure, rules of grammar, and sequencing force people to think like their language. You may have known persons whose thinking is molded by some artificial organizing system—computer specialists who organize much of their thinking in terms of binary, on-off, or digital categories; game-oriented minds who speak of winning, piling up points, going one-on-one; other people whose jobs enforce a vocabulary and way of thinking that they perhaps do not think about much.

Whorf's theory was that much of the language is made up of nouns and verbs, while in real life experiences happen in a *molar* way—the job, the raise, the nice boss, the elation are all part of an ongoing experience. Thus, when you try to relate that experience by word language alone, it disintegrates into somebody doing something and then something else happening and then your telling about it. In this way your mode of expression controls how you see things, just as your occupation might distort your world view into numbers, points, sales, and so on. Linguists such as Noam Chomsky assume that people somehow intuit a "deep structure" in a language through the exercise of a relatively small number of learned rules. You grasp the logic of these rules and generate significance from the endless combinations of sentences you encounter.

The dangers of applying the connections that exist between language and thought directly affect group work and group audiences and how they think.

THINKING AND REASONING BARRIERS

linear/mosaic thinking

Chapter 2 examined a few of the ways you think and perceive, and you have participated in tasks and enactments that revealed behaviors that affect how you communicate in groups. Figure 4–1 shows two different "routes" you might take to arrive at judgments. In linear thought you pass from one judgment to its neighbor following a single directional *line*. In mosaic thinking you pass from one judgment to another by *jumping over* "neighboring" thoughts and concepts.

Linear thinking means going from square one to square two. It implies a steady, methodical buildup of proved "knowns," facts that you test and retest, but that always seem to yield the same answers. Mosaic thought is *plasmic*—it builds up a big picture of a condition or concept

figure 4-1   Linear/Mosaic Thinking

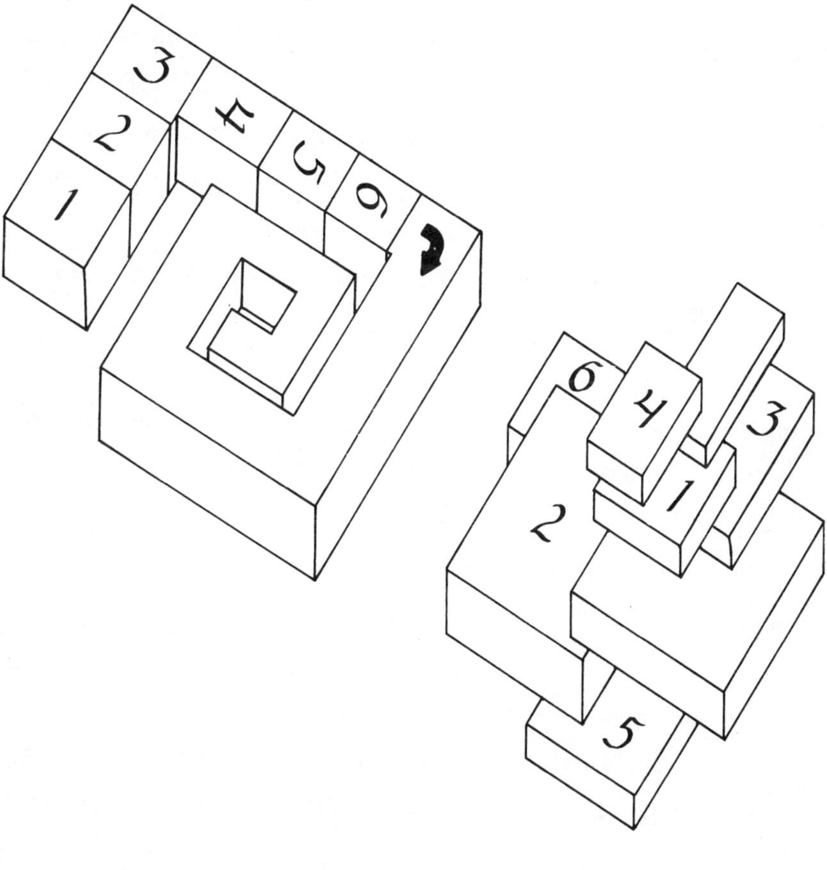

in a helter-skelter fashion, several squares at a time. Like a film, mosaic thought passes from one frame to the next—linearly—but with such speed that the directional impression is whole and instantaneous. When you "read" a face, you make an instant judgment. You seldom analyze all the muscle sets to form the conclusion that this is a happy or sad face.

task 2   LINEAR OR MOSAIC?

Think about these procedures as demanding linear and/or mosaic thought patterns. Which is the *better* way to make a judgment or complete the activity?

1. A group of 50 trainees is to be given a final training talk before assignment. The talk is given 50 times, once to each trainee. This is mosaic/linear thinking and is/is not the better procedure, because _____

_____.

2. The high school gym is filled to capacity with students who have come to hear why the school is eliminating its athletic program. The moderator recognizes members of the audience with hands raised for questions, calling on students starting with those seated at the end of the front row, then looking at those seated all around the bleachers, and next starting with the second row, then the third row, etc. This mosaic/linear mode is the better/worse method,

because _____

_____.

3. Union Bank and Trust Company wants to create a trademark/slogan as part of its drive to increase its accounts. Plan A is to use: "It makes more sense." Plan B is to give a "clearer pronoun reference," and a more "complete statement": "Union Bank and Trust makes more sense for everybody." Plan ___ is mosaic/linear and the better procedure, because _____

_____.

4. Voting precincts are reporting their vote counts. The national campaign headquarters plans to call each registrar of voters for counts beginning with Aardvark, Alabama, and proceeding through the alphabet. This mosaic/linear

procedure is a good/poor one, since _____

_____.

5. The agenda of a large group meeting calls for (1) opening remarks and welcome by Head, Cardiovascular Institute, (2) reading of minutes, (3) discussion of old business, and (4) new business, which includes a demonstration of a heart transplant. The heart recipient's condition is deteriorating; the patient's life signs are marginal. It is better for the agenda-keeper to think mosaically/ linearly, because _____

_____.

6. An extraterrestrial "visitor" appears while a region is suffering its worst drought on record. Public sentiment favoring quick, hostile action is growing. Linear/ mosaic thinking is necessary, because _____

_____.

7. A sudden vacancy occurs in a foreperson's position at a plant. According to the union, the three persons next in line by seniority are first an alcoholic, second a person who suffers dizzy spells, and third an MIT graduate in engineering. Linear/mosaic thinking will result in the best choice, because _____

_____.

deductive/inductive reasoning

When you deduce a judgment or conclusion in your thinking, you begin with one or more assumptions—propositions you take to be true and unchanging. As already indicated, the problem-solving group action assumes certain truths: (1) that there really is a problem (an imbalance or state of disequilibrium), (2) that it can be corrected, (3) that it should be corrected, and (4) that correcting it is worth any problems derived from correcting it. From these basic assumptions a group adopts a specific mode of ascertaining more truths or facts—deduction.

The inductive approach starts from scratch; it assumes nothing, starting with a clean slate—a tabula rasa. Figure 4–2 conveys the flow or direction of thinking (from left to right) in using deductive and inductive reasoning. The grouping on the left shows the steps in reasoning progressing from broad, general conclusions toward judgment of a

figure 4-2 Deductive/Inductive Reasoning

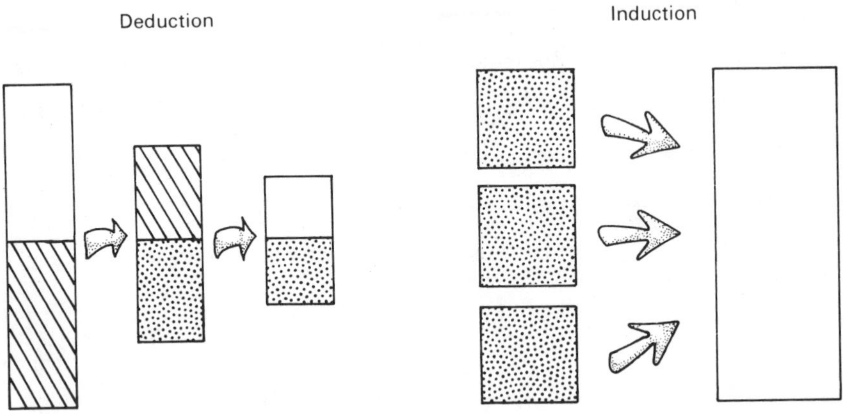

Deduction   Induction

specific case. This is deductive reasoning. The grouping on the right shows the steps in reasoning progressing from several specifics to a general conclusion. This is inductive reasoning.

Follow the train of deduction in the example of a corporate decision depicted in Figure 4–3. Can you pick out trouble spots in this judgment that might hurt communication between employees and management? Figure 4–4 depicts the inductive approach of collecting and examining specific data first, slowly expanding your judgments from the small and specific to the larger and general. What are the flaws in judging and making decisions from one employee's viewpoint and based on one person's judgment?

causality

"The stock market fell because of lack of faith"; "I was hired because I am good looking"; "We lost the game because of the weather." Each of these three statements claims specific causes for an event. Large groups are concerned with ways of proving cause and of estimating likelihood, but certain house rules—an early climate of objectivity—can help disarm the personal motives and emotionalizing tendencies, which you have read about and enacted. What rules exist for testing claimed causes of imbalance?

figure 4-3 Deductive Thinking

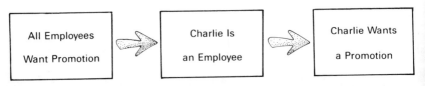

| All Employees Want Promotion | Charlie Is an Employee | Charlie Wants a Promotion |

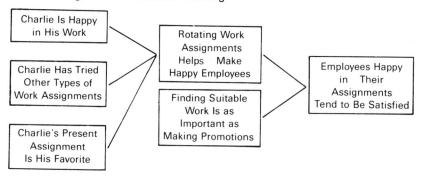

figure 4-4   Inductive Thinking

1. The *a priori* method of reasoning suggests that causes are centered in the way things were before the imbalance occurred. An a priori attitude toward imbalance holds that people start out a certain way, that the forces of nature and the universe exist prior to our experience with them.
2. *A posteriori* means demonstrating cause by assessing and guessing about effects after they appear.
3. *Empiricism* means living through an experience and noting how factors interact, so that you can reproduce the same conditions and obtain the same effect, if you want to test it.
4. *Method of agreement* is one test for determining the likelihood of causes and effects. If "lack of faith" has been common to a large number of stock market declines, then it is a good bet that lack of faith is either one of the causes or one of the effects. If lack of faith is not common to many examples, then that condition is probably an "innocent bystander"—neither a cause nor an effect, merely a component of a particular stock market drop.
5. *Method of difference* is a test to see if any single element is necessary for a condition to exist. If you take that element away and any change occurs, you know that the element is contributing to your original problem. Your friend who gets jobs through his or her "good looks," could, through use of makeup, eliminate the good looks to test whether jobs continue to be offered. Perhaps he or she would be hired regardless of appearances. If so, looks were not the cause.
6. *Method of instrumentality* is a test to see if change in one factor changes other factors. If wet weather changes the style of play in a game and has an effect on team attitude, then weather does, indeed, play an important cause or effect role in winning or losing a game.

syllogistic reasoning

A syllogism is a three-part test of a concluding judgment and is a form of deductive reasoning. Parts 1 and 2 are called premises and declare two statements to be true; part 3 is the conclusion. Look at the flow of deduction in Figure 4–5. Does it make sense? A little. Will such syllogistic thinking bring your business problems back into balance?

figure 4-5   Categorical Syllogism

> First Premise: All Money Is Valuable
>
> Second Premise: Dollar Bills Are Money
>
> Conclusion: All Dollar Bills Are Valuable

Can every term be defined so that members of a large group can agree on its meaning?

Another kind of syllogism hypothesizes or speculates about the reliability and sense of your conclusions; Figures 4–6, 4–7, and 4–8 contain hypothetical syllogisms. Each of the examples beginning with Charlie contain errors or fallacies of judgment, as you probably detected. *Fallacies* are those nearly true bits of information that people sometimes

figure 4-6   Hypothetical Syllogism

> If Dollar Bills Are Money, They Are Valuable
>
> Dollar Bills Are Money
>
> Therefore, Dollar Bills Are Valuable

figure 4-7   Either/Or Syllogism

> Charlie Is Either Happy or Unhappy
>
> Charlie Is Happy
>
> Therefore, Charlie Is not Unhappy

figure 4-8   The *Be* or *Not Be* Syllogism

> An Employee Cannot Be Happy and Unhappy at the Same Time
>
> Charlie Is Happy
>
> Therefore, Charlie Is not Unhappy

accept and pass along as evidence or proof of things. *Facts* are accurate measurements of predictability or condition; but even facts are limited to what you know about the basic nature of things. In preparation for Enactment 7, anticipate the problems that can be generated in discussing facts when the following fallacies are "thrown forward"—intentionally or not—into the group problem-solving proceeding.

The Fallacy of Misplaced Concreteness. Misplaced concreteness is the tendency to speak of faith, happiness, or "niceness" as if these words were really objects all people could sense, measure, and categorize in the same way. There seems to be a convenience in exchanging symbolic expressions such as *profit, good will,* or *economy* as if everybody knew what the speaker were talking about. This fallacy holds true for the use of language itself; the word is not the thing in itself; the picture is not the event in itself; the contract is not the transaction in itself; the money is not the value in itself.

The Pathetic Fallacy. Large groups—audience and participants—may sometimes project human motives, qualities, and characteristics into settings and problems that are not human. Check the human traits given to nonhuman objects in these phrases:

that stupid computer
that's a sexy car
that machine hates me
the weather is fickle
paperwork follows me everywhere
runaway inflation

The Fallacy of Authority. The character and expertness of someone will not alone make his or her testimony accurate and reliable. The biases and vested interests of expert authorities frequently make their statements dubious forms of support. You must take care to separate an individual's area of competence from areas of acquaintance. Everyone has opinions on most things, and problems call for authoritative opinion on matters within the authority's specialty.

The Fallacy of Numbers. The ability to quote statistics is impressive evidence of a speaker's ability to count. To be evidence of more than that, rigid comparison data, rigorously qualified, must be also introduced. The most scrupulously controlled studies and questionnaire tests provide information that can decay and become invalid even as it is being gathered. This is especially true of samples involving human response; meaning, again, is the elusive factor and must be carefully weighed as proof of a claim.

The Fallacy of Generalization. General, all-inclusive pronouncements distort objective appraisals and hinder consideration of the multiple causes of occurrences. "All," "every," "always," and most superlatives sound convincing and are compelling in their weight, but they tend to cancel out the balance sought in making important judgments. "Jumping to conclusions" and "going off half-cocked" are popular expressions that warn against hasty generalization.

The Fallacy of Sampling.   Another type of error-producing generalization is the attempt to assess and judge the entire quantity by sampling just a small part. This is also referred to as *pars pro toto*—a part for the whole. Professionals would never judge an organization by the demeanor of its main receptionist, whether their experience with that employee was good or bad. They would want a greater sample—more evidence of different types, at different times, etc. "Charlie" is just one of many employees; his situation can hardly reflect the situations of all employees and is certainly not valid evidence for reaching conclusions about past employees, employees' past experiences, or present employees' future prospects.

The Fallacy of Post Hoc.   The *post hoc* imbalance in thinking is sort of like the old idea of imitation. If you do something that imitates the effect you want, you will make it happen. *Post hoc, ergo propter hoc* means "after this, therefore because of this." The error is in attributing false causes to effects. Some people blame elected officials for everything that happens after their election; others blame everything on the weather. A new manager cannot be held accountable for all conditions that seem to follow his or her appointment.

The Fallacy of Card-Stacking.   Participation in large group discussions and business proceedings may occasionally make you feel that the "deck has been stacked" in favor of a certain point of view. Certainly all types of meetings require direction and restraint, but this must be publicly and openly explained so that a sense of "closure"—of being excluded—does not develop among participants. Linear procedure, as noted above, narrows the content and limits the direction of idea flows; applied unreasonably, linear thinking stacks the cards.

The Fallacy of Ad Hominem.   The discussion on listening in Chapter 3 noted that your priorities sometimes get confused and your listening curtailed if you devote your attention to the voice, the appearance, or the theatrics of the speaker. Inefficient listening may occur, if you judge the person rather than the words. *Ad hominem* thinking focuses too much on the person. Arguments and assertions that attack a person's frailty, personality, or physical characteristics have little or nothing to do with problems and their causes. You know the difficulties of ascertaining the "real" self beneath the images and roles people play; time wasted discussing personalities takes away from the time you have to get to the basic questions.

The Fallacy of Vox Populi. *Vox populi, vox dei*—the voice of the people is the voice of God—underlies many claims to "reasonable" problem-solving. This fallacy holds that the will of the people, the overwhelming majority, must somehow be right, because it is testimony to the will of God, or the nature of things, of the universe. This maxim leads to many different excesses and errors as justifications for solving imbalances: justifying questionable products because of the large market for them; reshaping of the environment because of a "national priority," or because it is the lesser of two evils; complying with the demands of our most primitive and basic needs, because they are common to all and therefore "must be okay."

The Fallacy of Transfer. Transferring is inherent to many types of fallacious thinking. The basic idea of transference is applying a set of characteristics from one situation to a second situation without thinking clearly about whether they belong or fit those circumstances. Sometimes the use of fallacious reasoning and argument is done in the hope that a quality will be transferred to you, to your audience, or to the issues at hand. In certain circumstances you hope, for example, that signs and symbols will have a sympathetic effect or be persuasive. You may remember incidents when people were assumed to be innocent because they associated with people known to be innocent; where red, white, and blue garbage cans transferred the idea of patriotism to the idea of refuse collecting; or where the VIP label was used to give glamour to a meeting or a gathering.

The Fallacy of Reducing to an Absurdity. Any really good idea, plan, suggestion, or person can be made to look ridiculous. The trick is merely to extend some aspect to its furthest, most extreme *possibility*. Anything is possible, but fewer things are likely. To argue against a plan because it is ridiculous if carried to extremes is fallacious. Carried to its own extreme, this argument would lead you to do nothing, because doing nothing cannot possibly offend or hurt anyone. If a wage contract calling for a raise is considered, the easiest opposing argument might be to assert that "soon, the employees will be making more than management is." Absurdities often take this "road to ruin" line of thought by extending a possibility and palming it off as likelihood.

The Fallacy of "One More Won't Hurt." The proverbial "straw that broke the camel's back" exemplifies this commonly heard fallacy. Variations of this line of thinking include: "You might as well go all the way" and "there's always room for one more," or "the more the merrier." As a problem-solving accommodation, the "one more" fallacy is sometimes an attempt to placate everybody and may have little or nothing to do with the real problem. In another sense this fallacy is like "going to the well once too often"—applying solutions and answers that worked before but are not going to work this time, because of the sophistication of the present problem or people involved.

The Fallacy of the Bandwagon. The error of bandwagon thinking is that very old fear of being left behind, of being excluded or closed off from the mainstream. "Everyone does it" can be a compelling argument for adopting a policy or solution to a problem; it carries the strong pull of being up-to-date, fashionable, in the forefront, and abreast of the competition. Much of business transacting is in reaction to others. Investment is in part a "reactionary" business, where instant information is mandatory. Hints of future decision-making and "where the market is going" determine the likelihood of risk variables. The tendency to imitate or judge on the basis of how an idea "plays in Peoria" should be balanced by its applicability to your own specific circumstances.

task 3 "OH, COME ON, BE REASONABLE"

Each of the following statements is heard in meetings, conferences, and situations where many people come together to answer questions and solve problems. List three good reasons why the statement might create a climate of poor thinking and unsound judgment:

A. "Why shouldn't we ignore it? That's always worked before."

1. _____

2. _____

3. _____

B. "People are interested in economy not quality."

1. _____

2. _____

3. _____

C. "Has he ever had an idea that worked?"

1. _____

2. _____

3. _____

D. "We don't want it good, we want it tomorrow."

1. _____

2. _____

3. _____

E. "You're either part of the problem or part of the solution."

   1. _____

   2. _____

   3. _____

F. "Just whose side are you on?"

   1. _____

   2. _____

   3. _____

G. "They're all alike: give them an inch and they'll take a mile."

   1. _____

   2. _____

   3. _____

H. "You can't have your cake and eat it, too."

   1. _____

   2. _____

   3. _____

I. "They're all counting on us to solve their problem."

   1. _____

   2. _____

   3. _____

enactment 7   ONE HUNDRED CENTS

This enactment, like Enactment 3, is a _reversed_ exercise, in which participants attempt the opposite of sound word use, clear definition, and reasonable assertion and proof. The intent is to try to create imbalance and disequilibrium, to "break the rules" in order to find out how necessary they are.

Can you "throw forward" these types of thinking problems in

poor definitions
connotative words
inappropriate linear/mosaic
    thinking
questionable deductions/
    inductions
causal fallacies
descriptive fallacies

**enactment 7: ONE HUNDRED
CENTS**

participants

A moderator is selected to enforce rules of procedure and order. The class is divided into four groups: (1) students of the college, (2) parents of students in the college, (3) alumni of the college, and (4) administration/faculty members of the college.

problem

A surcharge of "one hundred cents" has been voted into law by the state legislature and will be added to all fees charged by the college—everything except bookstore and student union purchases. The hundred cents is to be used and divided at the discretion of the college administration, and this large group "hearing" has been called by the administration to seek suggestions for a balanced method of determining a balanced division of the new income. All four groups are invited to the hearing.

need to talk

Each group feels it is entitled to a certain share of the one hundred cents and believes that a particular type of agency, committee, board, etc., will represent its interests best. The moderator's task is to order the flow of comment and to ensure some degree of reasonable thinking. This person may summarize, clarify, or ask for clarification of any statement made by a member of a group.

time/locale

The meeting takes place in a large auditorium with lots of space. Rules of procedure, for recess, and for adjournment are determined by the moderator.

critique 7   TROUBLESHOOTING

1. Did you feel that everyone had a chance
    to speak his or her piece?
2. Why would it be better to "hear" each

interest group separately and away from other groups?

3. Why not "hear" each interested person in private?
4. What commonalities were apparent between different interest groups?
5. Was each group "represented" in proportion to its influence in school affairs? In proportion to how much it spends on the school? In proportion to its "social status"?
6. Did any "happy mistakes" emerge from the discussion—statements that unintentionally might be very valuable as leads to solving the problem?
7. Was there a balance of "satisfaction" among the various groups?
8. Did explaining the house rules help the efficient flow of the hearing?
9. Which of the groups had done its homework best?
10. What effect did *distances*—proxemics— have on listening?
11. Did the four groups achieve a degree of cohesion? If so, how?
12. What problems would you consider essential for the next phase in solving this problem? What would you place on the next agenda?

WHAT MIGHT BE DONE TO IMPROVE IT?

OVERCOMING PROCEDURAL BARRIERS

Anticipation and readiness make a lot of ventures look easy; Hamlet's advice, "readiness is all," sums up a monumental secret of success. The previous sections have progressively aimed at this *readiness* axiom as an overall governing factor in communicating well in professional transactions. To work with groups, however, you must devote your attention to readying others as well as yourself. Several guidelines are offered here to help groups carry out their tasks in a professional way with professional results.

advertise meetings

Take pains to inform designated members or interested observers about what the meeting is for, what topics they should anticipate discussing, when and between what times it will be held, where it will be held, and who is sponsoring, ordering, or designating the assembly to meet. Unless it is common knowledge, describe the basic activity or task method to be used (negotiating, problem-solving, data-gathering, round-table discussion, orientation, crisis meeting, conference, etc.).

plan the environment

Anticipate the size of the group and the audience, if there is to be one. Locate and arrange seating that will be most conducive to interaction and decentralization of authority. Find ways to introduce the members of a large audience to each other; use name cards, badges, or place names, particularly if there is a chance of initial embarrassment or isolation—a feeling of exclusion. Repeated messages of welcome by word and sign help set the tone for productive disclosure and collective discussion and problem-solving.

Select several good methods of visual reinforcement, such as chalkboards, oversize flow sheets, or sketchpads. Individual tools will also indicate your thoughtful anticipation of professional exchange and may enhance the idea that this meeting is important. Aids that are supplied and ready can be a meaningful nonverbal clue that the competence factor is operating and is expected from members.

plan the format

Formats are systems of exchange that tell people: "Who's turn is it to talk?" "What kind of things can I say?" "How can I participate?" Symposiums, for example, offer a format of (1) expert testimony and expression of views, (2) an efficient and timed method of restricting the direction of talk, and (3) the opportunity for large numbers of people to see and hear and to ask questions and get answers.

Various types of closed meetings can accommodate invited guest participants, experts, or others considered necessary to enhance the discussion, reporting, or problem-solving. Special events may be structured into a group format, such as guest speakers, expert demonstrations, or professional presentations of slide, tape, videotape, film, over-head, or sketched reporting, use of models, mockups, schematic diagrams, or reenactments, and exhibits of many different types.

plan for the flow of ideas

Anticipate possible confusion among members about the purpose and scope of the meeting. A published and predistributed agenda or list of topics is a common method to allay this confusion. If your meeting is the second, third, or other follow-up in a sequence of meetings, try to bring everyone up to date before it begins. Use of both written and spoken summaries helps to start all participants off together and may avoid an immediate disadvantage to some that might create an

imbalance in the proceedings. This briefing may be an absolute necessity if some participants have missed a previous session or are new-
comers to the business of the committee.

Anticipate possible linear/mosaic patterns in order to help
everyone have an opportunity to speak. Some studies, notably those by
Thomas Schiedel and Laura Crowell,[1] indicate that, even though overall
discussion patterns tend to follow a linear pattern, each phase of discussion contains periods in which members "tread water." A timely question by the chairperson, such as "Well, let's see what we've got," will
help participants get their bearings. This type of confirming and verifying talk is a necessary pause, and if it is given indulgence it can help
decentralize authority and contribute to a free exchange.

Review the types of questions likely to be asked and the types
of statements that may be made. *Questions of fact* are provable, demonstrable. *A statement of value* is something that is true for the individual
who said it but not necessarily for anyone else. Value is a private
characteristic and cannot be assumed to be the same for everyone.
Statements of opinion are sometimes presented as fact, in which case the
omission may have to be publicly noted. Anticipate vocabulary difficulties; check the level of abstraction and special terminology before the
meeting and be prepared to clarify or ask for clarification or for a simpler
presentation.

Focus on information-sharing rather than judgment-making;
try to emphasize the exact description and extent of the imbalance rather
than what to do about it. The young Turk or firebrand (young or old) may
run away with the meeting by wrapping it up with a neat solution to
everyone's problem before an exchange can happen. This type of jumping to a conclusion might be contagious; it requires sensitive guidance
and leadership from each member to restore balance to the discussion.

plan for creative problem-solving

Meetings that arrive at the "proposal point"—the place where
action is to be considered—might benefit from two methods of what can
be called "creative problem-solving."

Brainstorming. Free-flowing, unrestricted, and unchecked
disgorging of ideas can be useful at any juncture of exchange and is
characterized by five rules.

1. All forms of criticism are suspended and dispensed with.
2. All forms of free-association, fantasy, and far-out notions are encouraged.

---

[1]Thomas M. Schiedel and Laura Crowell, "Idea Development in Small Groups," *Quarterly
Journal of Speech*, 50, no. 2 (April 1964), 140–45.

3. The goal is to get as many different possibilities stated as possible.
4. Everything must be recorded accurately.
5. Participants are urged to build on one another's schemes.

Brainstorming is one form of tapping unconscious activity that normally is held in check or pushed down and contained.

As developed and used by Alex F. Osborn, brainstorming was applied to problems in advertising, where a constant supply of fresh viewpoints is needed. The group attitude encouraged in this technique is that there is no such thing as a bad idea. In practice this nonjudgmental rule has the advantage of allowing expression to guide itself. Your experiences with brainstorming might reveal the grip that free association can exert on proceedings; it is rather like the frenzy of certain mob psychologies or the abandoned play of certain games and competitions.

Several adaptations may prove useful for brainstorming sessions. You might try (1) asking questions to keep the momentum and rhythm alive; (2) shifting categories of ideas and opinions from "What good things can you think of?" to "What bad things can you think of?" and then to "What could possibly happen if. . .?" (3) rotating the leader role or the interpreter function, so that a different idea "attack" is used.

Synectics. The synectic approach to creative problem-solving also tries to stir up participants' memory banks and to use the limitless combinations of words and word images their minds are capable of producing. The basic component in the direction of this type of discussion is the *analogy*—a comparison between two unlike objects, people, places, conditions, etc. Synectic flow charts, as described by George M. Prince,[2] use the following steps:

1. *Problem as given* (PAG): a description of existing or known quantities and relationships.
2. *Analysis and explanation:* an expert's statement of the problem.
3. *Purge:* a period for voicing immediate suggestions for a solution—getting your ideas off your chest.
4. *Problem as understood* (PAU): a period for you to write out a version of the problem as you understand it and explain your own "wishes"—no matter how farfetched—for its solution.
5. *Three kinds of analogy:*
   a. comparative or parallel characteristics, e.g., "friction between customer and employee is like friction between student and teacher"
   b. personal analogy, such as "If I were that person . . ."

[2]George M. Prince. "The Operational Mechanism of Synectics," *Journal of Creative Behavior*, 2, no. 1 (winter 1967), 1–13.

c. poetic or symbolic analogy—the use of key *connotative* words to form highly descriptive labels, called *book titles.*

6. *Examination:* a collective look at a promising bit of phrasing that seems to capture the imbalances within the problem being studied. During this focusing on a characteristic, an attempt is made to "force fit" the analogy into an area of the overall problem itself.

What is produced through synectics? The overall problem is examined from many angles—inside and out. It is stretched in every direction, so that hidden relationships and possibilities become visible. Figuratively, creative problem-solving forces you to "stand on your head," to see things from impossible angles in the hope that your fresh orientation may produce a fresh viewpoint or an important insight into people and their problems.

task 4 PEOPLE ARE LIKE RECEIPTS

Task 4 is an exercise in analogic thinking, the kind described in creative problem-solving. The object is to get your analogy to fit an idea that seems to be different from it but actually contains hidden parallels. Unveiling these parallels is useful in obtaining a fresh view and will help you get out of your set ways—the same old rut. The first item is completed as an example.

1. People are like receipts, because *they record transactions and exchanges*

   with others—noting time, place, amounts of "self-disclosure," so that

   communication experiences can be "stored" and "filed" away for future

   comparison and use.

2. My speech class is like swimming, because ＿＿＿＿＿＿＿＿＿

   ＿＿＿＿＿＿＿＿＿＿＿＿＿＿＿＿＿＿＿＿＿＿＿＿ .

3. Investing capital is like choosing a major, because ＿＿＿＿＿＿＿

   ＿＿＿＿＿＿＿＿＿＿＿＿＿＿＿＿＿＿＿＿＿＿＿＿

   ＿＿＿＿＿＿＿＿＿＿＿＿＿＿＿＿＿＿＿＿＿＿＿＿ .

4. Professionalism is like a rope trick, because ＿＿＿＿＿＿＿＿

   ＿＿＿＿＿＿＿＿＿＿＿＿＿＿＿＿＿＿＿＿＿＿＿＿ .

5. Large groups are like television commercials, because ＿＿＿＿＿

   ＿＿＿＿＿＿＿＿＿＿＿＿＿＿＿＿＿＿＿＿＿＿＿＿

   ＿＿＿＿＿＿＿＿＿＿＿＿＿＿＿＿＿＿＿＿＿＿ .

6. A communication invitation is like solar energy, because _____

_____

_____.

7. Your competence factor is like successful surgery, because _____

_____

_____.

8. The problem of interface is like the problem of running out of time, because

_____.

9. *Ad hominem* statements are like ashes, because _____

_____.

10. Listening is like having the flu, because _____

_____.

plan for follow-up

Nothing ends at the end of the meeting except the collective presence of the participants. Anticipation of "what to do, now" after the group is satisfied with carrying out its task is a "transitional" or bridging prerequisite. A plan for following up the exchanges *connects* group business with the next step in using what has been achieved—whether the group is to delay, continue research, advise somebody, recommend something, adopt a policy or course of action, or merely report.

Gerald M. Phillips's PERT method (program evaluation and review technique) of follow-up suggests placing each task to be done in a system or schedule of completion.[3] This is similar to the programmed countdown system used in complex sequences of tasks and checks. PERT is an outlined approach that coordinates quantities in space and time and is suited to statistical or logistical problems. The product of large group discussions takes a variety of forms and depends on the group's authority and goal. If the product is to be a report, it may be written by the leader or by a designated person or subcommittee, which then forwards copies to the leader. The leader in turn transmits the report to the sponsoring authority, makes it public, or both. Groups may have the authority to vote that a report be transmitted in a special way—by telex, telegram, position papers, white papers, a press conference, or media releases.

Steps should be taken to *evaluate* the workings of the group

[3]Gerald M. Phillips, "PERT as a Logical Adjunct to the Discussion Process," *Journal of Communication*, 15, no. 2 (June 1965), 89–99.

and to make a critique plan. Evaluating large audience response is our next topic and is part of the follow-up planning. A device such as the troubleshooting critiques used here or the PMR (a postmeeting evaluation sheet) may help assess the group techniques used and the degree of satisfaction enjoyed by participants. Enactment 8 tests the critique method of grading students.

enactment 8   SYN-STORMING

This enactment evaluates a currently used assessment or critique process, such as (1) grading evaluations, (2) taxation evaluations (tax assessment methods), (3) ecological evaluations, or (4) hiring–firing evaluations. Combinations of problem-solving methods should be tried and themselves evaluated in this evaluation of an evaluation.

Can these problem-solving patterns help you in...........
:   :
:   **enactment 8: SYN-STORMING**
:   synectics
brainstorming
planned environment
planned format
planned flow of ideas
planned follow-up

participants

Divide the class in half and then subdivide to form:

Two critique or observer teams.
Two groups who will assess two different evaluation areas.
Two panels of "experts," each with three to seven persons.
One moderator or leader for each group.
Two audience groups (each half of the class alternates as an audience for the other group).

problem

Each group wants to find out how a professional task force evaluates conditions. Each group wants to discuss how valid professional testing is and how it might be improved. Ideas for improvement might be discussed through brainstorming and/or synectics.

need to talk

Everyone knows a little about evaluating. You usually can find ways of checking on how things are working and how you are doing. Sometimes your thinking gets turned around when you decide to evaluate how you evaluate, how you have been checking your own standards of measurement. The panels of experts will briefly respond to questions about how evaluations are made and why certain techniques are used. The audience may submit questions to the panel and then audit or take part in the group proceedings.

critique 8   TROUBLESHOOTING

1. Describe what you think is the best way of transmitting the product of each group discussion.
2. Cite four unusual ideas or insights that came out of the creative problem-solving phase.
3. Should either of the meetings have been televised? Why or why not?
4. Which group was the better audience?
5. What evidence was there that each group recognized and observed the competence factor?
6. Which group ran the greater risk in forming judgments about evaluating in its area?
7. How did plural viewpoints help provide a stimulus to interaction?
8. Which moderator was the least visible and vocal?
9. Which moderator needed to be more visible and more vocal?
10. Which group would you hire to study the problem for your firm? Explain your reasoning.

HOW MIGHT YOU PLAN TO IMPROVE THE NEXT MEETING?

AUDIENCE BARRIERS

One reason colleges require "some kind of speech course" of their students is the belief that people are all inescapably both senders and receivers. Perhaps most of your experience has been in the role of audience member, listener, or auditor. Public education attempts to provide varieties of audience experiences for young people, but obviously more participate as audience than as speaker. Which of these audience experiences do you know best?

1. classroom audience: 10–100 members.
2. church audience: 20–300 members.
3. school assembly audience: 100–2000 members.

4. sports audience: 100–120,000 members.
5. concert audience: 200–200,000 members.
6. television audience: 1–90,000,000 members.

An audience may be defined as a quantity of one to infinity who are bound together by their collective receiving of a message source. Audiences send individual and collective messages, too; the members may or may not be physically linked, but they are psychically linked to the source—the source knows the audience is "out there" and responds accordingly. The corporation knows its audiences are out there, though it may receive their messages (feedback) days, weeks, or even years after the communication cycle begins.

does an audience know it is an audience?

Most often you are not aware of your role as audience. In the exercises and enactments you have experienced, you may have participated as an audience member, because you happened to be in class that day and happened not to be picked for another role—your audience membership may have been purely "accidental." To be more effective as a *speaker*, you must realize that a number of your auditors find themselves in an audience by chance or because they got "caught" and cannot get out. Communicators also realize that they must seek out ways of bringing a sense of cohesion to audiences. They search for ideas and modes of expression that will unite audiences or polarize their attention and their need to listen; they try to give their audience a "sense of being an audience."

The sketch in Figure 4–9 is a relational diagram, showing the sphere of influence exerted by the message and its source—the center of the audience orbit. Why do audiences become audiences? Combinations of self-interest and the attraction of the message/source unite to form a two-way *pull*—the receiver and the message/source need each other and are pulled together. If there is widespread need among several potential audience members, then a "sphere of influence" is created and lasts as long as there is a mutual need.

task 5 WHAT'S THE ATTRACTION?

What is the message in each of the following situations? What is the attraction?

1. An audience collects around a traffic accident, because _____

_____.

2. An audience collects around a bankruptcy sale, because _____

_____.

figure 4-9 Audience Sphere of Influence

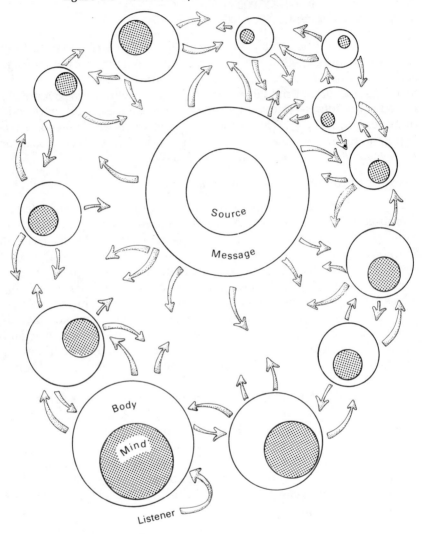

3. An audience collects around a football game, because _____
_____.

4. An audience collects around an unemployment office, because _____
_____.

5. An audience collects around a bulletin board, because _____
_____.

6. An audience collects around someone using a bullhorn, because _____

_____.

audience bindings

Certain patterns of human motive have been discussed in previous chapters under general topics such as why people communicate, why people think and perceive, why people work, why people listen. Business transactions, whether in goods, services, skills, or knowledge, must reflect a grasp of specific reasons for large audiences coming together. Figure 4–10 indicates a few of the specific reasons why groups of people become audiences and bind themselves together in "orbits" around a message/source attraction.

Elitism/Coterie. Professional exchange is sometimes made possible on the basis of elitism—exclusion. A product may be marketed to convey snob appeal, reverse snob appeal, or exclusiveness of some kind. Its consumption is communicated to mean: "You are special, you are an 'individual' if you buy this message." One of the many variations of elitism might constitute an orbit for audience members seeking individuality.

figure 4-10   Audience Bonds

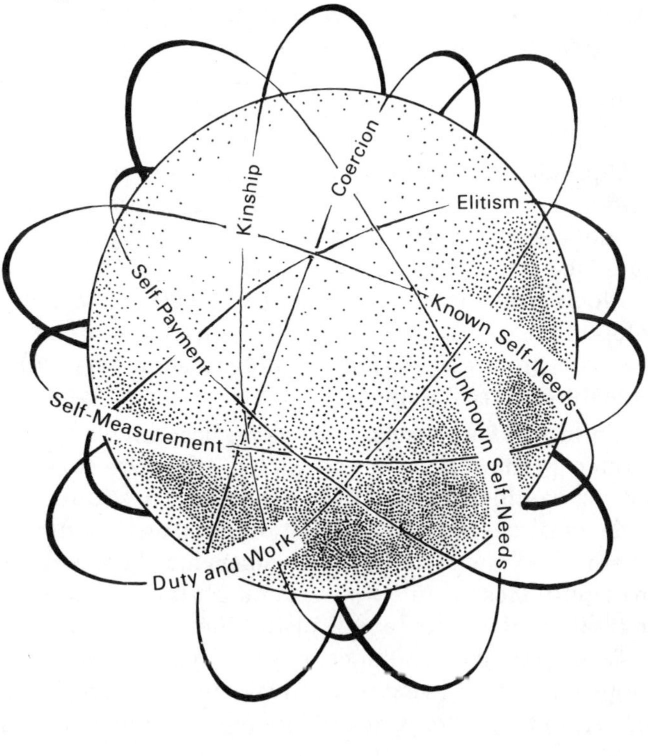

Kinship. You may find yourself attracted to the promise of feeling "a part of something." Kinship tends to bind separate individuals into an audience, because of their need for security in numbers. The need for comradeship, for being part of a team might be gratified by joining an audience. The attraction of kinship is seen when you think of yourself as a contributing member of a nation, state, county, etc., or when you strongly identify with your political, social, or cultural subgroups. You may associate your will and destiny with industry, commerce, geopolitics, agronomy, or any larger enterprise you feel has importance and impact.

Known Self-Needs. Audiences come together partly because of a shared, conscious desire to obtain—to be given something. They anticipate a "profit" from entering into the sphere of influence of messages and their source. Audience members may, for example, be seeking *direction.* They may ask: "Where do I find opportunities, and how do I get there?" They may want to be taught how to do something, how to improve, how to solve, how to obtain, how to develop the skills. Audiences may consciously recognize that help, in the form of the messages sent, will be profitable for them.

People align themselves into audiences, because they recognize a need for new experiences. They may wish to satisfy curiosity, to fill in gaps they have always wondered about. People may be intrigued by strange, unusual, mystifying, even grotesque messages and sources. This recognized need may be more of a desire for entertainment—to be intellectually, emotionally, or physically titillated in a safe way.

Another known reason people join an audience collective is that it might provide a better experience than whatever else is available; people participate in reaction against a worse alternative. They may prefer a certain message/source to others—they may want to *escape to* or *into* an audience from several worse evils.

Membership in an audience may be attractive because it is fashionable—the thing to do. You may derive a vicarious pleasure from associating with prominent figures or rubbing shoulders with "attractive" personalities, ideas, policies, or others in the audience.

Unknown Self-Needs. Needs for becoming a member of an audience often become blurred and mixed—they are reasons for behavior that you would just as soon not recognize. These unknown needs may include fears; the fear of being left out, of isolation, of getting too old, or of being too young. Audience members may be seeking a kind of remission of guilt. Most people want assurances that they are "doing the right thing," that other people will justify their own past behavior.

Belonging to an audience may be a type of proof or evidence that you hope others will recognize and take into account. In this sense you are on exhibit, visible. Audience membership may appeal to you because it is equivalent to receiving a testimonial of right thinking, attitudes, or behavior.

Self-Payment. People join audiences as a way of treating themselves. They may feel that "they have paid their dues," and they are entitled to belong and to participate. Membership represents an election and is a form of self-congratulation—patting themselves on the back.

Self-Measurement. "Do you stack up?" is a question implied by participation in some audiences. You may find yourself within the orbit of a message/source with the intention of comparing what is said and done with your own convictions and abilities. Some people devote time and energy to "checking out the competition," or scouting the opposition to get feedback and a standard of performance by which to measure their own proficiency.

Duty and Work. Some members of any audience join the group because it is their job. Some people feel obligated; they feel they "should" join, listen, participate, go to meetings, and so on. For others, audience membership is a job-related responsibility—part of their assignment or otherwise required by their occupation.

Coercion. Unfortunately, you may have found yourself as part of an audience because you have been forced into it. You owe it to somebody, you attend as a favor, you take part because there is no way out of it, or you find yourself "captured" there and cannot get out. One audience tendency you probably have experienced or heard about is the feeling that you might as well stick it out—see it through to the end. Sometimes you may feel, "I have come this far," and you accept your membership in the audience as your fate.

Coercion may take the form "accepting the bad in order to get some of the good." Messages and sources may be suffered because they are "slipped in" with something you really want. You may gladly put up with the red tape that is part of a project in order to arrive at the "prize"; you may patiently suffer the police officer's lecture, so that you can go on your way unimpeded. Audiences, too, may be coerced into accepting the bad as a step toward obtaining the good.

polarization

A sense of cohesion or mass response suggests that an audience is focusing on a single, shared notion. When this occurs, and to the degree that it occurs, it might be said that an audience has become *polarized* or clustered tightly around a given message; this is an instance when all eyes, ears, and minds are fixed on the signals being sent. Polarization implies a sense of expectation—something very important is about to be said or done, and it will be received with welcome (positively) or with reluctance (negatively).

fragmentation

Audiences may, of course, experience split polarization. Members may divide into several polarized groups within the large group. What is good news for some is bad news for others. You have probably heard of great historical rallying messages that "bound nations together," or turned the tide of war. Plurality, however, is the rule in most audiences.

peripheral membership

Large groups, because of their size, accommodate a kind of "transient" membership—people who drift in and out, who hang on the edges and never become full-fledged component members. There is also a type of splinter membership that may use the audience for other purposes; this subgroup "borrows" somebody else's audience in order to send its own message, though it is ostensibly composed of members of that audience. These individuals join in order to manipulate or use their audience membership for other ends.

Figure 4–10 depicts these eight categories of membership as being separate, though of course an audience's motivational patterns are very complex. They overlap and shift as members react to and accept the attraction of other orbits, other stimuli.

task 6   AUDIENCE ANALYSIS

Think back to the last class meeting you had, whatever class it was. Which of these audience characteristics did you experience?

1. The class seemed to contain___different subgroups or polarized groups with the

   following characteristics : _____

   _____

   _____.

2. One individual seemed to have been coerced into membership, because he/
   she appeared to _____.

3. One individual seemed to have joined the group to measure himself/herself
   because he/she _____.

4. One individual seemed to be giving himself/herself a treat, because he/she

   _____.

5. One person was obviously a peripheral member, because _____

   _____.

6. Several members seemed to have fears that membership in the class helped alleviate, because they appeared to _____

_____.

7. Several members joined this audience because it was a lesser of two (or more) evils, and their membership can be described as _____

_____.

8. Several members joined this audience because they felt they would profit from it, and their membership can be described as _____

_____.

9. Several members appear to have joined this audience because they have friends in the class, and their membership can be described as _____

_____.

As you have undoubtedly guessed, professionally prepared messages frequently attempt to reflect the personal motives and dispositions of audience members; the best messages have appeal and impact of this type. Certain kinds of professional transactions are quite open and blatant in fragmenting large groups and in using "friendly" competitiveness as leverage to attain a professional goal.

If you have ever participated in a form of competitive bidding, you know how audience motives help create a collective audience—a sense of oneness and of polarity. You may recall grammar school spelling bees pitting boys against girls, or the football rallies where freshmen challengèd upperclassmen to shouting and cheering contests— "managed" of course by cheerleaders.

According to Jean Patteson, one form of competitive audience bidding—the auction—has existed since the first appearance of slave trading in ancient China; she writes that "in 193 A.D. the Praetorian Guard . . . put all of Rome on the block and this grand prize was won by the highest bidder . . . Didium Julianus."[4] Auctions, obviously, create a gambling atmosphere; the stakes or winnings can be high, and you may be bidding against the future value of goods.

Audiences at auctions offer an opportunity for interesting case study investigation by students of business and professional speech. Attend an auction sometime, particularly if you have never been to one. You will be much more aware of the effects of rhythmic, ca-

---

[4]Jean Patteson, "People, Places and Things Are a Way of Life for Auctioneers," *Auctioneer*, XXV, no. 11 (November 1974), 11.

denced speech, the use of humor, the appeals to *ad hominem* thinking, the use of generalization, bandwagon, and other rhetorical tricks of hyped salesmanship. And you will witness audiences that feel the attraction and the compulsion to participate.

Enactment 9 is a practice audience situation that uses dynamics found in stock market, gold market, grain market, and other market bidding. Have your own auction and see what happens within the class in its role as audience.

enactment 9   "ONE-ONE-ONE, D'HEAR TWO?"

Watch for these types of audience bindings in . . . .

peripheral membership
self-measurement
kinship
known self-needs
duty and work

enactment 9: "ONE-ONE-ONE, D'HEAR TWO?"

participants

The *auctioneer* serves as a describer, agitator, pitch-maker, joke-teller, entertainer, and salesperson; the *bidders* are all members of the class.

problem

Structure a number of items in an ascending order of "value" for bidding; i.e., start with something of inferior value first and proceed with items of increasing value until you reach the "main event." You may want to "spice" the bidding with several mystery commodities of unknown value, but that are "guaranteed" to enhance or profit their new owner. The class may decide to trade in money or services or promises—just about anything that will get the audience to respond.

critique 9   TROUBLESHOOTING

1. At what point did the bidding become a *serious* contest?
2. What special kind of listening was required? Why?
3. What kinds and types of persuasion were used or generated that you might incorporate into a persuasive speech?

4. What "orbits" of membership appeared that have not been mentioned?
5. Describe how the audience characteristics differed at the close of the auction from those at the opening.
6. In what ways do all members of this type of communication exchange obtain "satisfaction"?
7. How does audience size and spacing affect "selling" of this type?
8. What are the differences between an auction event and a telethon?
9. Describe some of the polarizing influences in auctions and telethons that might be incorporated into professional business dealings.

WHAT HAPPENED?

afterthought GROUPTHINK

Group work in the professions is vulnerable to the same plodding and time-consuming effects of equal-time policy used in parliamentary proceedings. "Free speech" in the sense of ensuring everyone the opportunity to be heard is not as efficient as autocratic forms of decision-making. But if you stop to think about the effects of consensus (not to mention unanimity), you may find that the law of plurality tends to bring out sharper and more objectively weighed answers, and it is from the very differences among participants that you may locate interfaces. These do not necessarily lead to uniformity but rather to mutual respect and shared professionalism.

Groupthink is agreement at any price—consensus for its own sake; this attitude excludes variety, differences, creative thinking, and free expression. The erroneous belief that a group must somehow agree on everything, assent or dissent unanimously, is one of the sadder examples of either/or thinking. The concept of *balance* in problem-solving does not mean that everyone must cluster at one end of the scale or the other; nor must they be bunched on the fulcrum. Groupthink, however, gives the illusion of balance when in actuality it creates only top-heaviness.

Your experience as an audience member broadens your understanding of the communication process by suggesting the other point of view—active listening and silent talking. This reciprocating aspect in the process will be examined more closely in Parts 2 and 3 of this book, where you will have the opportunity to work in small groups and get the feel of problem-solving and idea flow as these processes might occur in your professional future.

READ FOR YOURSELF

ANDERSEN, MARTIN P., WESLEY LEWIS, and JAMES MURRAY, *The Speaker and His Audience.* New York: Harper & Row, Publishers, Inc., 1964.

BARKER, LARRY L., *Listening Behavior.* Englewood Cliffs, N.J.: Prentice-Hall, Inc., 1971.

CLEVENGER, THEODORE, JR., *Audience Analysis.* Indianapolis: The Bobbs-Merrill Co., Inc., 1966.

FREELEY, AUSTIN J., *Argumentation and Debate.* Belmont, Calif.: Wadsworth Publishing Co., Inc., 1971.

SMITH, CRAIG R., and DAVID M. HUNSAKER. *The Bases of* Argument. Indianapolis: The Bobbs-Merrill Co., Inc., 1972.

CHAPTER CHART

Key idea: A problem is a felt imbalance or state of disequilibrium

Language Problems
    Definitions should apply precisely to the way the word is used
    Definitions should not use the words they define
    Definitions should not connote
    Key idea: Language structure influences how we think

Thinking Problems
    Linear thinking progresses from square one to square two
    Mosaic thinking progresses in a helter-skelter fashion

Large Group Problem-Solving Assumptions
    A problem really exists
    The identified problem can be solved or ameliorated
    The problem should be corrected
    Correcting the problem is worth the effort

Types of Thinking
    Deductive: from the general to a specific
    Inductive: from the specific to the general
    Causality
        a priori: causes existed before the problem
        a posteriori: causes occurred with and after the problem
        empiricism: assessing causes through experience
    Syllogistic reasoning: a three- or four-part test for judging a proposition

Fallacies of Thinking
    Misplaced concreteness: stating abstract, intangible concepts in a way that
        assumes they are *real*
    Pathetic fallacy: giving human qualities to things
    Authority: applying an expert's reputation to unrelated subjects
    Numbers: juggling statistics and using them out of context
    Generalization: using *all, every, always* indiscriminately
    Sampling: jumping to conclusions from narrow evidence
    Post hoc: attributing the cause of a condition to factors preceding that
        condition
    Card-stacking: filtering out or selective use of data
    Ad hominem: judging the words by the person speaking
    Vox populi: assuming that if a thing is popular, it must be right
    Transfer: assuming that qualities in one area will "rub off" on another area
    Reduction to absurdity: making something look ridiculous by carrying it to
        extremes
    "One More": the mistaken notion that a solution can always accommodate
        "one more" factor or person
    Bandwagon: acting on the basis of group appeal regardless of individual
        circumstances

Problems of Procedure
Advertise meetings
Plan the environment
Plan the format
Plan the flow of ideas
Plan for creative problem-solving
Plan for follow-up

Synectics
Key idea: Put yourself in the other's place

Audiences
Spheres of influence (orbits)
Bonds
    elitism/coterie
    kinship
    known self-needs
    unknown self-needs
    self-payment
    self-measurement
    duty and work
    coercion
Polarization
Key idea: Individual audience members affect each other

PART 2

PERSON-TO-GROUP SPEAKING IN BUSINESS AND THE PROFESSIONS

chapter 5

PROFESSIONALISM

image-REFLECT   image-REFLECT   image-REFLECT
image-REFLECT

"Looking for a job?"
"Yeah."
"What for?"
"I need the money."
"What for?"
"Ya gotta live."
"What for?"

What for gets asked about everything. Why are you in school? Why are you majoring in that field? What are you doing in this class? Your answers reflect three self-judgments: (1) who you think you are, (2) who you do not want to be, and (3) who you would like to be. Chapter 1 offered some tentative answers to the question "Why communicate?" This chapter attempts to set the stage for business encounters further by grappling with another necessary question: "Why work?" A single answer for both basic questions might be: "Because it is impossible not to."

Somehow, everyone communicates and works. Your attitudes toward communication and work reflect who you think you are and want to become. If you are reasonably secure, your motive to work is the opposite side of the coin of your motive to communicate.

105

WORK

Work in its broadest sense means expending energy. People work at gambling, their marriages, their overhead smash, and many other activities. What does all this expenditure of energy reflect? Does it reflect who you really are or who you think you are? Does it reflect your desire to become somebody? One aspect of you that it reflects is your expectation that something will come from it. A brief look at work theories might provide an approach to the question "Why work?"

expectancy theory

The motivation for work is described by Victor Vroom, John Campbell, George Strauss, Leonard Sayles, and other theorists as the desire to receive rewards through worthwhile activity. This idea suggests that your degree of effort will depend on how badly you want something. Using factors such as, "Can I do the job?" "Can I expect a reward?" "Can I expect that doing the job and getting the reward will satisfy my needs?" you can develop an index of probability when facing a set of tasks. "Who needs it?" is the key issue. Is it worth it to clean lavatories in order to "make" Latrine Specialist 1?

n Ach theory

David C. McClelland has worked with tests that measure "achievement needs" or (n Ach). He notes that workers scoring a "high n Ach" work mostly to accomplish something for its own sake; they like the "doing" and enjoy tinkering or messing around with problems, dilemmas, people and things that need fixing. Accordingly, these workers are less mindful of monetary and esteem rewards, but they are sometimes driven to lick one problem and then move on to the next. These persons are achievers, accomplishers, and surmounters.

need gratification theory

The idea of need gratification is central to all explanations of why we do what we do. It is the notion behind the *what for* questions—that work is a step-by-step ascent or path toward a goal (satisfying a need) that is the achievement of those steps on the way. You may study to pass, you may pass in order to graduate, and you want to graduate because it is prerequisite to something else. You may sometimes be oblivious to next higher rungs on your fulfillment ladder. Perhaps you are not certain that your work is significant enough or that your next goal is sufficiently obtainable.

equity theory

There are some indications that people have a learned sense of fairness or equity.[1] Work is worthwhile if, for example, you are rewarded no more and no less than what you feel you should get. If you are significantly overpaid or underpaid, you may develop a cynicism about your job and see it as demeaning or unworthy of your sense of fairness, balance, and proportion. This is one reason why the old Marxist slogan, "From each according to his[or her] ability; to each according to his [or her] need," gained some acceptance with equity-conscious "have-nots" early in the twentieth century.

Equity is also another spatial judging phenomenon. If "bigger means better," you might have to work harder to fulfill expectations that accompany a larger paycheck. "How much do you make?" and "How much do 'they' take out?" are questions used to measure the fairness of your rewards for work.

needs

Psychologist Abraham Maslow put forward a graduated list of the human needs that underlie attitudes toward work.[2] Starting with the most basic needs and ascending to the "highest" category, Maslow cited these groups: physiological needs, the need for safety, the need for love, the need for esteem, and the need for self-actualization.

Physiological Needs. Your needs for nutrition, clothing, shelter, sleep, and sexual satisfaction are in the physiological category. These bodily needs are primary or basic to your homeostatic or balanced animal existence. They are listed first, because they must be met first.

Safety Needs. You expend energy or work in order to maintain security from hostile forces, disruptive factors that affect your physical and emotional well-being. You work to safeguard your home turf, to maintain who you are—the several faces that reflect your condition.

Love Needs. The need for love in all its forms and complexities is transactional—its energy release forms a bridge from one person to others; it is a social need of belongingness, acceptance, inclusion into a collective that is greater than yourself alone. Love as a basic need was mentioned earlier in the discussion of feedback. You seek situations in which to obtain "stroking" and work to structure events and people so as to receive your needed amount.

Esteem Needs. Maslow felt that people also need to receive evidence or recognition. Your individuality, sense of importance, and worth to people

[1]For a more complete explanation of equity theory, see George Strauss and Leonard R. Sayles, *Personnel: The Human Problems of Management*, 3rd ed. (Englewood Cliffs, N.J.: Prentice-Hall, Inc., 1972).

[2]Abraham H Maslow, "A Theory of Human Motivation: The Basic Needs," *Psychological Review* 50 (1943), p. 394. Copyright 1943 by the American Psychological Association. Reprinted by permission.

nourish your self-image, because they are a reflection of your own good opinion of yourself. Thus, work must somehow be considered worthy of attention and worth the effort. Esteem, like love, is other-placed—it must be known or testified to by others.

Self-Actualization Needs. Maslow considered the "highest' need to be self-actualization: becoming, by your own effort and thought, what you are capable of becoming. Simply, self-actualization is growing, making your own choices, learning from others, and learning to be your own boss. In communication, this need can be seen as the motive for working to synthesize languages, thinking, face/voice/hand/body, space, and time into an integrated impulse of exchange.

If in your work you worry about losing what you have—your family, love, and esteem—you are forced into working to defend these things, to protect them or keep your store of them "filled up." In terms of the double helix figure in Chapter 1, you may feel compelled to stop with what you have, rather than go forward to meet, exchange, and communicate.

According to some psychologists, this stand-pat attitude toward work tends to weaken your prospects for gaining the richer, more complete satisfactions of human existence: the conviction that you do not have to worry about your wholeness and your competence.

working to defend, working to grow

Another way to think of your work is to see if it is aimed toward defense or offense, existing or living, stasis or movement. Do you work to defend? Do you work to grow? Maslow saw growth as a progression, in which each step was better than the last. As a student, you might feel that your work is better for you than whatever else you could be doing. You may have internalized your work, so that it seems right for you, and you trust yourself to know what is right and wrong for you.

Some people work so that they will not have to work. They look upon their needs as feelings and work to get rid of these feelings. Need creates tension and anxiety, so it must be reduced or eliminated. They work to avoid a deficiency. Work for them is a necessary evil, but a lesser evil than the deficiency. The reward or pleasure obtained from working to overcome a deficiency is a kind of relief from strain, tension, or discomfort; the pleasure derived from working to grow is the elation felt in operating smoothly, functioning competently.

The pleasure of overcoming a deficit tends to be episodic, a satisfaction followed by "Well, what's next?" This kind of short-term pleasure is expressed in the old joke: "The only trouble with eating well is that it spoils my appetite." Growth-motivated people enjoy "living through it" for its own sake.

Growth-motivated workers are not as dependent on the favor,

allegiances, and loyalties of the organization they work for; these rewards are conferred by the self on the self. Growth-oriented people go fishing just to go fishing; they work at climbing mountains because the mountains "are there," but also because they like climbing.

The viewpoint that pleasure is somehow related to erasing deficits by getting applause, recognition, and other rewards tends to define people as objects of use. In this view people exist to be used, manipulated, or handled as tools or props. Misfortunes, tough breaks, and messes are "caused" by others. The growth-motivated person is less susceptible to this dehumanized outlook. Depending less on others for gratification and reward, self-actualizers are better able to see and understand people and their problems. They are less afraid to "give up a little" to seek a harmonious attitude and interface, because they know they will not be losing something or creating a deficit in themselves. Work for actualizers is closer to play; it is freely expressed, spontaneous, and part of an integrated outlook.

The attitudes toward work described here lead up to a definition of two terms that have been loosely used in previous pages but not defined: *professionalism* and *competence*. The professional communicator, you may already know, does not refer only to the gifted, silky-throated performer who is paid to communicate. Professionalism and competence reflect your self-image, how you approach work, and your personal hierarchy of needs.

enactment 10   WHAT FOR?

In this enactment try to trace the path of your motivation by asking *what for* questions thoroughly and honestly. Converse as you normally would, expressing wishes, examining circumstances, and discussing alternative choices for working in your profession.

Try to reflect honestly in . . . .

enactment 10: WHAT FOR?

why you want certification
how badly you want it
whether certification will allow
    you . . .
  to keep something?
  to get something?
  to have something?
  to do something?
  to be somebody?
  to get away from something?
  to be better than somebody?
  to risk something?

to attempt something?
to avoid something?
to buy something?
to make something?
to express something?
to create something?
to help somebody?
to show somebody?

participants

State board certifier, a state-appointed agent, expert in and representing one of the following professions: accounting, architecture, banking, beauticians, cabaret-entertainment, education, engineering, food handling, health services, home construction, insurance, law, livestock management, manufacturing, medicine, public utilities, real estate, retailing, social work, or urban planning; applicant, a person seeking formal state recognition and licensing of his/her competence and motivation in some specialty of a profession.

need to talk

Each wants something from the other. The applicant seeks a license certifying that he/she has met the qualifications for a specified period of time to practice the chosen profession. The certifier must find out and identify the applicant's attitude toward work in the interest of properly serving citizens and maintaining high standards of service in the profession.

time/locale

The interview takes place after a preliminary application has been made and training and skill competence have been established and documented. The locale is the board certifier's office.

critique 10   TROUBLESHOOTING

1. What was the applicant's opinion of himself/herself and of the profession?
2. How would you rate each person as a listener?
3. What opinion of the applicant did the certifier reflect back to the applicant?
4. Which language was used most effectively?
5. What evidence did you see of defensive and of growth motivation?
6. Would you license the applicant? Would you hire the certifier?

CAN YOU DEMONSTRATE WHAT WENT WRONG?

PROFESSIONALISM

Manipulator, exploiter, hustler, manager, entrepreneur, professional: all of these labels may fit persons who are gainfully employed, pay taxes, contribute to the gross national product, vote, raise families, share in community projects, participate in all forms of social exchange. Each person typified by such a name may reflect broad skills and knowledge; each may operate within legal boundaries, as do some professional transients, panhandlers, freeloaders, and assassins—for example, route salespeople, promoters and fund raisers, certain welfare recipients, and various armed employees. Most people are part or all of these stereotypes, just as they possess all or part of need complexes and work motives discussed above. Which characteristics might you include in your profile of a professional?

Manipulator. The manipulative professional knows the range of thing-variables and people-variables. Although this person may perform the tasks of everyday living, his or her transactions are with "clients, accounts, votes," nonhuman quantifications. The goal of manipulators is *control*. Their skill is in developing a repertoire of attitudes or roles that they are adept in using to control people and events. Generally, you manipulate because you do not trust yourself to be effective and acceptable the way you are (or think you are). Manipulators rig circumstances, they stage events and relationships for effect.

As a communicator, you may manipulate in many ingenious ways that you can recognize:

1. *Coattail-hanging:* merging your wants with those of a "front-runner" who runs interference for you with friends, relatives, bosses.
2. *Using scapegoats:* using intermediaries to accomplish your objectives so that if they fail, they, not you, take the rap.
3. *Message relaying:* using the strategy, "I'm just telling you what 'they' told me to tell you."
4. *Passing the buck:* asking "Why doesn't somebody do something about it?"
5. *Righteous law-giving:* using rules, if convenient; if not, interpreting them to fit your convenience.
6. *Self-effacement:* pleading incompetence, inability, illness, insufficiency, ineptness, so that action will be taken by someone else.

Exploiter. Exploiters rush to fill a vacuum. Speed and quick maneuvering are essential. The exploiter sees personal gain and profit in barrenness, disarray, and chaos. This person lives for the future, promising and fantasizing deferred dividends. Like the manipulator, the exploiter trades in half-truths, rumors, possibilities. Exploiters hope for a quick turnover of their dream schemes to somebody else—at a profit, of course. As communicators, they deal in grandiose big lies that might be true, such as:

1. *Early-birds:* "If we can just get our foot in the door . . ."
2. *Pioneers:* "Look around! Opportunities are everywhere."
3. *Record-setters:* "Being first means being the best, the most permanent, rooted, successful."
4. *Simplifiers:* "I say, give them what they want."
5. *Pacifiers:* "I say, give them what they think they want."

Hustler. People hustle by overcoming resistance with wit, charm, élan, nerve, and sheer energy. Hustlers are gifted compromisers; if they cannot get it all, they will take half, a third, whatever. They are perfect agents for exploiters and manipulators, because they are highly effective salespeople in certain situations and with certain types of personalities. They hustle products, schemes, ideas, candidates, anything—with superficial proofs, questionable testimonials, inaccurate statistical data, and gross exaggeration. Sample message techniques include:

1. *Documenting evidence:* "Look, the proof is all there. Two years ago it was at 50, a year ago, 100. This year it's bound to . . ."
2. *Gambling:* "Where would we be if we didn't take a chance once in a while? Take a chance! What can you lose?"
3. *Psyching:* "I'm only mentioning it to you, because I thought you might be the kind of person who could handle it."
4. *Begging:* "What are the alternatives? What reasons are there for *not* going forward with it?"

Manager. Managers lead, conduct, and supervise programs leading to a prescribed condition. They coordinate flows of people and things, usually on behalf of and sometimes in participation with organizations—the company, the firm, the foundation. When you manage, you frequently adopt a procedural viewpoint; you monitor systems and networks of activity for bottlenecks, slowdowns, and snags. Once the model of efficient productivity is workable, newer and better sections are sometimes introduced—while the old system is still in operation. Managers replace and update personnel and procedures in trying to make the whole thing work. Much has been said about management communicators and their problems, but at this point, it might be noted that they manage only as well as they monitor. And, while managerial skill consists of juggling varied factors, the managerial role is largely listening, assessing, and gauging the interplay of systems.

Entrepreneur. Most people share in entrepreneurship in the sense that they own something; they therefore execute ultimate decisions regarding its use and shared ownership. In business you may own franchises, limited rights to access and use; you may own leases allowing you an executive privilege over the organization of space and materials. Generally, owners wish to maintain the relative value of their property and business structures. They wish to effect growth—expansion of the line, trademark, market, or service. Some owners are collectors of properties; they accumulate cars, books, houses, just about anything. Ownership, of course, may be a means to gain larger, overall or *telic* rewards that, in turn, serve to advance you toward a terminal goal-condition—freedom, political power, truth, beauty, or justice.

Professional. Just as each person finds combination of needs, motives, and behaviors in all these stereotypic "professionals," the definition of *professional* offered here also encompasses a spectrum of attributes, all of which are decidedly human. We suggest that a professional is a person whose main task is helping others to find themselves and to assume competence.

Much is said about businesspeople learning to get along with others, but professionals have developed the prerequisite to smooth social exchange and communication: They are good at getting along with themselves. Their motives are no better than those of others, and their piety and virtue do not impress people, because professionals do not intend them to. A professional is very good at certain things. Using Maslow's *eupsychian* manager as a model,[3] some of these strengths are:

1. Professionals are adept at *trusting*. They understand that their indications of trust will help create a self-trusting tendency in other people who are capable of trust.
2. Professionals assume that you like to know where you stand. You probably prefer an objective appraisal of matters that affect your job and your goals; you like to know what is happening.
3. Professionals project a demeanor and position that tells you, "I know that you know your job and want to perform it well." Professionals take for granted your desire for achievement, while recognizing that many people could not care less at this point in their growth.
4. Professionals attempt to minimize dominance–subordinate relationships in dealing with people. Their outlook accommodates pluralities of people first, and rank and job-title last.
5. Professionals extend their own views to include the total organizational structure by passing beyond the parochialism of clique, office, department, division. They are enterprise-oriented, organization-centered, and identified with the larger cause they feel is worth supporting.
6. Professionals believe that most people find "getting along well" less painful than animosity, envy, and jealousy and that, given a choice, people will tend to choose the easier alternative.

[3]Abraham H. Maslow, *Eupsychian Management: A Journal* (Homewood, Ill.: Richard D. Irwin, Inc., and Dorsey Press, 1965), pp. 17–33.

7. Professionals like themselves well enough to appreciate others' successes and genuinely find pleasure when their colleagues excel, even when colleagues surpass them in achievement and contribution. They know that excellence in others does not subtract from their own.

8. Professionals receive ill-humor, hostility, and animosity as temporary outbursts of the moment; their attitude is that negative feelings expressed are not necessarily ingrained in the speaker's nature and not endemic to that person's personality.

9. Professionals take risks on people's ability to be tough, to find unknown ranges of endurance and the capacity to function and solve problems creatively.

10. Professionals believe that most people prefer to feel esteemed, loved, and proud, rather than beaten, degraded, and manipulated.

11. Professionals suspect that people would also prefer to respect and admire their bosses, though they may not.

12. Professionals recognize that nobody likes to be afraid of other people, though you may often respect those you fear more than those you love or feel tenderness for.

13. Professionals look at people as potential leaders. They assume that most people would rather be the motive force behind an enterprise than merely a cog in a wheel.

14. Professionals believe that people generally prefer constructive work; that they tend to want to fix, improve, grow, and enhance their environment and the general human condition.

15. Professionals feel that people often get bored, that novelty is a refresher for them, and that they grow when they are stimulated.

16. Professionals accept the premise that most people know what they are doing and that personal choices—acts of choosing—contribute to self-actualizing in general.

The other term that has been left undefined so far is *competence*. As we use the phrase *competence factor*, its meaning is a reflexive one. You demonstrate competence or ability by *acting as though it were true*. In communicating, your competence or ability asserts itself, if you allow it an opportunity to be there. If you try it out and think professionally, your behavior will reflexively provide you with the feedback that you are functioning competently. Your belief in what you transact, as we said, is catching. Your professionalism will also be reflected in how others respond. They too will see evidence of your belief and accept those cues as part of your overall message. The competence factor, then, means *practicing professionalism, working at it, living it, communicating it*. Test your understanding of professionalism and the competence factor in Task 1.

task 1   PROFILING THE PROFESSIONAL

Choose the *most likely* "is or isn't" verb for each of the following statements about professional communicators. Write one good reason to support your opinion. Professional communicators . . .

1. do/don't laugh too much, because _____

_____.

2. are/aren't married to their jobs, because _____

_____.

3. can/can't always finagle a way out, because _____

_____.

4. do/don't tell you what you want to hear, because _____

_____.

5. do/don't like to take time off, because _____

_____.

6. are/aren't mainly concerned with themselves, because _____

_____.

7. do/don't worry about income or fringe benefits, because _____

_____.

8. do/don't do a lot of talking, because _____

_____.

9. do/don't always know what to say, because _____

_____.

10. are/aren't leaders, because _____

_____.

11. are/aren't team players, because _____

_____.

12. are/aren't mavericks, renegades, loners, because _____

_____.

13. do/don't give in easily, because _____

_____.

14. do/don't stick to the subject at hand, because _____

_____.

15. do/don't try to get everyone else to be a professional communicator, because

_____.

16. do/don't tip their hand, because ——————————

————————————————————————————.

17. do/don't have answers for every question, because ——————————

————————————————————————————.

18. do/don't gamble, because ——————————

————————————————————————————.

19. do/don't "feed" on feedback, because ——————————

————————————————————————————.

20. do/don't know who they are, because ——————————

————————————————————————————.

enactment 11   TRINARY

The purpose of this enactment is to acquaint you with multiples of the manipulative, exploitive, hustling, and professional attitudes that assert themselves in everyone under certain circumstances. Try to present the biases described but also project what you would probably say if TRINARY were a real situation.

Try to reflect these roles in . . . . :

enactment 11: TRINARY

manipulator
exploiter
hustler
professional

participants

Researcher A, a person of any age, sex, or personality type who has successfully isolated and artificially produced one component that, when combined with two "triggering" elements, forms a product of incalculable significance to mankind; Researcher B, possessor of the second ingredient, who feels it is the most important, greatest, most indispensable contribution to the three-part compound; Researcher C, a person who claims credit for all three components and feels they should be made freely available to the world; Manager, the person in charge of the research unit that produced the compound, who represents the organization's interests and those of its stockholders.

need to talk

Each is interested in protecting his or her interests, and in having a say about how each component is used. None of the three components is meaningful without its complements; thus each researcher needs the other two.

problem

The participants come together for a crucial meeting. Can differences of motive, aim, need, and professional attitude be reconciled so that collective action may be generated by collective decision?

time/locale

The three-part product has yet to be assembled or mixed, but its effect, tested mathematically and through simulation, is certain. The nature of the three-part discovery is such that combining any two components will prolong the life span of those components, whereas left alone each component deteriorates in a matter of hours and becomes worthless. This meeting takes place in the laboratory, late at night, only an hour or so before decomposition will begin.

critique 11   TROUBLESHOOTING

1. Which participant communicated respect, esteem, and tolerance best? Which seemed to *need* these reflected back the most?
2. Pick out an exploitive phrase and a manipulative phrase that were used.
3. Who adopted the most professional attitude?
4. How were participants forced into responding in one or more of the four characterized modes?
5. What nonverbal languages seemed characteristic of any of the four "professionals"?

   CAN YOU DEMONSTRATE HOW IT MIGHT BE IMPROVED?

6. Which messages tended to push the four participants toward harmonious behavior?
7. Do you feel it is more important to have highly intelligent employees who discover or produce brilliantly or employees of average intelligence who communicate well? Why?
8. Explain why it might have been easier for ten persons, each possessing something the others needed, to transact and find interfaces smoothly and equitably than for four people to do so.

IMAGE-MAKING

I believe . . . that [skin] was the organ that was the sole medium of self-betrayal in the early stages of evolution. Originally . . . it was . . . the skin that showed what was going on within. It was the earliest organ to reflect mental processes. Blushing and turning pale still betray our feelings, and perspiration still breaks out when we are afraid. All self-betrayal makes its way through the pores of the skin.[4]

The first part of this chapter explored questions that dealt with who you really are, how you assess your work prospects, and strive to defend and/or grow as a professional. Image-making, as Theodore Reik suggests, has to do with the facial display of how you would like to be seen—the difference is the difference between "looking good," and "being good." In your enactments you "put on" several faces; you may have tried one out when this class first met, and you have used several since that first day. But the point of this section is not *surface* appearances—an outward symptom. These next pages consider your whole personality complex, the total effect that is called role-playing and image-making.

Think back to the participants in the enactments you have witnessed. You saw students—all different types—assume various set attitudes. They were teachers, students, community representatives briefly personified. Whom did you believe? You knew they were not behaving as they really do, but something came through that *was* really part of them and really believable. This believable or *credible* aspect of the images was the undeniable character those students are and have.

People in the professional world send and receive image and ethos signals constantly, instantaneously. You wear many hats, many disguises, thousands of faces. Why? A few reasons have already been mentioned, but one that has not is the necessity of finding efficient, shorthand emblems that honestly convey the true part of yourself. This need motivates your search for personal trademarks—signatures.

task 2 YOUR PERSONAL TRADEMARKS

A. In the spaces that follow, *force* yourself to experiment with a totally new personal

signature of your name, a professional trademark. Circle the one that you feel

best reflects your self-image.

1. _____

---

[4]Theodore Reik, *Listening with the Third Ear* (New York: Farrar, Straus & Company, 1948), p. 143.

2. _____

3. _____

4. _____

B. In the spaces that follow, *force* yourself to rearrange your name—use initials, reverse names, invent a new professional name. Circle the one you feel best reflects your projected professional image.

1. _____

2. _____

3. _____

4. _____

C. Write your new name as a signature _____

D. Show your new signature name to a friend and ask if it projects what you think it projects. Give your friend feedback on his/her new trademark. Talk over whether your new signature names came through in your last enactment. Discuss whether your new name signatures are consistent with, opposite to, or radically different from the way each of you dresses for class and your other nonverbal styles of expressing self-image.

Another reason why people play roles goes back to prelogical times, before human beings developed vocal languages to any extent. An early "science" and major profession was magic. People reasoned that to gain the power of things, they should imitate the outward signs of those things. To have the power of a sabertooth, a person imitated it, dressed like it, made noises and "music" like it, moved or "danced" like it. This was an instance of the harmony principle operating and a very early example of the intrinsic urge to communicate and to find meaningful ways of symbolizing forces in nature.

James Frazer's landmark study of myth and religion, *The Golden Bough*, contains numerous examples of primitive people's attempts to enhance their self-esteem, provide for their basic needs, and find signatures and emblems with which to communicate a believable professional image. Frazer noted two basic types of magic: the law of similarity and the law of contagion. The law of similarity argues that "like produces like." Magicians inferred that they could produce an effect or outcome, if they could find the appropriate way of imitating it.[5] Their techniques of movement, speech, and dress attempted to manipulate people and things by copying their exterior movements, speech patterns, and dress. In short their belief was: you can be a winner, if you act like a winner.

The law of contagion is the belief that people and objects continue to act on one another—to communicate—even though they may become separated. The magicians of old traded in the knowledge of charms, amulets, and potions in the belief that these objects somehow retained connections with their original contexts or sources.

Today, people use calling cards, mementos, souvenirs, and "keepsake" diamonds as links with people and events. A child's tooth beneath a pillow "attracts" a reward or a blessing in the form of money; a lock of hair keeps you in touch with a loved one. The use of substitute or surrogate tokens shows a vestige of belief in or reliance on this law. Shredding a photograph or burning letters is a symbolic act of terminating or destroying a relationship link, of stopping communication.

A third reason why persons role-play is hinted at in the word *person* itself; it is derived from the Greek term *persona*, meaning *mask*. Thus, in a sense, the roles you play, the scripts or scenarios you rehearse, the costumes and lines of dialogue you use are masks. They are cover-ups—symbolic attempts to have the powers you need and work for rub off on you. Role-playing uses the several selves you develop, enact, orchestrate, and stage as surrogates for your real self.

A role-playing example might be found in people who value their anonymity, people who like being lost in the crowd. They value and work to play the role of being invisible. They may feel more protected, less vulnerable, and less susceptible to the demands of communicating. This role-playing is yet another variation of selective seeing, of people insulating themselves, protectively coloring and shielding themselves behind anonymity. You may hide behind your desk nameplate, your job title, your books—the list is endless. In business, being turned down by a prospective client is a rejection that you can avoid feeling if you interpret and organize "No, thank you" as being aimed at your firm or at all salesmen, rather than at you, your real self.

PROFESSIONAL REPUTATION

Your professional reputation is like the gold that backs up paper money. The "paper" is all the roles you play, but your profes-

---

[5]James George Frazer, *The New Golden Bough*, rev. and ed. by Theodore H. Gaster (New York: The New American Library, Inc., and Mentor Books, 1964), p. 35. Reprinted by permission of S. G. Phillips, Inc. from *The New Golden Bough*, ed. by Theodore H. Gaster. Copyright © 1959 by S. G. Phillips, Inc.

sionalism is the solid foundation that supports your masks, trademarks, and emblems. Developing professionalism is an exercise in growth and believability. How do you learn to trust a firm, a product, a person? One way is through honest self-disclosure, letting your own self be seen and heard. Chapter 8 includes self-disclosure as part of Enactment 23. How do you test a person's credibility? How do you develop a trusting interface? Task 3 suggests a few standards commonly used as a check of a person's professionalism.

task 3 PROFESSIONALISM: "DO YOU REALLY MEAN IT?"

Using the six tests that follow, check the professionalism of the persons making the statements listed below.

Test 1: Do your actions match your words?
Test 2: Is what you say and do consistent over a period of time?
Test 3: What biases, prejudices, motives, and external forces determine your words and actions?
Test 4: Are you temporarily influenced by health factors?
Test 5: Who can you rely on for recommendations and testimonials?
Test 6: How do you know your humor, sense of irony, and intentional ambiguity is not misconstrued?

1. The president: "I'd rather be right than president."
2. The head football coach: "Building character is more important to me than building winners."
3. The university president: "I believe there's no such thing as a 'poor' student."
4. A used-car salesman: "I'd buy this little honey myself, if I wasn't prohibited by law."
5. An unmarried person: "Marriage is the best hope mankind has left."
6. A short, 300 pounder: "My advice is to follow my sure-fire, guaranteed, ten-day, way-to-lose diet."
7. A billionaire: "Believe me, I know what poverty is."
8. A three-time convicted felon: "Your honor, I'm a changed person."
9. A four-year-old: "It was red and had ten eyes and ten ears."
10. Your speech teacher: "I want you all to do real well."

Words and Actions. A good, common-sense test used consciously or not is whether your actions are extensions of what you say: "By their fruits you shall know them" is a pretty reliable check of your own professionalism and credibility.

Consistency. People hesitantly extend trust to strangers, because consistency of character takes time to demonstrate. Hasty engagements, decisions, and choices receive criticism; time is seen as a measure of surety. Consistency also implies a varied set of conditions and situations in which to assess a person's character, competence factor, and credibility.

Bias.   The biased person has an axe to grind, a profit to turn, a vote to get, or some other motive that tends to overwhelm whatever he or she might say or do. Most people are guarded in their acceptance of messages from those who have obvious vested interests in winning that acceptance or who stand to gain from it.

Health.   Many studies are presently trying to isolate factors that temporarily affect our capacity to judge and think clearly. A health influence can be anything from overeating and indigestion to mind-affecting medication. Some people—and their messages—are directly affected by weather, season, sense-acuity, and a variety of other factors. Questionable states of health may contribute to questionable professionalism, and a reputation for erratic health undermines credibility.

Opinions of Others.   As a first test, you may rely on "what you've heard" about a person. Your professional reputation precedes you before you say a single word, and it may depend greatly on your "track record" in the dealings and transactions you have had. This seems to represent a vicious circle of acquiring a reputation before you prove you have one, but people frequently transfer evidence of character from other categories of activity. Your grammar school teacher learned something about you from your parents; your parents probably sought explanations of your personality from their parents and grandparents; and so on.

Humor.   Wit and cleverness have a two-edged effect. Everyone is supposed to like a funny person, but often people question the credibility or intent of the humorist. Humor arises from a collision of different logics and referents; it sometimes has a valuable influence in reducing the tensions of transacting. Chapter 7 touches briefly on the uses of humor, the risks of joking with literal-minded receivers, and the confusion caused by intended ambiguity. Self-deprecating wit is sometimes seen as a sign of genuine self-effacement, which is considered to be a form of honesty and self-disclosure.

Professionalism can be described as a molding task, because it represents a growth process. Your professional character is formed by layering trial and error lessons to create a fiber of self. Good communication reveals this fiber. The relationships that are so important in communicating are equally essential in obtaining a grasp of your professional self. Perhaps the relationships of your needs, work motive, self-image, range of roles, and emerging professionalism will be further molded in Enactment 12.

Enactment 12 is intended to give you practice in combining all the factors discussed so far affecting professionalism. Using the lead-in phrase "pardon me, but haven't we met somewhere before?" try to find out who your partner really is; why he/she works at his/her job; what he/she thinks of himself/herself; how trustworthy he/she is.

enactment 12   "PARDON ME, BUT HAVEN'T WE MET SOMEWHERE BEFORE?"

Try to reveal these characteristics in ....

your credibility
your self-image
your attitude toward work

enactment 12: "PARDON ME, BUT HAVEN'T WE MET SOMEWHERE BEFORE?"

participants

Person 1, a student of any description; *Person 2*, a student who seems to recognize Person 1.

need to talk

Person 1 has no need to respond to Person 2, other than to answer questions civilly, but he/she may get socially involved, feel compelled to "straighten Person 2 out," pretend to be who he/she is mistaken for, or otherwise pass a few moments of pleasant chatter. Person 2 genuinely believes that if Person 1 really is the person he/she thinks, the encounter is very much worth pursuing. Person 1 may be a famous person, a friend, an enemy, a person "worth knowing"— whomever Person 2 decides he/she looks like.

time/locale

Midday, any meeting place on campus.

critique 12   TROUBLESHOOTING

1. What evidence was there that Person 2 made a "happy mistake"?
2. Did Person 2 appear to be professional in his/her "interest"?
3. What roles did Person 1 adopt?
4. Did Person 2 see through the role-playing to the self within?
5. Which tests did either take of his/her partner's professionalism?

6. Was either defensive about his/her background, esteem, or identity?
7. Who would make the better manager? Why?
8. What did you detect about image and professionalism in the faces of the participants?
9. How did each participant find common grounds, common languages with the other?
10. How would you rate each participant on listening?

HOW WOULD YOU IMPROVE THE EXCHANGE?

afterthought **COMMUNICATION: WHAT IS IT? WHY IS IT?**

The tasks and enactments to this point have attempted to get you to explore your communication skills and to reacquaint you with many common-sense truths about communication that you have probably experienced. The examples and illustrations offered were sequenced to stimulate your own findings about the nature of communication and your role in the process.

As you conclude the preliminaries—your personal inventory and practice—you may discover that no single book can tell you everything and that the most important and usable guides are those you uncover yourself and tailor to meet your individual needs and purposes. The contexts of discussions and enactments that follow, therefore, are practical extensions of the material so far presented. You have experienced some basics, and you are ready for the field problems of communicating in business and professions.

READ FOR YOURSELF

HANNEMAN, GERHARD J., and WILLIAM J. MCEWEN, eds., *Communication and Behavior.* Reading, Mass.: Addison-Wesley Publishing Co., Inc., 1975.

MASLOW, ABRAHAM H., *Toward a Psychology of Being* (2nd ed.). New York: Van Nostrand Reinhold Company, 1968.

MCCLELLAND, DAVID C., *The Achieving Society.* Princeton, N.J.: D. Van Nostrand Company, 1961.

SHOSTROM, EVERETT L., *Man, the Manipulator.* Nashville: Abingdon Press, 1967.

CHAPTER CHART

Theories of Work
> Does the reward seem sure, and is it worth it?
> Do you *need* to achieve, dominate, or subdue?
> Do you see work as a means to an end?
> Do you elect to work out of a sense of fairness?
> *Key idea:* Effective communication helps you to work in order to grow

Maslow's Hierarchy of Needs
> Physiological needs come first
> Security and maintaining the status quo are second
> Love needs, including needs for acceptance, belongingness, and feedback, are the next highest
> Self-actualization or learning to like yourself as your own boss is the last need
> *Key idea:* Effective communication helps you develop into a self-actualizing professional

Types of Professional People
> Manipulators control people, treating them as objects
> Exploiters capitalize on and trade in potentials
> Hustlers are agents and high-energy salespeople
> Managers regulate and coordinate the flow and sequence of systems
> Entrepreneurs own and determine the use of properties and resources
> Professionals facilitate others to find themselves and assume competence
> *Key idea:* The competence factor is the degree to which you practice professionalism, work at it, live it, communicate it

Image-Making
> The undeniable character you are comes through in all your images and roles
> Your personal trademarks reflect your idea of yourself
> You play roles in the hope that something of the role will rub off on you

Professional Reputation
> Your professionalism is molded through the trust others have in you
> You can test the professionalism of others by:
>> matching their words with their actions
>> testing their character over a period of time
>> recognizing their biases
>> recognizing health factors that impair them
>> assessing the opinions of others
>> assessing their use of humor and ambiguity
> *Key idea:* Building a professional reputation is a growth process

chapter 6

chapter challenge

Understand the public speaking contract

Inventory your private speaking skills

Use tension-reducing methods

Practice maintaining contact with your audience

Improve the variety in your speaking performance

Find ways to overcome distances

Recognize public speaking occasions that require spontaneity and/or manuscript skills

Cultivate a sensitivity to "exposure time" in the use of visual aids

Involve your audience and encourage participation

THE SPEAKER

voice-CALL   voice-CALL   voice-CALL   voice-CALL   voice-CALL

As a member of the business or professional community you will have numerous opportunities for person-to-group (public) speaking. When you rise to speak, you call attention to the many aspects of your professional image. When you are called on to present an idea, your performance reflects the hours you have spent developing your competence factor in tasks, discussions, and enactments. Chapters 6 and 7 of this book examine the professional occasions when you call on an audience to listen, when you call on yourself to voice your plans and opinions; when you call on your knowledge of and sensitivity to the communication process.

PUBLIC VERSUS PRIVATE SPEAKING

A public speaking occasion might be defined as any instance where an individual speaks to a collective group of listeners face-to-face. The situation calls for a specific set of rules applicable to speaker and listener. These rules are:

1. One person speaks *to* an audience of listeners.
2. The speaker should be prepared and speak with conviction.
3. Both speaker and listener have particular roles to play.
4. Speaker and listener share responsibility for the success of the presentation.
5. The speaker has the responsibility for determining whether or not an oral presentation is the best method to convey the message.

Let us examine and compare these rules of the public speaking contract.

speaking to the audience

When you rise to speak, the things you say and your mode of saying them must somehow match or fulfill the expectations of your audience. Your presentation of known symbols in a novel way performs a communication task for your audience; you think, organize, generalize, and interpret for them through the message. Your visual and audible "voice" calls forth images and sensations for them, as well.

Private speaking may contain some of these traits, but ordinarily private speaking follows a reciprocal pattern of give and take or dialectic; each participant speaks for himself or herself, sometimes thinking out loud, ruminating, and talking without much planning and rehearsal. Private speaking tends to be spontaneous, whereas the public speaker's audience is most often served best by a planned presentation.

a worthwhile message, spoken with conviction

You must have something worthwhile to impart, if you assume the responsibility of a speaker. Your conviction (or lack of it) is catching. If you do not believe in your topic and purpose and have to fake it, your attitude will become part of your message. Insincerity will be heard by someone in your audience—perhaps by many. Even the highly skilled actor will have difficulty convincing an audience if the message is out of sync with his or her convictions. For example, a speaker who tries to persuade an audience to do something without demonstrating belief in the subject will not have much power to convince.

In private conversation testing of ideas and attitudes is understood and accepted. You may talk just for the sake of talking. Private speaking may be recreation, wild fantasizing, bragging, ridiculing, and game-playing. A public presentation must generate a reward for the audience for listening; that reward comes from the speaker's adequate preparation and demonstrated conviction.

role agreement

The public presentation dictates separate roles for speaker and audience. Roles determine seating, distances, attention, and behavior over a period of time. In private speaking roles are fluid and interchangeable.

mutual help

A public speaking event invokes the assistance of both speaker and audience. Speakers help their audiences adjust to the message; they work to compensate for distortions and other obstacles that impede efficient, vivid transmission. Communication is two-directional and simultaneous; you speak as eloquently when listening as you do when you talk. Both audience and speaker should participate in the public speaking contract if the communication is to be a success.

the speech is necessary

The responsibility of proving that the oral presentation is necessary lies with the speaker. The force and momentum of your message should be compelling and made to seem necessary to your audience.

A public presentation calls for certain communication dynamics. When you rise to make a presentation, you do so under the condition that a speech is the best possible way to convey your message. Your audience agrees to listen only as long as this contract is fulfilled. As a representative of a business or profession, your individual way of speaking cannot really be duplicated, but your message can. If your message would be more effective taped, filmed, or mimeographed, why should anyone take the time to listen to your speech? You the speaker must be convinced that your presentation is the most effective way of sharing the information with your audience.

Task 1 is a check of your skills in private and public speaking. Part A asks you to list some of the advantages of a public presentation. Part B gives you the opportunity to complete the personal communication inventory you began in Chapter 1 by completing the phrases that show whether you can use in public communications the effective speaking skills you already apply to your private speaking.

task 1 TAKING INVENTORY OF PRIVATE AND PUBLIC SPEAKING SKILLS

Part A: "A public presentation is more effective than other formats."

1. A public presentation indicates the speaker cares more, because _____

_____.

2. A public presentation offers a better opportunity to self-disclose, because

_____.

3. A public presentation is remembered longer, because _____

_____.

4. A public presentation allows for involvement of all the senses, because ____

_____.

5. A public presentation is suspenseful, because _____

_____.

6. A public presentation is more controllable, because _____

_____.

7. A public presentation is easier to understand, because _____

_____.

8. A public presentation is more efficient, because _____

_____.

Part B: What do you do in private communication that will work for you in a public format? Write a phrase or two describing speaking skills you already have that can be used as strengths in public speaking.

1. _Nonverbal languages:_

   a. I use my hands and arms to help _____

   _____;

   b. I use my head and face to _____

   _____;

   c. I use my body so as to _____

   _____;

   d. I laugh in order to _____

   _____;

   e. I'm conscious of heights, and I usually _____

   _____;

   f. I sometimes change my voice, when I _____

   _____;

   g. I'm conscious of being too close or too far away, and I _____

   _____;

h. I look at my listener only when I want to _____

_____;

i. I meet my listener's eyes only when I _____

_____.

2. *Vocal expression:*

   a. I try to make sounds that are as pleasant as I can, because _____

_____;

   b. I try to say words as clearly as I can, particularly when _____

_____;

   c. I sometimes distort or muffle words intentionally, because _____

_____;

   d. I try to give my listener a chance to take in everything I say by _____

_____;

   e. I try to give my listener clues about words I want to emphasize by ___

_____;

   f. I try to give my listener clues about words and ideas that are not too
significant by _____

_____.

3. *Nervousness:*

   a. When I get tense, I usually _____

_____;

   b. When I think my listener is nervous, I _____

_____;

   c. My own embarrassment and nervousness usually go away, because I

_____;

   d. I usually become more nervous whenever _____

_____;

   e. My listeners help take my nervousness away when they _____

_____;

f. When I forget what to say, I just _____

_____ ;

g. If I ever become aware of my breathing, it's usually _____

_____ ;

h. If I ever become aware of my hands, it's usually _____

_____ ;

i. I never feel that I'm risking something when I _____

_____ ;

j. I never feel I'm being judged when I _____

_____ .

4. *Message encoding:*

a. I sometimes ramble on and repeat things in private speaking, because

I know that _____

_____ ;

b. I use the latest slang expressions so that _____

_____ ;

c. When I hear vocabulary words that are new, I _____

_____ ;

d. The kind of proof I most often use is _____

_____ ;

e. In private speaking, I stick to the point by _____

_____ ;

f. People always know I don't mean it when I _____

_____ ;

g. My listeners like to hear my stories, because _____

_____ ;

h. My listeners know when I'm joking and when I'm serious, because I __

_____ ;

i. Certain kinds of occasions dictate how I talk, for example, _____

_____ .

The student who asks: "Why should I take a course in speech? I've been talking all my life," is making a fundamental point about public speaking. The effective public presentation exhibits all the positive skills people use throughout their personal lives in communicating. Everything you do well in private speaking can help you fulfill the speaker/audience contract in public speaking. Keep your inventory in mind during the following list of suggestions for applying private speaking skills to public speaking situations.

NERVOUS TENSION

The condition commonly labeled nervousness, stage fright, or "butterflies" is a kind of conflict of opposing energies. When your body gets ready to perform extraordinary tasks, you may sometimes associate the change in feeling with *fear*—a panicky state of disorganization and a conviction of impotence.

In other sections of this text, a lot of space is given to situations where communicators work to defuse or disarm conflicts, because competitions, one-up strategies, divisiveness, and similar forms of unprofessional behavior undermine human coexistence. Another view is possible, however: tension or oppositional pull might best be seen by the professional communicator as a type of *plurality*—to be accepted for its productivity and not considered a weakness.

One source of incapacitating tension when you are a public speaker may be misunderstanding your contract—your license to speak. If, for example, you sense that a contract exists and that you cannot fulfill your responsibility, tension will grow with the fear of failure and the guilt of knowing that you have not made adequate preparations. Thus, Axiom 5 provides a testable guideline for business transactions . . .

**axiom 5:   THE PROFESSIONAL COMMUNICATOR REDUCES
UNPRODUCTIVE TENSION BY FULFILLING THE
COMMUNICATION CONTRACT**

reduce your tension by being extremely well prepared

Generally, your audiences will want you to succeed; they do not want to see failure or "half good" presentations. They will fulfill their part of the bargain as long as you prove (or at least do not disprove) that you deserve their faith in your message.

If your inventory showed a discomfort with private speaking, then overpreparation is all the more essential. Practice the presentation out loud; break down each phase into separate components and try 20 or 30 enactments, so that your live assemblage of the parts is smooth.

Approximate the distance if you can. Reconstruct the speaking arrangement you will be using—the lectern, the chair-back, the table, or whatever speaker's space you will have.

reduce your tension by using it up

Physical work of any kind helps to relieve unchanneled, bunched-up energy by getting it to circulate. If your inventory indicated a problem about "doing something" with your hands, feet, and so on, plan to incorporate opening movements, gestures, hand games into the beginning part of your presentation. If your breathing gets out of sync, try taking several deep breaths just before you reach the speaker's space.

Body movement will allow you to release pent-up tension. Your study of the hand gesture chart in Chapter 2 might suggest how you could brush up your natural inclination to use hands and arms in private speech and make it work for you during a public speech. The gesture should be the outward growth of an inward feeling, however, and never a mechanical movement.

reduce your tension by channeling it

When you reach as high as you can to touch something—the ceiling, for example—you consciously *focus* your energy. There are many objects into which you might channel or focus energy during a speech; here is a partial list:

Focus Your Energy

into gestures
into clothing
into your jaw, mouth, and smile muscles
into your audience's eyes
into your throat, voice-box, and nasal cavities
into hand objects
into other body parts
into the floor through your feet

reduce your tension by passing it along to your audience

Public speaking, like private conversation, is a participatory event. Speaker and listener work together and participate in the exchange, so that tension is sometimes generated by and in all the participants. From your inventory you might have noted that it is easier for you to talk with people you know. It therefore would be worthwhile for you to get to know your audience. Making the acquaintance of just one or two persons before you speak will give you "friends" to talk to. This lets you channel energy to those people and pass it along to them.

Try to find ways to "turn the tables" on your audience. Mention something that you have found out about them that they did not know you knew. Knowing a few names helps; perhaps you know an incident or some personal item you can mention or allude to without offending anyone. Your arm and hand gestures will, of course, point energy toward them. Some presentations lend themselves to partitioning the audience. You may divide the group by row or section or cluster and create small group identities within a very large audience, through your use of gestures and body movements.

Another technique for reducing your tension and for passing it along is use of handouts. Any object that is distributed or made available to audiences can help them participate and provide a release for everyone's nervous tension. Handouts have a positive function in providing needed information and reducing tension; however, the distribution of handouts during a presentation tends to redirect the focus of the audience from the speaker to the handout. Offering the handout before or after the oral presentation may be more suitable, unless the material to be presented warrants inclusion in written form for the audience's inspection during the speech but will lose value if revealed beforehand. Thus, the use of handouts should be planned carefully to be sure their purpose is fulfilled and aids you in completing your speaking contract.

Supplementary "listening aids" are used for many types of large audiences. People carry transistor radios to ballgames, they are given programs, agendas, prayer cards and hymnals, even ticket stubs; each of these serves as a tension drain and a kind of membership badge that binds audience members together.

The speaker's attitude should be one of giving. Just as you might incorporate the exchange of tactile and highly engaging objects, you will certainly plan to give members of your audience rhetorical gifts. You will ask that they conjure pictures in their minds, visualize stories and anecdotes, follow reasoned plans and assessments, keep track of numbers and statistical patterns as you present your ideas. These and many other tasks are offered in the speech. They may serve to place responsibility with your audience and reduce your nervous tension.

MAINTAINING CONTACT

In its broadest sense, speaker/audience contact is maintained through any of the potential interfaces explored in the early chapters of this book. What methods do you use in private speaking to gain and keep your listener's attention? Task 2 lists some common attention-getting elements in public speaking. Explain why they would or would not be effective in a business presentation.

task 2 "MAY I HAVE YOUR ATTENTION, PLEASE?"

1. Use of visual and auditory aids might get and maintain an audience's attention, because _____.

2. Quoting poetry would/would not help, because _____ _____.

3. Looking your audience straight in the eye, would/would not maintain attention, because _____.

4. Speaking very loudly would/would not help, because _____ _____.

5. Revealing something personal would/would not be effective, because ____ _____.

6. Repeating key words and phrases would/would not be effective, because _____.

7. Maintaining distance between you and your audience would/would not be effective, because _____.

8. Using shocking statements does/does not maintain attention, because ____ _____.

9. Keeping your audience in suspense—promising them something later— would/would not be effective, because _____ _____.

10. Quoting from today's newspaper might/might not be effective, because ____ _____.

11. Mentioning members of the audience by name in public will/will not help gain their attention, because _____.

12. Flattering the audience individually or collectively, would/would not maintain attention and contact, because _____.

13. Threatening the audience, individually or collectively, would/would not be effective, because _____.

14. Using humor does/does not help contact, because _____

_____.

15. Speaking spontaneously—off the cuff—would/would not help maintain contact,

because _____.

16. Being an "authority" does/does not help bind contact, because _____

_____.

17. Having taken this course would/would not help you maintain contact, because

_____.

Maintaining contact is, of course, part of the public speaking contract. If there is a better way to impart the message, then that other format should be used.

VARIETY IN THE SPEECH

Speaking length is "understood" rather than stated in your contract. A 12-reel saga with a dinner break will not help communication, but a respect for brevity and conciseness will. You probably realize that prolonged exposure to patterns tends to lull the senses. Flickering lights and the hum of machinery are often sleep-inducing. When you are speaking publicly, you should take great care to inject a variety of patterns into your speaking performance, as detailed in the following pages.

variety in images

Most people take delight in being addressed several ways. During a speech, for example, your overall effectiveness will be enhanced if you use different ways of projecting images.

A projected image can be thought of as the link between the speaker and the idea. It is the "place" where the audience should direct its attention. Think about these examples of helping an audience to know where to "look" and how to adjust its thinking in various ways.

1. *Projecting an image into the audience:* "I want to thank each of you for your help in gathering these research data." You may have seen a speaker slowly fan a hand, palm facing the audience, during this statement. The link is shown to be between the speaker's hand and those indicated.

2. *Projecting an image into the past:* "Recall, for a moment, our last meeting." You may have seen a speaker gesture with a hand to some side space. By gesturing to a location for the link, the speaker gives the audience a place to think of as "the past" and helps it to participate more fully.

3. *Projecting an image into the future:* "Let's look ahead to see what might lie in store for our profession." You may have seen a speaker use a throwing gesture over audience's heads. The image can be "thrown" in any direction except perhaps straight up, as long as the idea of the future is projected into a different area.
4. *Projecting an image into the speaker's space:* "Here, I have proof that will affect all of us." You may have seen a speaker gesture to a space close by. The link between image and speaker provides a bit of variety to the public presentation.
5. *Projecting images thought of by others:* "It was Lord Keynes who first described the trick, and he said it this way." The speaker turns his or her body to indicate the image is coming from another person. Quoting or story-telling is enhanced and variety is attained by projecting the image of a second speaker into a space, showing the audience that the image is beside you and that you step out of yourself to quote or assume another person's viewpoint.

The possibilities for image and gesture are limited only by how much time you spend trying out various combinations. Check your inventory and previous enactment experiences for instances when you have used a variety of image projections without thinking about it much.

vocal variety

You are probably expert in the kinds of vocal traits that put you to sleep. Whether or not you are gifted with a beautifully modulated voice, you probably have a number of vocal characteristics you might improve.

The *pitch* is the highness or lowness your voice reaches. People generally have and use a comfortable range of pitches. With a little help from your colleagues in class, you should be able to find the range of your voice in Enactment 13.

Rate is the second vocal trait through which varied patterns are produced. Your rate is the speed at which you talk, and this speed shifts between words and syllables. You control your rate by speaking in one or more of the following ways:

1. Waiting until all eyes are locked on yours before saying something. You may do this several times in your presentation.
2. Elongating or stretching a vowel sound, as in "Ooooo-kay."
3. Breaking syllables for emphasis or for clarity, as in "con-cat-en-ation."
4. Playing on the expectation usually associated with terms such as "because," "however," and "finally." Pausing for one or two seconds after these words adds variety to your rate patterns.
5. Speeding up whole phrases and lists of words to show their unimportance or to ridicule their length, for example, "all kinds of beans and bean products: split, whole, round, string, yellow, black, brown, green, dried, freeze-dried . . ."
6. Sometimes stopping in midphrase, after a preposition, for example: "The greatest change is somewhere in . . . this area." Pausing this way may help

you accommodate visual aids or movement to another space and may add variety to cadenced speech.

The *volume* of your voice is the third trait and is controlled by speaking loudly or softly. It is important for you to understand that "loud" and "soft" are comparative descriptions. Since you are the only one speaking, you can set your own standards of variety. Most audiences will adjust their listening from speaker to speaker as part of their contract. Wide variances between speech patterns are reduced by use of amplifying equipment, so that the volume levels of the voices heard before and after yours will tend to be kept consistent.

The study of speech production is a specialized area, but a few hints on making your voice sounds as pleasant as possible may enable you to provide your audiences with a more satisfying communication experience.

Open your mouth. Sound energy needs air between it and the receiving eardrum. Any obstacle will color or distort the original sound patterns. Dropping your jaw and showing your teeth does wonders to end mumbling, slurring or mushing of your words or trying to keep your voice sounds in your mouth.

Exaggerate sounds begun or ended with the tip of your tongue. Practicing with tongue-twisters and with whispered speaking will help bring your attention to muddy articulation.

Give yourself *air*. If you are short of breath, open your mouth and suck in air; it is the main carrier for speech energy. Once you have air in your lungs, do not be afraid to release it and use it.

variety in posture

Your aimless twitching and squirming, bouncing from side to side or forward and back may create a "predictable pattern" for your audience. If it begins to swing and sway with you or even think rhythmically, the public speaking event turns into something different from what was intended. Select places in your speech where the distance between you and your audience *should* be changed. In private speaking, after you have become acquainted with someone, you feel a little more inclined to close distances, if that is warranted. In public there may be this same "get acquainted" period in which you spend a few phrases just to help the audience become familiar with the situation. In the public presentation you symbolically close or open space by leaning toward or away from the audience and by pulling your head back and up or forward and downward; any gesture toward or away affects proximity.

variety in facial animation

"Smile!" is a very old word of advice for people speaking in public. It may be particularly applicable to those who are unable to smile

figure 6-1 Expressive Faces

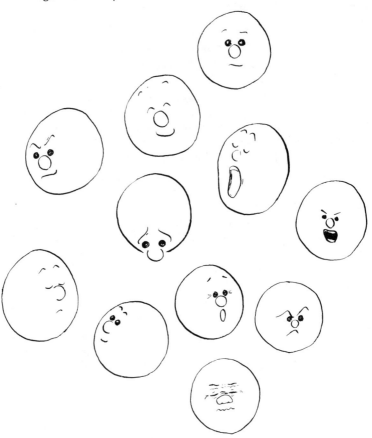

at themselves when they do or say something stupid or inept. Audiences prefer a human being to a machine that emits canned noises. Your candid recognition of self-limitations will tend to humanize your relationship with most audiences. A smile should not be put on, but when appropriate—smile.

Use your facial muscles and explore your range of facial expressions. The eye area is perhaps the most important conveyer of messages and states of mind.

task 3 HARMONIZING

Match the phrase from a famous speech with the eye and mouth expression that you feel is harmonious with the state of mind revealed in the phrase. Draw them below.

1. Abraham Lincoln: "The ballot is stronger than the bullet."

2. Mark Antony (Shakespeare): "I come not, friends, to steal away your hearts . . . I am no orator . . . but . . . a plain, blunt man."

3. Charles Dickens (*Nicholas Nickleby*): "At Mr. Wackford Squeer's Academy, . . . youth are boarded, clothed, booked . . . instructed in all languages living and dead . . . no extras, no vacations."

4. Talleyrand: "War is much too serious a thing to be left to military men."

5. Swift: "I have ever hated all nations, professions, and communities, and all my love is towards individuals."

6. Sir Andrew Undershaft (Shaw): "I am a millionaire. That is my profession."

enactment 13   FINDING THE RANGE

This enactment is meant to do two things. First, it asks you to prepare a professional presentation in a speech format that most people do fairly well—*story-telling*. Your story may be entirely fictional, partly fictional, or true, but whatever the combination it should meet your standard of conviction: You have to believe it is worth telling.

Review what you have read about being a speaker; think back to how you have told stories in private and the speaking techniques that have worked well for you. Practice your presentation, plan your nonverbal expressions, anticipate the class arrangement.

The second objective is to find your vocal range. Figure 6–2 shows a sample graph that can be used by your colleagues to draw a picture of your pitch, rate, and volume *variety* as you tell your story. Each group, assigned to one vocal dynamic, listens and graphs the highs and lows or loudness and softness of your voice, by placing a pencil or pen (stylus) at the x and letting the arm move freely to the end of the graph. After allowing you a little warm-up period, your colleagues

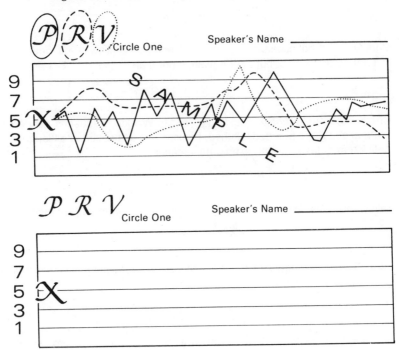

figure 6-2 Vocal Variety

should graph your storytelling presentation and give you their graphs showing a general picture of your vocal ranges in it.

Try to exhibit these traits in ....

enactment 13: FINDING THE RANGE

knowledge and commitment to
the speaker-audience
contract
private speaking skills
release of tension
focusing energy
maintaining contact
varied projection of images
varieties of pitch, rate, volume

critique 13 TROUBLESHOOTING

1. Why was this the best possible way to convey this particular message?
2. At what points should the distance between you and the speaker have been changed? Why?

3. In what ways should a public presentation be similar to a conversation between two people? Why?

4. How did your participation-by-graphing help or hinder you in fulfilling the speaker–audience contract?

5. Which aspects of the presentation helped bind your attention?

6. How does the concept of invitation fit into public presentations?

7. What audience needs are met through story-telling?

8. What might story-telling have to do with reports that rely on numbers and other digital codings?

9. How did facial animation help you to know where to look?

10. Which gestures helped the speaker project images clearly?

HOW WOULD YOU IMPROVE IT?

SPONTANEITY

Some businesses take great pains to treat their customers and associates as individuals. Certain segments of the professions are criticized for their mass-produced service, and you may have already found that you gain credibility, persuasiveness, and personal respect from others only by taking the time to be a good communicator. As a public speaker your need to convey this special consideration of individual audiences and individuals within those audiences is shown in many ways.

Audiences recognize and respect the hard work you make evident by your preparation and your performance. They also appreciate the "speaking load" that you take from their shoulders. In these two respects, members of an audience might sense that you are treating them as individuals. Another characteristic that professional presentations need and often lack is *spontaneity*—the audience's belief that you are speaking directly to each member as a person and that you are trying to speak especially for this one occasion.

Spontaneity is one symptom of self-disclosure and is perhaps the most distinguishing feature that separates private from public speaking. Your credibility may be weakened, for example, if a listener arrives at the conclusion that you "say that to everybody," or "I know what that speech is all about; I've heard it enough times." Segments of your public audience may be hard pressed to believe in your sincerity, even though they may credit the facts and figures offered in support of your opinions.

Your real message may thus become: "I am *performing* a message for you." When this occurs, your speaking role changes from the professional who is speaking to the professional who is performing a speech.

Task 4 compares speaking and performing, to provide you with a guide for determining the degree of spontaneity that may be expected in your speaking contracts for different occasions.

task 4   SPONTANEITY AND THE PLANNED MESSAGE

Circle what you believe is the most appropriate degree of spontaneity and explain why.

1. I would propose marriage by speaking/performing with a low/medium/high degree of spontaneity, because ————————————————.

2. I would deliver a stockholders' report by speaking/performing with a low/medium/high degree of spontaneity, because ————————— ——————————————————————————.

3. I would make an after-dinner speech to a service organization by speaking/performing with a low/medium/high degree of spontaneity, because ———— ——————————————————————————.

4. I would make a damage report of a major fire to a municipal committee by speaking/performing with a low/medium/high degree of spontaneity, because ——————————————————————————.

5. I would make a floor speech to the state senate by speaking/performing with a low/medium/high degree of spontaneity, because ——————————— ——————————————————————————.

6. I would make a welcoming speech to new club members and officers by speaking/performing with a low/medium/high degree of spontaneity, because ——————————————————————————.

7. I would make a technical report to assembled department supervisors by speaking/performing with a low/medium/high degree of spontaneity, because ——————————————————————————.

8. I would give a sermon to a large congregation by speaking/performing with a low/medium/high degree of spontaneity, because _____ .

9. I would give a televised interview about my company's views on pollution control by speaking/performing with a low/medium/high degree of spontaneity, because _____ .

10. I would give a campaign speech for a political candidate before a large audience by speaking/performing with a low/medium/high degree of spontaneity, because _____ .

11. I would present a briefing of a problem to a small group by speaking/performing with a low/medium/high degree of spontaneity, because _____ .

12. I would present a eulogy or testimonial speech to a large audience by speaking/performing with a low/medium/high degree of spontaneity, because _____ .

THE MANUSCRIPT SPEECH

Some speech contracts specify that the speaker may read and/or refer to a script or copy of the speech during the presentation. The presentation in this case is neither speaking nor performing, as previously described, but lies somewhere in between.

The purpose of this kind of presentation is to adhere to an exact phrasing and word choice. Sometimes a public speech reaches a mass audience before it is given; for example, prepared government statements are distributed to the media in advance of their performance. These news releases may present very fine articulations of policy, and, because they may be read by people all over the world, they are carefully depersonalized and digitally encoded to ensure maximum clarity and precision.

Task 4 may have suggested a few of the problems associated with the degree of spontaneity in public speaking. One such difficulty is time. A manuscript may help shape your presentation to meet a specific time limit, such as six or ten minutes—no more, no less—that is prescribed by television program directors or radio producers. Genuine spontaneity may not provide this kind of precision.

Manuscript reading may also hinder speaker–audience contact. Television studios use several methods of helping speakers to give the illusion of eye contact and spontaneity, including teleprompters and cue cards. If you give a television speech, the director will determine the techniques that best serve the type of message, speaker, format, and occasion that you are involved with. To some degree the camera lens provides angles and proximities that will aid the illusion of spontaneity and contact.

It may help you prepare for Enactment 14 to think through the following suggestions about reading manuscript speeches:

1. Is reading a manuscript the best possible way to convey your message?
2. Try to memorize lead-in phrases and short, key sentences, so that your eyes can leave the page and reestablish audience contact.
3. Type or print your copy extra large, and do not skimp on the paper; you must be able to read without seeming to read.
4. Try different page layouts for your speech, such as block phrasing or writing words in clusters, in order to find the word arrangement that fits your individual way of scanning a line when you read it.
5. Memorize the opening and closing of a manuscript speech and practice these crucial parts so that contact is assured and a high degree of spontaneity is conveyed.
6. Try to compose your manuscript to fit a particular audience. If you adapt a speech given before, do so with your new audience in mind.
7. If you continue to lose your place during practice sessions, alternate the use of fingertips to help you scan and keep your place in the manuscript. Use of alternate hands will give you more freedom to gesture.
8. Remember to write your manuscript in "talk" language, not in "read" language. Your audience will be a listening group first and a reading group second.
9. Plan a method of turning pages unobtrusively, unless you want part of your message to be the spectacle of your turning, holding, and creasing the pages, with all its noise.
10. Remember, you must vocally *punctuate* your text for your audience. Use pauses and full stops to regain contact and to help your audience ingest what you have said.

enactment 14   "LADIES AND GENTLEMEN, BOYS AND GIRLS . . ."

As president of a large company, you are addressing a television audience on "the state of the industry." Write a manuscript speech that accommodates both the group in the television studio and the viewing audience. Do not be concerned as much with what the camera "sees" as with incorporating remarks that you want your television audience to hear.

Try to use what you have read about these concepts in ....

spontaneity

manuscript speaking

enactment 14: "LADIES AND GENTLEMEN, BOYS AND GIRLS . . ."

critique 14 TROUBLESHOOTING

1. How did the reading make it easier for you to listen?
2. Although you knew the speech was not entirely spontaneous, which parts gave the illusion of spontaneity? Why?
3. How does an audience believe a speaker when it knows he/she is paid to say certain things?
4. Why is contact particularly essential at the beginning and end of a speech?
5. What method was used to project images? Was the audience sure of where to look?
6. What problems does manuscript reading cause in attaining pitch/rate/volume variety?
7. Did you feel the need to interrupt this type of speech? Why or why not?
8. Describe any patterned speaking behaviors that drew your attention.
9. Did the speaker's appearance fit the occasion?
10. Did you ever forget you were in a speech class listening to a student? Should speakers strive to achieve this effect on their audiences?

HOW WOULD YOU IMPROVE IT?

PRESENTING TECHNICAL DATA ORALLY

The preparation and oral presentation of what may be termed *technical data* can often be a problem to a business or professional speaker. In general, technical presentations may be classified as either *informational* or *analytical.* Informational presentations include facts and specific findings in an area. Analytical presentations include informational data interpretations, conclusions, and recommendations. Eliciting audience understanding is of prime importance in either type of presentation. Thus the technical speaker should give careful consideration to the following:

1. *To whom will the presentation be made?* While audience analysis is critical in preparing for any speaking situation it has an added dimension in the technical presentation. You must decide whether to use jargon (a technical vocabulary) peculiar to the field or profession. To make this decision, you should clearly identify the target audience. Then you can adopt appropriate language and ensure clarity of your meaning (giving examples, definitions of terms, etc.) by evaluating your listeners beforehand. The term *dichlorodifluoromethane* may be clear to the engineer, but the use of *refrigerant* might be more appropriate when discussing a new line of refrigerators with a Midwest marketing group.
2. *What oral style characteristics can be adapted to the presentation?* Oral presentations of technical data are often based on written reports. For you to simply read a written technical report aloud serves little purpose. You should use language that is concrete and referential and has direct application to a specific audience. (See the discussion of manuscript speech.) While it is common to use initials and acronyms in technical reports the speaker should explain them fully the first time they are used. LTD, for example, would be recognizable to a chemist working with pesticides as Lethal Test Dosage. However, to the newly hired agrichemical salesperson attending a first trainee seminar, LTD might have no meaning at all or a meaning entirely different from that intended, until the technical speaker explains the term fully.
3. *What supplemental aids can be used?* In addition to your oral presentation of a technical speech, you should consider using visual and/or auditory aids to assist in eliciting understanding. Clarity and impact of statement are enhanced when these aids are used appropriately. (See the discussion in the next section.)

In general, as the presenter of technical data you should ask yourself: (1) *What* am I presenting? (2) To *whom* am I presenting it? (3) *Where* will I be presenting it—in what physical surroundings etc.? (4) *How* can I best elicit understanding?

USING VISUAL AND AUDIO AIDS

Whatever your future experiences might be in making presentations, you will want to consider the use of signs, graphs, exhibits, and hand objects as aids for your audience. To help and not confuse your listeners, your choice and use of objects should follow a few common-sense controls.

aids that aid

Your selection of a picture or graph must actually help the audience understand a point, fix its attention, or otherwise translate your verbal message into a more immediate sensory experience. It may serve to confuse or lose the audience's attention by its failure to meet any of the following requirements.

Simplicity. Whatever you choose to show must be seen and/or heard by a number of people, each of whom sees, hears, and thinks differently from you. Try to think of your display object as a single exposure whose effectiveness lasts for a given period of time and then decays, becomes less effective, or even changes its message. The longer people look at or listen to a stimulus the more time they have to read something into it. They see that it is only paper or plastic, that it is peeling or scratched or has a hundred other qualities that are revealed by prolonged exposure.

Keep your graphs simple and large enough for everyone to see. If your presentation is complicated, break the exposures down into phases or steps, so that each exposure will not compete with the others but will present an *accumulative* effect—each building on its predecessor. An example is a set of charts that show the listener past conditions, the present situation, and your own predictions of future conditions.

Coherence. Visual and aural aids should "hang together" with the rest of your presentation. Objects are not the presentation, and they are never a speech. If the mix of aids becomes the central attraction, then the objects turn the presentation into a performance or show. Professions commonly use shows or demonstrations of products and techniques to good effect; sometimes they use a live speaker to accompany the demonstration or use a "voice-over" narrative to help convey the images in a slide, film, or filmstrip presentation.

The best use of aids produces what is called in film a *montage* effect: the sum of the parts is different from each individual element. Coherence is achieved by mixing a variety of elements into a single effective presentation. The total environment must again be kept in mind. You must reconstruct all the speaker–audience factors to smoothly mesh your "cast of characters"—you and your equipment. Check lighting and sound characteristics; be sure you have proper AC outlets and ground adapters; find storage space for equipment before and after its use in your presentation.

Ask yourself if there is a balance in your demonstration. If you rely on technology to do the talking for you, it had better operate superbly. If you make comparisons between old and new, big and little, cheap and expensive, etc., be certain that the differences are sufficiently dramatic to impress the point of the comparison on the audience. All these questions will help you, your audience, and your message cohere to produce an effective public presentation.

Mobility and Focusing.   Demonstrators need to plan for the entrances and exits of their equipment. You may have been part of classroom demonstrations where you spent most of your time focusing on an animal or some piece of apparatus, because you felt compelled to watch that element although other parts of the demonstration were going on. You may have missed whatever else was planned in the presentation, because your attention was riveted to the wrong "character."

Try to plan a way of providing "selective" viewing and hearing for the members of your audience. You should be able to control where they look and what they listen to. You may want to use a system of shrouds, cloth covers, or collapsible boxes, or perhaps have a simple demonstration counter with storage space below.

Some presentations use assistants to carry objects on and off the speaking space, and you may wish to encourage your audience to participate in this way. Some presentations, however, are improved by the use of storage-through-assemblage; this means that each succeeding object is combined or assembled into an arrangement with preceding ones, producing a specific accumulative effect. For example, a component may be introduced; then another is brought in and added to the first; later a third is added; and so on, until the total assemblage forms a computer or engine or whatever. Flat objects such as charts and pictures may be arranged in a similar way to evoke an important, conclusive impact.

Speaker mobility should not be hampered by use of aids. Sometimes you will want to "enlarge" yourself by using pointers, raising your level, or using paraphernalia such as rotating tables to extend your control over the exhibits or aids you are using. The key standard for you should be the old question of dominance and focus: Is your speaking function to aid the aids or are they used to aid you?

Involvement.   The purpose of using aids is ultimately to help you and your audience share what is on your mind and to satisfy one another's respective communication needs. A picture of an animal involves the senses more than a one-sentence description; a stuffed animal on exhibit may involve your audience even more; a live animal is again more persuasive; and a live animal in your audience's lap is very, very impressive.

Find ways to involve the members of your audience; plan things for them to do. Remember that listening is not passive. It requires a specific set of tasks in order for a transaction to be possible. Help your audience get involved by incorporating some participatory tasks. Have the members of your audience:

1. answer questions
2. ask questions
3. compete against the object or each other in some form of game situation
4. aid you in the demonstration
5. participate in a group experiment
6. try to find or locate problems, omissions, key factors
7. take handouts, free samples, something to link them with you and your message (but remember that, while handouts etc. may be useful in eliciting greater understanding, they may also hinder communication by directing attention away from your presentation; plan their use carefully)
8. alternate their focus from speaker to object or speaker to image.

The many types of audiovisual aids offer support for almost any kind of presentation. The more frequently used aids are explored below.

Models.   A model is a three-dimensional rendering of an idea, plan, organization, process, person, place, or thing. A working model duplicates the dynamics of the real object. A sectional model is a cutaway portion of the object that reveals internal aspects and workings and the relationships among them. An example is a toy doll's house. By removing the front walls, you reveal what is inside and how living patterns relate to the overall house design.

Charts.   A chart is usually a two-dimensional drawing of a condition existing in time. Bars, lines, and dots can be used to give an instant picture of a quantifiable concept or factor, such as growth or income. Like all speaker–audience aids, charts must be recognizable by the most distant listener/viewer.

Chalkboards.   The chalkboard is a venerable tool with the advantage of being available in most classrooms; its limitations are therefore well known to most students. At best a speaker must turn partially away from the audience to use a chalkboard and reduce or break off contact, but the board offers many possibilities for presenting pre-planned drawings and writings. Incomplete sketches or writings, can be set down before the presentation, allowing the speaker to turn quickly

figure 6-3 Types of Graphs

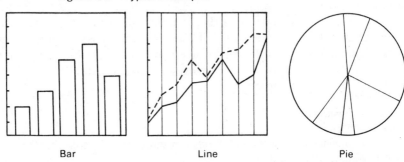

Bar   Line   Pie

and complete a key word or line. Another method is use of assistants to write or erase material. Material may be written completely in advance and then covered over, so that the speaker can expose it bit by bit to the audience.

Sketchpads The large sketchpad mounted on an easel is also a commonly used device for aiding public presentations. Pages drawn in advance may be lifted back for easy control of exposure while the speaker maintains eye and face contact with the audience. Variations of this method include the use of sequenced cards or posters that fall away or can be easily removed.

Film and Videotape. Films are excellent communicators. They involve audiences with their spectacle and penetrate even the most abstruse subject matter. Videotaping has the advantage of offering instantaneous playback of a filmed event.

Both film and videotape give the speaker the ability to freeze the presentation to place emphasis where it is needed and to maintain a balanced contact between speaker, spectacle, and audience.

Audiotape. Tapes of sounds, music, or voices introduce another "speaker." Voices, particularly, will offer competition to your voice, and, unless you introduce this type of material in a careful way, you run the risk of being outdone by a taped voice.

Frequently a tape is introduced as support for a plan or point of view. It may be a reading of conference minutes, a sample poll response, or sounds recorded in the field and under difficult circumstances. Aural fidelity to the original is essential, but more important for you as the speaker is careful preparation of your audience for either good or bad playback. Tell your listeners the limits of the playback before they must make up their own minds. If the voices are at all overpowering, make the comparison to your own voice, so that the contrast will not weaken your presentation to the point where your audience prefers to listen to the tape.

Environments and Dioramas. Occasionally you may be part of a presentation that simulates an experience. You may be familiar with the sightseeing bus that transports its audience around an interesting locale, while a speaker narrates an account of what is seen.

Dioramas and environments are aids that surround an audience and immerse it in an artificial set of conditions that represents some real situation. Certain types of exhibits are organized this way—boat shows, display rooms for furniture suites, or reconstructions of historical contexts are familiar examples.

Sometimes dioramas can be effectively used as part of a larger event, one that may feature public speakers as well as other communication channels. Planned and structured well, these multimedia events can be effective presentations of your idea, product, or plan. They are rich in various sensory stimuli and call on audiences to participate. Enactment 15 gives you the chance to use your resources to make an effective audiovisual presentation to your colleagues.

enactment 15 PICTURES SPEAK LOUDER

Try in this public presentation to mount an array of different aids that help you involve your audience and to persuade them to accept your recommendation. Organize a public speech around your audience's need to follow your recommendation on a plan of action or a product. Your intention in this speech is to sell them your solution to a conscious or unconscious need/problem. Review your performance in previous public speeches; work toward variety, spontaneity, and sustained audience contact. Examine carefully what you now know about your colleagues in this class, the collective wishes they have expressed, and the imbalances they experience.

Use some of these aids to provide a vivid and graphic plan that convinces your classmates of their need to "see things your way" in . . . . .

models
charts
chalkboard
sketchpad
audiotape
diorama

**enactment 15: PICTURES
SPEAK LOUDER**

critique 15 TROUBLESHOOTING

1. Did the speaker compete successfully with the various aids?
2. Explain how the aids helped or hindered your listening.
3. Would the presentation have benefited from the help of an assistant? If so, how?
4. How would you evaluate the "exposure time" of each aid?
5. Explain why you would/would not accept the recommendation in this speech.
6. In what way did the aids "speak louder" than words?
7. Describe the rhetorical gifts the speaker "gave" to the audience.
8. What kind of questions might tough-minded businesspeople ask of this speaker?
9. Which gestures would you consider a kind of invitation to communicate? Why?
10. Was the speaker convinced of the recommendation? How do you know?

WHAT WOULD YOU DO TO IMPROVE IT?

afterthought ONE TIME ONLY

A public speech is a once-only occasion. The many variables are never really the same on any two speech occasions. Although the axiom that you will have second and third opportunities to communicate is valid, each public presentation (like other formats of exchange) is a finished contract and should be completed with that finality in mind.

This obvious principle means that the speaker must pare unnecessary verbiage from the presentation. Aids that are hackneyed or obviously weak contributors to the message should be seriously measured against the damage they might do to the fragile links between the speaker, the concept, and the audience. In the next chapter, you will examine the task of the message itself and will look at the many ways in which what you say relates to how you say it.

READ FOR YOURSELF

ANDERSON, MARTIN, WESLEY LEWIS, and JAMES MURRAY, The Speaker and His Audience. New York: Harper & Row, Publishers, Inc., 1964.

EISENSON, JON, Voice and Diction: A Program for Improvement (3rd ed.). New York: Macmillan Publishing Co., Inc., 1974.

WILCOX, ROGER P., *Oral Reporting in Business and Industry.* Englewood Cliffs, N.J.: Prentice-Hall, Inc., 1967.

WILSON, JOHN F., and CARROLL C. ARNOLD, *Public Speaking as a Liberal Art* (3rd ed.). Boston: Allyn & Bacon, Inc., 1974.

WIRKUS, T., and H. ERICKSON, *Communication and the Technical Man.* Englewood Cliffs, N.J.: Prentice-Hall, Inc., 1972.

WISEMAN, GORDON, and LARRY BARKER, *Speech—Interpersonal Communication* (2nd ed.). New York: Chandler Publishing Company, 1974.

CHAPTER CHART

Public Speaking Contract
>
> One person speaks to an audience
>
> Speaker should be prepared and speak with conviction
>
> Both speaker and listener agree to stick to their respective roles
>
> Speaker and listener share responsibility for the success of the presentation
>
> Speaker determines that the oral presentation is the best method to convey
> the message

Private Speaking Skills Used in Public Speaking
>
> You care about your listeners
>
> You do not hesitate to self-disclose
>
> You use your entire body and personality
>
> You use greater variety and spontaneity
>
> You use a lot of energy
>
> You adjust your mode of speaking to the listeners and the occasion

Reducing Nervous Tension
>
> Be extremely well prepared
>
> Use energy
>
> Channel nervous energy into gestures, parts of your body, objects
>
> Pass nervous energy along to your audience

Maintaining Audience Contact
>
> Use visual aids
>
> Try to maintain eye contact with somebody
>
> Vary your volume, pitch, and rate
>
> Self-disclose
>
> Vary the distances between you and the audience
>
> Promise your audience something to look forward to
>
> Reveal something that your audience does not know you know about them
>
> Experiment with forms and degrees of humor
>
> Use imminence or topicality in some references and citations
>
> Give your audience a place to "see" the past, present, future, or other persons
> referred to

Vocalizing for Effect
>
> Cultivate variety in pitch, rate, and volume
>
> Open your mouth
>
> Exaggerate sounds made with the tip of your tongue
>
> Give yourself air

Visual Variety
>
> Avoid any patterns that an audience might predict
>
> Use movement and posture to emphasize or punctuate your message
>
> Cultivate facial animation

Spontaneity
>
> Give the illusion of speaking for your immediate audience to strengthen
> the communication bond

Key idea: The impression of spontaneity strengthens the speaker's image of integrity

The Manuscript Speech

Read material that must be clearly and precisely conveyed

Read material as a form of support for your contentions

Practice ways of appearing not to read

Use selective memorization and a high degree of familiarity

Use copy that is extremely easy to read

Write your manuscript speech in "talk" language

Punctuate your speech vocally when you deliver it

Presenting Technical Data Orally

Identify your target audience clearly

Use language appropriate to your audience

Adapt written reports to oral style

Visual and Auditory Aids

Make aids simple

Control exposure

Provide for entrances and exits

Prove to yourself that the aid will work before the presentation

Use aids that complement and fit in with your speech

Use aids that are mobile and that allow you to be mobile

Use aids that involve the viewer/listener

Types of Aids

Models

Charts, graphs, pictures

Chalkboards

Sketchpads

Film, videotape, audiotape

Environments and dioramas

chapter 7

chapter challenge

Explain the significance of speaker and audience motives in preparing the message

Use an efficient plan for choosing a topic

Use the four basic methods of the speaker's craft to change your audience

Recognize the necessity of knowing your audience

Explore the possibilities of patterning a message

Develop the habit of partitioning thesis statements

Begin to collect a repertoire of binding beginnings and clinching closes

Discover how transitional phrases and words help your listener

Identify the locations of supportive materials and opinions

Formulate a personal style of persuasive message-building

Cultivate a respect for the differences among fact, value, taste, policy, justice/fairness, and cause

Understand how forms of humor can help establish the speaker–listener bond

THE MESSAGE

message-SEND   message-SEND   message-SEND   message-SEND

When does the message begin; when does it end? As you think about your recent communication experiences, you could probably claim that your messages began when you first started to organize your thoughts and feelings with the intention of sharing them with someone. You may have begun with a visceral urge to impress your state of mind on someone, to induce a similar condition or to effect some change in a listener. You may have wanted to inform, enlighten, prove, persuade, inflict, correct, impress, defend, teach, disarm, entertain, or affect an audience.

The preparation of your message begins with a realization of your intent—why you want to send a message. Task 1 asks you to analyze speakers' intentions.

task 1 GOOD INTENTIONS

Try to supply two things in the following examples: (1) a description of the change the speaker might want to produce in the audience, and (2) why the speaker might want that change.

1. A manager of a supermarket might prepare a message for a chamber of

commerce meeting in order to change _____,

because the manager wants _____.

2. An attorney might prepare a message for a political rally in order to change

_____, because the attorney wants

_____.

3. A grammar school principal might prepare a message for a transit authority

meeting in order to change _____,

because the principal wants _____.

4. A retiring military officer might prepare a message for a community college

student-government meeting in order to change _____,

because the officer wants _____.

5. A union steward might prepare a message for a meeting of newspaper

publishers in order to change _____,

because the steward wants _____.

CHOOSING A TOPIC

The question of which comes first, the speaker's intent or the topic choice, is unanswerable, because topic and intent are inseparable. The following guidelines may help you to select a topic that will effectively send the message you want and elicit the desired audience change.

choose a topic you are committed to

The subject for your presentation must be very close to your own values and commitments. Your dedication to a subject helps your projection of professional integrity and credibility. If you speak about something you know well, this closeness to the subject will be communicated to the members of your audience. They may not agree, or even choose to listen, but a kind of admiration or respect will probably be given to you if you show that you love your subject.

choose a topic that is manageable

Narrow your general subject down to fit the time limits imposed on the speaking occasion. This is one area where your intent may dictate which ideas and details to leave out and which to emphasize. Another determining factor is, of course, the time you have to prepare. When you are scheduled to speak with very little advance or lead time, you may have to fall back on a topic for which you already have an abundance of material.

choose a topic that harmonizes with your audience's interest

Your message—taken as a whole—is an invitation to communicate. One reason you rise to speak is that you have been called to "fill a vacuum" in the experience of your audience. Part of your unstated contract to speak is your agreement to provide something new or something old in a new way to your audience. Your choice of topic must reflect the analysis you have done of that audience. More will be said about this important part of message preparation later in this chapter.

choose a topic that supports your intent

If your intent is to instruct an audience in selecting a product, because you wish to change their buying habits in a particular consumer market, your topic must provide them with a comparative description of products now available. Of all the possible combinations of things you could say, your topic should be the one best able to carry your intent. Knowing what you want to have happen within your audience and why you want it helps you cull examples and bits of information that will provide the best possible chance for that change to take place. A topic that supports your intent is one that makes assembling and organizing your message easier.

CHOOSING A METHOD

How do you assemble a message that will stimulate a change? Traditionally, three types of speeches are defined by *purpose*: the speech to inform, the speech to persuade, and the speech to entertain. As you know, communication exchanges are not that simple. Any signal you receive has all three properties to some degree, and most speeches will inform, persuade, *and* entertain. It might help you as a professional communicator to prepare your message by considering methods by which the change you wish to effect may occur.

instructional method

Instruction can be built into your message by asking yourself these questions:

1. What does my audience need to know in order to duplicate an action?
2. What special terminology does my audience need explained or demonstrated before it can make the change on its own?
3. Does it want to be instructed? If so, why?
4. What method of feedback can I incorporate into the message to show my audience it is successfully receiving instruction?

5. What connections can I provide to link what my audience can do to what I want it to be able to do?

The instructional method is sometimes called *show-and-tell* because it allows for a progression of changes among audience members. Checkpoints, pauses for self-testing, summaries, and two-way exchanges are often used in this method of effecting a change in the listeners. The instructional method of producing change is most often used in training sessions, where a concept, process, or object is taught or explained to a group.

demonstration method

The idea in the demonstration method is to perform the wanted change for your audience. Thus, you might show a series of arranged products with their various markings and list of ingredients, union labels, and coded dating, and simulate the problem of actually selecting the best buy. Rather than talking about it or asking your audience to do it, you do it for them. Demonstrations may be incorporated into the smallest bits of a message. You may literally demonstrate the consequences of not heeding a warning message by making an unpleasant face.

informational method

The informational method of effecting change is simply telling an audience about a subject. You organize the material so that it can be narrated or told as you would tell a story or experience. You then proceed to relate the sequences of names, facts, occurrences, and insights that you wish to pass along to the audience.

subjective method

Everything you do carries your personal signature and is *subjective* in that way. To affect an audience subjectively means to mount your materials so that they closely approximate your personal state of mind. You do this by imprinting facts, figures, and other data with a vivid personalized treatment. Your treatment might be dramatic, filled with personal images and phrases that spellbind your audience. You may reveal your particular view of data through humor and irony.

Speeches of this type send the message with the force of your unique viewpoint and style. Among the presentations using this method of change are some sermons, after-dinner speeches, orations, commencement addresses, and political talks.

persuasive method

Speakers may attempt to affect an audience by persuasion, offering a close review of conditions, their causes, and their effects.

Carefully selected intellectual and emotional appeals are directed toward satisfying known audience needs. Comparisons are made among alternative routes of action and states of mind, through which the excellence of the persuader's idea is proved to the audience.

the basis for choice

Figure 7–1 depicts four basic questions that you might ask yourself as you approach the preparation of a message:

1. What are the wanted changes in my audience?
2. Why do I want those changes?
3. Which methods can help the transaction?
4. What are my audience's needs?

Wanted Changes.   There can be no complete list of wanted changes but the following are commonly sought by speakers:

1. a change from stranger to friend
2. a change from indifference to involvement
3. a change from unawareness to enlightenment
4. a change from misunderstanding to comprehension
5. a change from habit or set behavior to reflective choice
6. a change away from boredom, hostility, self-preoccupation, passivity, intolerance, or some other negative frame of mind.

figure 7-1   Message Preparation

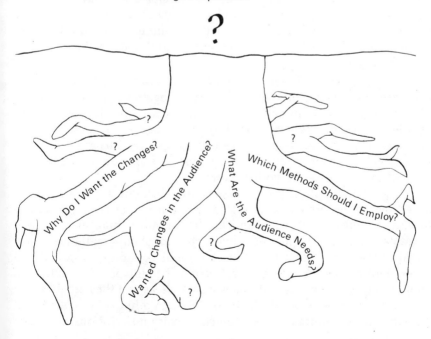

Reasons for Wanting Change. Your honest assessment of your personal motive for wanting change in the audience will help you prepare and deliver your message, because this self-knowledge forms the core of your professional character, which in turn affects your credibility and esteem. This is one reason why students may find it difficult and artificial to speak in class. The classroom of speech students is not a genuine random audience. In one sense its members are compelled to listen as you are compelled to speak, and the underlying motive is completion of your course requirement. All the messages sent in class are at least partially an enactment and not what might really happen in a business or professional situation.

Knowing your personal motive can also help you make a firmer contact with your audience by leading you to topics and materials that are mutually compelling of attention and consideration. As a professional communicator you want to harness your skills and energy to make a strong, uninhibited expression of your views. Knowing your motives may reduce certain tensions by allowing the unimpeded flow of spontaneous, sincere speech.

Methods That Will Help. The basic question of choice of method should follow from your recognition of why you want the change in your audience. Some speakers initially ask: "What method do I perform the best?" You will want to select a combination of methods that you are good at or that you feel comfortable in using, just as you would in your choice of audiovisual aids, encoding, and so on. Ideally you will become proficient at all of the methods, because a message transaction is seldom based on just one or two of them but encompasses variations of all five.

Audience Needs. Chapter 4 discusses the factor of audiences and notes 11 reasons why people come together to form audiences. The reasons binding an audience together were described as benefits people receive through membership in the audience; these binding motivations were seen as *group* needs. In preparing the organization of your message to a large audience, you must also consider why *individuals* will need to listen to your message.

It will help if you review what you know and have experienced regarding human value systems. You may want to refer back to Maslow's hierarchy of needs and the list of eupsychian management characteristics in Chapter 5. Always try to obtain audience information—the ages, educational backgrounds, genders, occupational types, political biases, and organization membership patterns of those in your audience. Generally audiences want to hear that they are doing "a good job" as parents, as students, or in some other role they play as human beings. Audiences need to hear precise descriptions and notations; they require concrete ideas that they can "grab onto" or "get their teeth into."

Audiences seek *confirmation* of their individual acts and beliefs. They possess enormous appetites for flattery and good news, but they also wish to hear constructive suggestions and messages of hope to balance bad news, criticism, or negative statements. You can look on your organization of the message as a process of balancing positive and negative concepts—consider it a form of qualifying or buffering, perhaps disarming an audience's tendency to disagree, reject, or attack the speaker who is a source of unwanted commentary.

Message preparation in professional exchanges seldom requires the time and reflection that reading these few pages on planning have demanded of you. Experience and the development of your professional roles will give you quick and generally accurate skill in approaching a topic, so that you may seldom have to consciously think out your own motives or reasons for wanting an audience change. The next section suggests a few ways to pattern your message to give it impact and to make it consistent with your speaking aim.

CHOOSING A MESSAGE PATTERN

Vocalized communication demands that word follow word and phrase follow phrase; your speech must have a linear organization. Your choice of a *message pattern* means that you give the flow of sounds and words a *shape* or structure so that an audience may not only comprehend the sense of it but also receive a word picture of the design of your message. Your speech, in other words, will be seen as having a beginning, a middle, and an end. You may choose, however, a pattern that divides these three main divisions into several other parts.

Another way to look at the major parts of a message is to think of five tasks that the speaker and the message perform: (1) get the audience's attention, (2) show a need for audience change toward the topic, (3) satisfy the need by proposing a remedy, (4) help the audience visualize the effect of the proposed change, and (5) direct the audience toward some action. Alan H. Monroe suggested this "motivated sequence" originally as a patterning device in persuasive speeches, and frequent revisions have included a briefer way to pattern a message. The ANSA sequence is one such scheme.[1]

---

[1]See Alan H. Monroe and Douglas Ehninger, *Principles and Types of Speech Communication*, 7th ed. (Glonview, Ill.: Scott, Foresman & Company, 1974). pp. 353–78, for a complete discussion of the "motivated sequence."

ANSA (attention, need, satisfaction, action) omits visualization because that step is implied in the other steps. Need in ANSA refers to the audience need to listen and what has been said about the speaking contract in Chapter 6. The speaker has the task of meeting or satisfying that need. Action is the change the speaker seeks in the audience.

Following the ANSA organization in a talk about shop safety, for example, you might tell a story of an accident and gesture by holding down your little finger while telling it. This might complete the attention step. Your reminders to your audience of shop mishaps and current statistics could establish the need for machinery operators to listen. You might then satisfy that need by giving a simple three-step way to avoid accidents, and the action step would be your advice to your listeners to follow the safety plan the very next time they work with machinery.

ANSA patterns give you a linear, four-step organization to follow in almost any message situation and emphasize your responsibility to speak for your audience. Use of the ANSA pattern starts you out with four main chunks of message. Your next step might be to dice each piece and label the portions by writing a sentence about each. Task 2 gives you practice in doing this.

task 2   DOING YOUR HALF

Look at the ten thesis statements below. Each main point has several possible divisions and half of one possible division has been written for you. Can you supply the other half of the idea?

A. People need a roadmap to get around a supermarket.

    1. Aisles are designed to aid the flow of traffic.

    2. _____

B. Reading labels is confusing.

    1. _____

    2. The type size is so small.

C. Some people buy products from habit.

    1. _____

    2. People look for familiar labels.

D. Manufacturers are trying to help you to be a smart consumer.

    1. _____

    2. Products could not exist for long without a consumer.

E. All products have substitutes.

  1. Many products have a fascinating early history.

  2. _____

F. Experts have several ways of grading products.

  1. _____

  2. Government agencies enforce certain minimum standards.

G. Your kitchen is the perfect research and development lab.

  1. Kitchens contain energy and raw materials for consumer experimentation.

  2. _____

H. What happens to the product after you use it is important.

  1. _____

  2. You can reclaim and reuse some products.

I. Consumers are geniuses at finding ways to beat inflation.

  1. Some people purchase only damaged goods and buy them in quantity.

  2. _____

J. There are two essentials of good consumership.

  1. Rate your purchases by priority.

  2. _____

By dividing the ten thesis statements, you provide yourself with twenty subparts or a total of thirty ideas; if you partition the subparts into examples, anecdotes, statistical support, authoritative statements, and comparisons, you have given yourself a basic framework for a speech. You can test each subpart's relation to the thesis statement by using these four guidelines:

1. Each subpart should be a "for instance" of the thesis idea.
2. Each subpart should seem to have a proper place under only one of the thesis ideas.
3. Each subpart should answer the questions your audience might have about that particular thesis statement.
4. Each subpart should make sense when connected to the thesis by phrases such as "for example," "inasmuch as," "because," and "so that."

Can your thirty ideas be adapted to fit the instructional, demonstration, informational, subjective, or persuasive method? By adding subparts and collecting evidence, support, and vivid illustrative materials, you gather almost everything you need to present an effective message. The crucial missing element is *form*—the overall shape of the message. Check to see if you can get some usable ideas from considering the suggestions below.

the form of cause and effect

Each of the ten thesis statements can be given a cause–effect form. For instance, you can cite what causes people to need a roadmap in a supermarket and the effects of not having one. You might demonstrate what causes a label to be confusing, and so on through the ten ideas. You may want to reverse the order and use effects-to-cause. A relatively simple form such as this is an excellent help to the audience, because it allows people to see clearly what you are doing with the speech pattern, and it encourages them to think ahead and in a sense participate in the development of the presentation.

the form of problem–solution

The problem–solution form of a message consists of developing the main problem areas that need remedy. You follow this with your plan for solving the problem and with a defense of your plan. Again, each of the ten thesis statements in Task 2 can be developed in this form; for instance, you would show the need for intelligent consumership and then present your plan for the essentials of good consumership. The problem–solution form has the appeal of making your position on an issue clear. It may aid the audience in obtaining a better picture of you and will certainly shorten the distance between your major points and what "you are driving at."

the torm of time

The clock, the calendar, the seasons, day–night, infancy–old age, and many other time forms may help to structure your message into a unified and effective listening event. Your "product speech" might be presented in chronological order of events, from discovery to reclamation of the product. Audiences understand and respect time orders. Many of us partition our days into shower, breakfast, commuting, working, lunch, working, commuting, dinner, recreation, bed, or something close to this form of daily living.

Several literary speakers also use the time form. It may incorporate new patterns into certain types of messages. The log or diary account, for example, is often used, and the "countdown" or reversal of a time sequence is now overused. With a little thought, you may be able to employ flashback and flashforward forms of time schemes, recalling the past and jumping ahead into the future, or perhaps present your conclusion or "clinching close" first.

the form of space

Each of the ten major statements in Task 2 could be given a specific locale, and your speech could take the form of a travel guide. You would begin, for example, by talking about the supermarket, progress to the home, then to the plant, and then to the inspection laboratory.

Other spatial forms involve objects-in-space, such as the shopping list in the hand that reaches for the product with the label, and so on—grouping ideas according to their major objects, in a spatial pattern. Each of these categories might be given a size grouping. Commonly used forms are small, medium, large, and local, state, federal, international. You probably recognize the logic in these two examples as inductive logic; you might also invert this form by starting with large places, groups, or concepts and progressing to the small examples.

the form of comparison

Certain audiences are especially familiar with local concerns and pursuits; others are predominantly guided by specialized interests and backgrounds. Urbane and sophisticated listeners obviously have different points of reference from people living in rural areas. Your message form can be shaped by comparing ideas to something well known by your audience. The great teachers—Lao-tse, Confucius, Socrates, Christ—all taught by use of comparisons or analogies. If you can compare technical aspects of the subject to a familiar object or process, your audience may have a better chance to make the change in behavior you want.

The analogy contains its own form and makes whatever it is you are comparing easier to assimilate. A speaker could, for example, make a comparison in the ten-point message in Task 2 to a game of chance. You take a chance, when you buy, that when you get home you will find what you wanted in the package. The analogy might include the "risk" of paying for the product first and later finding out whether you "won" or not. The same "chance" is taken by those who manufacture the product, license it, and sell it.

Analogies can often be found in well-known stories, parables, nursery rhymes, or historical events—battles, political campaigns, cultural changes. Your consumer message might be organized by depicting a "cold war" between the poor defenseless consumer and the subliminal tactics of a monolithic "they" who are bent on brainwashing uncommitted buyers.

Imaginative speakers can find analogies in almost anything; a deck of cards offers suits, color and shape symbols, high cards, trump cards, face cards, even jokers; a book, a piano, a typewriter can suggest a multitude of similarities that will help to give form to a message. Perhaps the most frequently used analogy is to human characteristics— the use of *personification*. You may speak of things and places as if they were human, giving them eyes, legs, mouths, limbs, needs, and emotions in an attempt to organize the relationships.

the form of journalistic questions

Like the analogy pattern, the eight standard journalist's questions can fit certain types of speeches and methods for changing an audience's viewpoint or behavior. The eight questions are: *who, what, when, where, why, how much, how many,* and *to what degree.* As an *internal* pattern, this set of questions can help structure the subparts of the thesis headings, so that every major point might be explained in terms of who, what, when, etc. If, for example, you want to prove that manufacturers are trying to help people to be smart consumers, you would relate evidence of how, why, and to what degree, to support your contention.

Regardless of which forms you give to your message, these basic questions will help start you thinking about details and ways to enable an audience to visualize concrete instances. Routine briefings or information updates can be patterned with this form, because with practice you will become adept at cutting away nonessentials and relaying the precise messages required in such exchanges.

the form of the human equation

Sometimes your message will be mainly about the human factor or you may want to place strong emphasis on how people are involved in or react to a topic. If your message is primarily about humans, your form in the message can be patterned after the five categories of human thought and expression: the physical, the mental, the emotional, the psychic, and the spiritual. These human classifications are large enough to accommodate almost any selection of details, and when combined with analogies or journalistic patterns these factors in the human equation offer a way to relate your message to even the most diverse audience.

Subdivisions for these five classes can easily be found in either time or space patterns also. You could, for example, arrange a cluster of remarks that describe how shopper traffic affects emotional states or how a shopper's emotional state affects the traffic flow in a supermarket. Perhaps it could be argued that a shopper goes through several phases of emotional states in the course of a shopping day, so that you will use chronology as another pattern of assembling your message.

the form of numbers

Many messages are best conveyed through a simple enumeration of subparts. "Let me point out three important benefits of comparative pricing . . ." is an example of a lead-in phrase that contains numbering as an organizational form. Number forms easily combine with the other forms described. Many speeches are given titles such as "My Six Crises," "Ten Steps to Better Health," or "Thirty Days That Shook the World." Each numbered subpart in its turn might accept still another organizational form to fit a particular message situation.

the form of the acronym

Abbreviations for words and initials arranged into a short form that stands for a phrase, name, or title are popular ways to form signatures that are easy to remember and identify. ANSA, PERT, and BLAB are three acronyms used in this text. In Task 3 you have a chance to try your hand at this form of organization.

task 3   TEN STEPS TO A BETTER GZJXWWQVT

Condense the ten basic thesis statements listed in Task 2 so that a single important word can be used as a key for the rest of the phrase. Try to arrange the key words so that their initials form a significant acronym. Write the key word in the space and place the first letter of each word in the box. Explain why your acronym might satisfy your requirements for a suitable form in this specific message.

[ ] ———————————————   This acronym would provide a

[ ] ———————————————   satisfactory form for a message on

[ ] ———————————————   consumership, because ————————

[ ] ———————————   ————————————————

[ ] ———————————   ————————————————

[ ] ———————————   ————————————————

[ ] ———————————   ————————————————

[ ] ———————————   ————————————————

[ ] ———————————   ——————— ————————

[ ] ———————————   ————————————————

With a little experimentation you can probably find a variety of acrostic and alphabet gimmicks that may aid organization. These samples might get you started toward an effective pattern:

1. LOVE spelled backwards is EVOL.
2. SIN is abhorrent, but looked at the right way it can be awfully NIS.
3. No matter how you spell it, if you GO with this project, you are going to end up with an O.
4. A SMILE will take you a -MILE.

the form of the catch phrase

You may find occasion to use a famous quote or cliché phrase on which to build your thesis statements. Bumper sticker slogans often enjoy a certain vogue, particularly during a national election year. Sometimes current song, movie, or book titles can be divided into parts or labels for sections of a message. A frequently heard bit of advice for speaking uses only six words grouped by twos: stand up, speak up, shut up. The brevity, repetition, and alliterative use of s create a catchy effect.

In Enactment 16 try to give yourself answers to the basic organizational question: What would be the most effective way for a professional communicator to assemble a message about organizing a message?

enactment 16   HOW I WOULD ORGANIZE MY SPEECH ABOUT MY CHOSEN PROFESSION

Use these techniques to explain your thesis in . . . .

instruction
demonstration
information
subjective interpretation
persuasion

enactment 16: HOW I WOULD ORGANIZE MY SPEECH ABOUT MY CHOSEN PROFESSION

participant

A student speaker.

problem

The speaker explains how he/she would proceed with the organization of an informative speech about his/her chosen profession. The speech about organizing should, itself, reflect good organizational planning.

critique 16 TROUBLESHOOTING

1. Did the speaker say or do anything that showed he/she was seeking and getting feedback?
2. What did the speaker do to get and keep your attention?
3. What evidence was there that the speaker had too much or too little support for the thesis statements?
4. Which *method* worked best for the speaker? Explain how this method matched the topic as well as the personal style of the speaker.
5. Why did you need to listen to the presentation?
6. What changes might be needed in the organization of this speech for effective presentation to experts in the profession discussed?

WHAT WOULD YOU SUGGEST TO IMPROVE IT?

7. Describe three places in the presentation that would be ideal locations for use of visual or auditory aids.
8. Explain how the speaker's pitch, rate, and volume variety did or did not give the impression of organization or shape to the presentation.
9. Why would this type of message require a high or low degree of spontaneity? To what extent would spontaneity depend on the audience needs and the motive of the speaker?
10. In what ways did the speaker invite a response from the audience?

BEGINNINGS AND ENDINGS

binding beginnings

The beginning of your message is designed to accomplish an important task: to bind the audience to you as a speaker. One general principle for the binding beginning of a message is for you to say and/or do the unexpected. You may have known teachers who seemed to wait endlessly for the class to be quiet before beginning the lesson. Even after everyone was quiet and apparently listening, the teacher may have waited still longer before speaking. Regardless of what may have happened later, for those few moments at least, the speaker had bound the audience to the message. This technique, though used over and over, was probably effective, because you were never absolutely sure what to expect when the silence was broken. Think about the unexpected in the following attention-getting devices.

Self-Disclosure. Some speakers confess some harmless fact or event—half true or not—about themselves to bind the audience to them. You might admit to being scared or make a comment about the remarks introducing you or what someone said to you as you arrived for the occasion. The key element is to pass along an intimate bit of personal experience that most of your audience will appreciate for its candor, honesty, and sense of humanity.

Shocking Statement. It is difficult to shock certain kinds of audiences, and speakers may run the risk of failing to shock or their attempts may be so transparent that sophisticated listeners "see through" this strategy and react in a negative way.

The shocking statement may be combined with self-disclosure to form an effective attention-getting device. An example is the speaker who says, "Ladies and Gentlemen, I feel ashamed . . . because I have nothing to give you except . . . words and promises. . . ." You must, however, exercise taste and discretion in your choice of shocking revelations, and the reference used should seem to grow out of your method and topic.

Rhetorical Question. You probably have heard rhetorical questions used as binding beginnings many times. If used in a well-stated series, such a question can help you set the tone for a speech in a variety of situations. It may help involve the audience in silent answers and may stimulate routes of thought. An example is: "Have you ever thought about what you would wish for if you had three wishes?"

Direct Question. Occasionally you may wish to ask a direct question of the members of your audience to involve them in an immediate way. You should indicate how they are to respond—by a show of hands or a collective "Yes," or "No," or other reply.

Crisp Quote. Check your reference library for books of quotations such as Hoyt's *New Cyclopedia of Practical Quotations* or Stevenson's *Home Book of Quotations*. These offer a wide variety of appropriate sayings that may help you bind your audience's attention.

Quotes may serve as an overall theme for a message; a preacher often chooses a Biblical passage as a text, for example. And a famous slogan, such as "Rum, Romanism, and Rebellion," can be used, as we pointed out above, to partition material into blocks of manageable ideas.

Announcing the Point. A startling statement of what you intend your audience to do or think fits the principle of doing the unexpected. Blurting out your intentions may serve to rivet attention and provide your audience with proof of your credibility.

Joke. Humor as part of the content and style of your message will be discussed in later pages, but the common, garden-variety of joke requires little sensitivity to humor and is an easy and often-used ice-breaker in many informal speaking situations. Your joke selection should be in good taste, topical, and universally understandable.

Prop. Frequently, you can relate an object to your topic and let it stand for your overall message. Used as a binding beginning, an object can be a strong symbol and can unite the various thesis statements in your message. Audiovisual aids fall into this category of attention-getting devices when used to begin your presentation.

Eye Contact. A binding beginning that is similar to the unbearable silence technique is the speaker's attempt to look each member of the audience in the eye before beginning the speech. In small or medium-size groups this method acts as a silent introduction—a quiet "Hello." Even with large groups, this scanning of faces can be used to establish contact with significant segments of the audience.

clinching closes

The end of the message mirrors to some extent the beginning. It brings the listeners and the speaker full circle—to the point where they began. Some clinching closes are simply binding beginnings repeated in an inverted way.

A few experienced speakers insist that the beginning and end of a speech are far more important than what is said in between and that an effective opening and closing are what an audience will remember most. Actually the ideal message will contain a number of beginnings and closings—one of each for every central thesis statement the speaker includes. For example, each segment in the consumer speech might use a binding technique at its opening and a clincher at its conclusion.

The main idea in the clinching close is to use your last chance to accomplish the purpose of the message. The close is your final opportunity to abstract or "boil down" your chunk of material to the very essence you want to leave with your audience. Many clinching close designs are similar to binding beginnings, but you may want to examine and try out some of the following variations.

Proverbs, Aphorisms, and Morals. Much of philosophical and religious literature is filled with pithy summaries that capture bits of wisdom in very few words. Scientific truths are often contained in fables, folktales, myths, and legends. Technological presentations given to lay audiences can often be summarized through use of famous theorems, formulas, and laws. One popular economic concept used in many unrelated fields in Gresham's Law: Bad money drives out good money. Folk equivalents to this law might be: One bad apple can spoil the barrel, and a chain is only as strong as its weakest link.

Punch Lines.   The effect of the punch line is that it surprises the audience and has impact. As a clinching close, this method is similar to saving your trump card or holding your fire until the end. Sometimes important announcements or important policy decisions are saved until the end of a speech for added punch and to avoid coloration or distortion of the main text. A speech in favor of a course of action could end with "and this is why I am resigning my job to run for the office of president." Protocol officers and public relations people will often deliberate over the merits of early versus late revelation of an important announcement in a speech. Like overexposure of a speaking aid, an early revelation of important news can "steal the thunder" of whatever is to follow, because the audience may devote its energy to digesting the import of the announcement.

Dares.   You may use a dare as a form of clinching action step. This technique of challenging your listeners takes the form of a direct proposition for action. You might select a type of challenge you ask your audience to accept, such as "for every man-hour you contribute, my organization will match. . . . Who'll be the first?"

Some individuals are threatened by aggressive questioning of their competence or sportsmanship and resent this type of appeal. Foreknowledge of your audience is essential for this reason, particularly if the audience's answer to the challenge is to be public—a monetary contribution or a personal signal such as standing up to be counted.

Forecasts.   Your summary of main points should include some reference to the future, and a prediction based on your supported assertions can provide you with an effective close. It may help to personalize your forecasts and to include your audience's projected behavior in these hypothetical contexts. An example is: "I know when your wife or husband asks you when you get home, 'Well, was anything said?' you'll have made your decision. I think I know from looking at your faces what your decision will be." Or, "My own prediction is that in the next decade we'll all be eating less and enjoying it more, partly out of economic necessity and partly to live longer, more productive lives." Another variation is to quote expert opinions about future expectations and insert your personal amendments to fit your message.

transitions

"I'm sorry, you just lost me" is a common listener reaction to messages and parts of messages that are not linked well. There are dozens of words and phrases that the professional communicator can readily call on to avoid just such a response. Some of the more useful phrases fall into four general categories.

Inference. When you want to demonstrate that you have drawn a conclusion from your examples, transitional words or phrases that help link this inference include:

For this reason . . .	On that account . . .	As a result. . .
To this end . . .	The consequence is . . .	It follows that . . .
In this way . . .	By looking at it this way . . .	Naturally . . .
Thus . . .	Accordingly . . .	In order that . . .

Change of Time. Because most people have had lots of experience dealing with narratives that chronicle events, the transitional phrases that show time are probably familiar to you. How many of these transitions do you routinely use in telling an account of an experience?

Now . . .	Meanwhile . . .	At present . . .
Immediately . . .	At last . . .	Since then . . .
After a short time . . .	Afterwards . . .	Not long after . . .
Instantly, . . .	Quickly . . .	In the meantime . . .
Before this . . .	Shortly after . . .	At this point . . .
Later . . .	Whereupon . . .	Suddenly . . .

Comparison and Personal View. Many times you will search for a way to compare an idea to something else, but you may also wish to show your own posture in the comparison or your manner of approaching the differences and/or similarities. Some of these phrases might help:

Equally important . . .	More effective . . .	Quite as necessary . . .
Not so obvious . . .	In like manner . . .	Of even greater appeal. . .
Just as surely . . .	Likewise . . .	In similar fashion . . .
As you would expect . . .	Quite as evident . . .	Accordingly . . .
On the other hand . . .	Conversely . . .	In contrast . . .

Doubt or Certainty. Transitions that lead into a state of doubt or of certainty might be introduced with one of these words:

Possibly . . .	Perhaps . . .	It may well be . . .
Probably . . .	Obviously . . .	Undoubtedly . . .
Surely . . .	Of course . . .	However . . .
Still . . .	Yet . . .	Nevertheless . . .
Furthermore . . .		

Transitional words provide that necessary second or two for an audience to adjust its thinking and shift gears with the speaker. Often the *ah*s and *uh*s of the inexperienced speaker are really well-intentioned attempts to connect ideas. With a little practice, especially in private conversation, anyone can gain the habit of using these more polished and meaningful transitional phrases. And, just as the listener gains time to absorb a change, you the speaker benefit from those moments of transition. They give you an extra second to check a note, adjust your physical attitude, make a new personal contact, check the feedback from some sector of the audience, or move to an aid or manipulating apparatus.

Finally, a well-placed transitional phrase carries expectation. The lists offered here are followed by a series of periods (ellipses) that indicate something is to be added. When you say "For this reason . . ." followed by a two-second pause, the brief silence can engage your listeners' sense of expectation. The fragment and the pause form a *pregnant* moment, binding your audience; this aids both speaker and listener to ingest what has been said and share what is to come.

task 4   SHIFTING GEARS

The following shortened text of a subjective, informational speech has six blank spaces where transitional words or phrases may be used. Read it carefully and insert a phrase that fits and that would simplify an audience's task of shifting gears from one idea to the next.

I recognize many colleagues here, and I would like to say hello to each of you.

But after this one-minute speech—you have heard of the Minute Waltz and

the one-minute egg? Well this is a one-minute speech—I'm not so sure you'll

want to be seen talking to me. (1) _____ I want

to tell you about a critical minute in your professional career. (2)

_____ the first critical 30 seconds for you will

be that time when you sit down to tell your boss exactly what you feel about

the state of things in your department. Will you begin by telling a funny anecdote about a coworker? Maybe you'll ask a string of questions to show you really know what's happening. Or . . . maybe you'll listen . . . Just sit—that's easy enough—and listen—that's pretty easy, too. Or is it? (3) _____ Listening skills are one of the main predictors of professional success. Why? (4) _____ during those first 30 seconds you establish your credentials as a human being . . . a receptor of other people's need expressions, and a seeker of commonalities. (5) _____ the last 30 seconds may contain your first opportunity to prove you were really listening. What evidence will you give? What might you say in support or in contradiction? . . . Will you try a question? (6) _____ my minute is just about up. I know because I've been listening to myself, and that's my one-minute speech. A professional career is built upon listening—half the time to others and half the time to yourself. Shall we listen to each other's questions, now?

SUPPORTING MATERIALS

When you send a message, it goes from person to person. Often some additional emphasis or *support* is inserted before it is sent along to others. A fundamental strength of a verbal message lies in its *own* supportive material, its proofs and illustrations. Most professional people believe that supportive data in great quantity are valuable, but in preparing a message your job is to extract what is important and effective for your particular audience occasion. It is a good idea, then, to begin with an abundance of "for instances."

What does it take to instruct, demonstrate, inform, persuade, or narrate a message to an audience? Where can you find supporting materials? The audience analysis you make may help answer the first question, because it provides some examination of the basic speaker–audience contract. To answer the second, materials may be found in many of the source areas listed here.

Experts.   Expert opinion is usually as close as a telephone. Your work on interviews to get information in Chapter 9 may sharpen your skill in obtaining supportive material. Do not hesitate to consult with government agencies at all levels. Much of the work in bureaucratic offices consists of gathering and disseminating information, and most are willing to provide data.

Basic Reference Books.   Many libraries have the latest editions of these and many other invaluable information sources:

Trivia and Curiosities

Famous First Facts
Guinness Book of World Records
What Happened When

Statistical Data

Information Please Almanac
Statistical Abstract of the United
   States
World Almanac and Book of Facts

Current Events

Time
Newsweek
U.S. News & World Report
Facts on File
Congressional Quarterly Weekly
   Report
Keesing's Contemporary Archives

Biographical Data

Dictionary of American Biography
Current Biography
Who's Who in America

Background Surveys

Collier's Encyclopedia
Encyclopedia Americana
Encyclopedia Britannica
World Book Encyclopedia

Local Businesses.   Current trends and patterns of business can often be supported or qualified by checking with local businesspeople. Some will exchange information with you personally, others have staffs to answer public requests for information. Manufacturers will often loan apparatus and sample materials, provided they understand how they will be used.

Local News and Media Agencies.   Many local newspapers and television network affiliate stations work hard at "taking the local pulse." These papers and stations can provide you with valuable facts, contacts, and trends in a variety of areas.

Personal Experience.   Speakers sometimes overlook the wealth of supportive material they have collected through their personal observation of and contact with events. Always inventory your own storehouse of lived-through facts for usable support for a message.

PERSUASION

Persuasion can be defined as *receiving in the guise of giving*. Most of the discussions and tasks in this text deal with forms of persuasion and emphasize the development of your professionalism as the most important factor in effective business communication. We said, for example, that when offered advice people tend to assess the performance record and the reputation of the person giving the advice.

You are probably aware of having to "give up something" when you accept advice, a plan, or a solution to a problem. The person who asks "How much is that free sample going to cost me?" is alert to the persuasive transaction in which a swap of some kind is expected. In addition to having credibility and trustworthiness, as a speaker who would persuade, you must know the needs of your audience and what it will take to satisfy those needs. You must ask yourself: "What can I say that will invite my listeners to make a swap?" The suggestions given here review material presented in earlier chapters, but they may help remind you of the main principles of bringing about changes in listeners.

establishing a need for change

Audiences must be made aware that a change is beneficial for them and that the "price" is not too high for them to pay; their shifts in viewpoint or behavior must appear to be possible at bargain rates. Whether the shift desired is a change of political administration or a change of diet, the persuader must prove that change is necessary. It's an easy task, for example, to show that everyone is dying but more difficult to demonstrate that this need not be pointless. The following aspects of persuasion may be used:

Existing Conditions Are Deteriorating. By assembling expert opinion, statistical support, and published eyewitness accounts, you may develop a picture of the status quo (existing conditions) that shows a need for remedy. For example, you may show the decay in the upkeep of certain buildings and streets.

Existing Conditions Are in Danger of Deteriorating. Frequently, a case can be made for potential or incipient needs by depicting the *potential* deterioration of existing conditions. As an aspect of persuasion, the potential need argument is based on previous experiences and causes known to have produced undesirable conditions, such as wars and depressions. You may show what has happened to other groups who have neglected to act when they had the chance.

Existing Conditions Are Satisfactory but Could Be Better. You may appeal to the need for improvement and for constant refinement in existing policies or attitudes, when you cannot show that they are either bad or in danger of worsening.

Existing Conditions Are Satisfactory but Require Changes to Maintain Them as They Are.   This is the "vigilance" notion—you must work to stay beautiful, stay young, stay fit, etc. Arguments are often based on the appeal that states: "You have come this far, you can go the rest of the way."

Existing Conditions Are Satisfactory, but Are out of Your Control.   This aspect of persuasive argument suggests that the audience may be living in a fool's paradise. This position argues that things may seem to be all right, but, if you do not know *why* they are all right, they might change at any moment and you could lose everything. Change is needed to provide controls.

If you present some variation on these basic arguments or try to establish all these points, you help your audience see that the need exists for change. You may then turn your attention to what can be done.

comparing alternatives

Once the need is established, as a persuasive communicator you examine available solutions or remedies for the problem. The superiority of your proposal may be demonstrated if testimony and evidence are given to prove that alternative plans are unworkable, too expensive, good for only the long or short term, "more of the same with a new name," or somehow associated with a cultural taboo.

Alternative Plan Is Unworkable.   Factors are related or demonstrated to the audience that strongly indicate that alternative plans will not work. Support for your assertion might come from past experience, documented testimony from a variety of people, or close analysis of the competing plans. Sometimes a plan can be shown to be workable for certain groups in specific circumstances that do not fit the present set of conditions.

Alternative Plan Is Too Expensive.   Usually evidence of cost or projected cost will help convince the listeners that alternative solutions are too expensive and should be rejected. In some instances, however, people associate cost with merit and react favorably to an appeal to "go first class," or to the argument that "you get what you pay for." It behooves you as the persuader in these cases to prove that your audience can receive a service that is just as good at no extra cost.

Alternative Plan Is Good for Only Long or Short Term. Your audience analysis will provide you with estimates of the climate of opinion or general state of mind within the group. Few answers to problems can be shown to "work" immediately and for a long period of time. You may want to show that your solution can operate within the existing machinery for action. The merit of your plan should be compared to that of the others available. Whichever need is present— short- or long-term solution—might be satisfied by your remedy with relative strength compared to the alternatives.

A main area of attractiveness for many ideas is that they do not require radical change. Few people are willing to swap their general pattern of living even for assured improvement unless a crisis demands it. A plan that is promising but that requires radical shifts in behavior is often seen as "too high a price to pay." Conversely, a radical plan may be exactly what your audience is looking for.

Alternatives Are "More of the Same with a New Name." Like the persuasive strategies outlined above, the more-of-the-same argument shows that competing plans contain nothing new. Listeners who are tired of the old palliatives, will give such plans little chance for success. Sometimes this "frills" tactic will appeal to groups who have chosen remedies that looked different but that proved to be similar to past plans.

Alternative Plans Are Connected with Cultural Taboos. A questionable stratagem in persuasion, but one that you will probably encounter, is a speaker's attempt to link competitive plans with undesirable or negative reference points. Your review of thought and perception in Chapter 2 will remind you of the twists and turns people's minds take, mixing up objective data with wishful thinking, personal biases, and prejudgments.

Most ideas, plans, or products can be connected to or made to seem part of ideas that people generally wish to avoid. For example, competitive plans can be made to seem harmful if the speaker can associate them with pollution. The same process occurs if you know a despicable person named Adolf and automatically shun anything or anybody related to that name or what it connotes to you.

In presenting your proposal you can, of course, use a positive transfer—try to associate your idea with the "good guys," with things that are valued and treasured.

showing the superiority of your proposal

The superiority of your proposal is bound up with your *appearance* of superiority, the sympathy you seem to have for your audience's plight, and the sympathy you can elicit from your listeners toward your personal motives in speaking.

An old song by Kurt Weill tells of a girl who declined the attentions of several attractive boys but simply couldn't say "No" to a bedraggled, lonely nobody. People always have a degree of sympathy for the underdog, but the lesson to be applied is that listener sympathy will often go to the person who is what he or she purports to be. Your conviction that what you are offering is better than known alternatives will be communicated with your message.

As you organize your message, try to be aware of your professional integrity. You should honestly reveal to your audience your fair attitude and judgment of the following six types of personal beliefs.

Questions of Taste.   Hasten to point out that what you believe is a reflection of your personal taste in fashion, color, leisure activity, and so on. If the point or issue you are comparing is one of taste, label it such, and avoid ascribing some universal standard to matters of personal choice.

Questions of Cause.   Convey the posture that there are many causes that affect the way things are. Assert a broad-mindedness about how and why conditions "got this way." Cause is usually very difficult to demonstrate and not always possible to prove. The message a persuader wants to convey is that he or she is trying to be fair in citing multiple causes.

Questions of Policy.   In discussing proposed changes, you will encounter two types of policy or procedural statements that are followed by authoritative bodies—de facto policy and de jure policy (policy "in fact" and "by law"). De facto policy is a procedure for doing something that is not written down but is just the usual or habitual procedure. De jure policy is an officially adopted procedure, usually written down and often made public. Sometimes a de facto policy will become official procedure after a period of testing to see if it satisfies everyone's interests. An unstated policy may in this way remain in effect until it is challenged, at which time an official decision can be made or steps taken to "legalize" what has always been done.

Your reputation as a professional may be enhanced if you make your references to policies very clear. If you are in the position of defending a policy, try to present an accurate chronology of how the procedure was determined, what the latest official attitude is, and what the prospects are for change.

Questions of Justice and Fairness.   Speakers and audiences must make a distinction between what is fair and what is legal. Sometimes laws on the books are so discriminatory and/or unworkable that procedures are set up to appeal and adjudicate special cases. Decisions and choices that are felt to be unfair are often controlled by statute, and little can be done without appealing to other avenues of redress.

Always make the effort to describe conditions affecting persuasion with this distinction in mind. Speakers may succeed in convincing an audience of legal questions, but lose their sympathy when it comes to fairness or the sense of what is "right." It is possible for the persuader to be on both sides, as long as this distinction is clearly recognized and communicated.

Questions of Value. Like taste, value is a personal preference. Generally, American culture adheres to Judeo-Christian ethics as enunciated in the sanctity of the person and property rights, but within this broad area of value there are many hierarchies of value. Some people place the highest value in God, country, and family; some ethical systems prescribe that the individual comes first. As you present a message, you should be careful to avoid ascribing your particular values to everyone else. Nor should you assume that there exists a single list of values accepted by everyone in your audience.

Your audience analysis will determine some of the general values held by your listeners—most people believe in playing by the rules and mutual respect between people, but even here you must take care to check before you assume these beliefs to be fact.

Questions of Fact. A fact is provable, demonstrable, predictable. To document your facts you need authoritative affidavits, test results, broad opinion affidavits, photographic or auditory copies that bear witness to an occurrence. Facts passed along to listeners without documentation should be called something else—hearsay, opinion, speculation, or the like. Again, the test should be one of fairness. Try to assert an attitude of fairness on questions of absolute certainty. Hedging or qualifying your assertions may dull the hard edge of certainty, but in the long run it may help you establish a firm image of professional integrity, which is the basis for effective persuasion.

task 5   FACT OR OPINION?

How sensitive are you to questions and statements of taste, cause, policy, justice/fairness, value, and fact? Fill in the blanks with the type of statement and explain why your choice is valid.

1. "Everybody knows that men are better drivers than women" is a statement of

_____, because _____.

2. Everyone has equal protection under the law is/is not the de facto policy in my

community, because _____.

3. "The design of that building is a mistake; it looks like a chicken" is a statement of

_____, because _____.

4. "Here is the bank statement that shows exactly one dime in our treasury" is a

statement of _____, because _____.

5. "The board of directors should look after itself first" is a statement of

_____, because _____.

6. "The sign said '25 miles per hour' and I was going 25 miles per hour" is a

statement of de _____ policy, because _____.

7. "The sign said '25 miles per hour' but all the traffic moves at 50" is a statement of

de _____ policy, because _____.

HUMOR IN THE MESSAGE

Diplomats will tell you that persuasion demands logic, charm, wit, selflessness, luck, lots of work, and repetition. Seldom will a single communication encounter produce a permanent change in an audience. Promotional campaigns, for example, continue for months and even years, featuring repeated appeals in a variety of formats and channels. Humor, however, may begin the process of change, because it affects the inherent differences of speaker and listener and brings participants closer together.

types of humor

Humor is an attitude toward living. It ranges from the cynically bitter to the most bemused and joyous. The potent effect of humor is that it levels differences; even our highest or most aloof concepts of things can be brought closer and made to seem more human or less frightening through novel twists of viewpoint. In this sense, application of the comic viewpoint can relieve the tensions associated with strangeness and new experiences. Humor is not a persuasive technique, but it can prepare an audience for a related experience, relatively free of anxiety, suspicion, and preoccupation with the seriousness of professional activity. See if the following discussion helps you to see humor in communication as an attitude that most people appreciate as a smoothing ingredient in a message.

Ridicule.   Ridicule is a type of humor in which everybody gangs up on something or somebody in order to poke fun at, chastise, or in some cases punish the object for being aloof. You may have learned early in life that self-ridicule or making fun of yourself tends to "steal the thunder" from your critics and enemies. They have nothing left to shoot at. Some audiences feel relieved when you reveal some universal fear—a folly such as taking yourself too seriously. It helps listeners themselves feel less pompous and less guarded—less aloof. Light, painless ridicule is often enjoyed because it is universally experienced. Members of the audience have been there, on both ends of the joke, and this gives you a solid basis for finding other commonalities and interfaces.

Exaggeration.   Most things are transformed when they are enlarged or reduced. Exaggeration does this and makes a thing or person seem ridiculous in comparison with normality. Part of the humor of exaggeration is catching the speaker in the act of doing it. He or she then looks foolish for trying to get away with something, which is another universal experience—everybody knows what that is like. You may grossly exaggerate the size of a fish you claim to have caught, and then gradually reduce the size to near normal, admitting to the exaggeration. You are, of course, allowing yourself to be found out for the sake of the joke.

Incongruity.   You may have had experiences where something was said or done that was totally unexpected and illogical but fit in perfectly with whatever preceded the intrusion. Incongruity is a kind of collision of logics. Saying "I love you" through clinched teeth is a collision of the word sense with a universal gesture of anger—grinding your teeth. It is totally out of place, but still shows a universal truth, that people love and get angry at the same time, that they often say one thing but mean something else, and that they are sometimes tripped up by their own absurd behavior.

guidelines for humor in professional encounters

It has been said that everyone loves the humorist, but nobody will lend him any money. Levity reflects your respect for precision in speech. Digital encoding tries to bring mathematical exactness to messages, and, if it can be said that analogic encoding was invented, then its discovery was probably meant to balance, complement, and soften the hard-edged reality of digital language. Humor as a type of analogic expression does not detract from or cancel the advantages of being impeccably precise in assembling messages, but it can be used with taste as another kind of buffer—a sugar coating—for the harsh and implacable realities of day-to-day living.

Some of the most commonly held misconceptions about humor are listed and discussed here. Consider them in relation to your personal speaking style as it has developed through the use of this text.

Being "Funny."   A speech student will sometimes say "I can't be funny, I'm not a comedian." Using humor does not mean being humorous; It means *talking about* something humorous. You probably do not expect your physics professor to be physical when talking about physics. You need not become a buffoon to describe buffoons or absurd behavior.

Laughter as Success. Some people equate humor with making people laugh. If you make an attempt at humor that does not "get a laugh" you may consider this a sign of failure. That is a harsh standard for success, one not many people could meet. There are degrees of laughter and only certain manifestations of it are overt or can be monitored as feedback. A smile or even a tendency to smile is evidence that you have communicated something truthful.

"I Can't Tell Jokes." You may have had the feeling that telling a joke is risky, because you are not sure whether your listeners are laughing at you or with you. Actually, they are doing both, and this is how they begin to have respect for your humanity. They realize they are being asked to share a viewpoint; they see attempts at humor as something being given to them.

The belief that you "can't tell jokes" can actually help you. Humor is detached; telling a joke in a detached, straight-faced manner is in itself the comic view. A deadpan facial expression, understatement, and irony add the humor of incongruity, because they are just the opposite of the view you are expressing.

Humor as an Icebreaker. In your professional encounters you will want to exercise caution using humor to break the ice, but ridicule and sarcasm directed at yourself can help launch a satisfying transaction with even the most sensitive person. Self-ridicule sets a model to follow. Although it may not be followed, it can be appreciated and noted even by those who lack a sense of humor. Humor directed at a common problem or frustration hurts no one and can provide a basis for mutual understanding and respect.

Subjects that May Not Be Humorous. Most people can appreciate word play—puns, double meanings, and comic juxtapositions of words. When your own name is used, however, you may react negatively. The same is true when ethnic, racial, or denominational "name-calling" is used at your expense or when humor demeans bodily functions and physical anomalies. Numerous targets for criticism are bigger and more worthwhile puncturing with the professional communicator's wit.

enactment 17 THE CHOICE IS YOURS

Select an issue of current controversy in your major field of interest. Assemble a message that reflects your analysis of one of these types of audiences: a national labor union convocation, a medical society, a merchants' organization, a public school administrators' meeting, a television journalists' meeting, a regional political rally, a consumer group, a manufacturers' convention, a military organization. Prepare a message that attempts to persuade the members of your specific audience to change the way things are, change some aspects of their behavior, or change their attitude toward the issue.

participant

You, the concerned student, are the individual speaker.

need to speak

Your audience is on the verge of adopting a position that is the opposite of everything you believe to be best for your profession. Can you dissuade them?

time/locale

Your speech will be the last utterance before your audience votes on a resolution that you completely reject. The locale is a national convention of your profession.

critique 17   TROUBLESHOOTING

1. What evidence was there that this message was meant only for this particular audience?
2. How was this proposal shown to be superior to alternative solutions?
3. Was the use of humor appropriate and effective for this particular audience? Why or why not?
4. Explain how facts, opinions, and value judgments were kept clear and separated by the speaker.

HOW MIGHT IT BE IMPROVED?

5. Why would this particular audience need to listen to this speech?
6. What was said that tended to strengthen the speaker's credibility?
7. Did the clinching close give you a feeling of completeness and "rightness"?

afterthought   THE PROFESSION IS THE MESSAGE

Marshall McLuhan's famous dictum about television, "the medium is the message," suggests a final reminder for students who would approach their careers with a ready-made professional outlook. Communication in business and the professions is a matrix—a total condition that is its own message. Through innumerable transactions you contribute to this emerging message being sent by your profession.

We said very early in this book that communication is a form of coexistence, a sharing of the human condition. In describing communication this way, we are seeking to show the place of the individual within the framework of the professional world. Your genuine respect for differences is perhaps the most important message you can send. This message, sent through the medium of your profession, becomes associated with your profession; your profession is the message.

READ FOR YOURSELF

BREMBECK, WINSTON L., and WILLIAM S. HOWELL, Persuasion: A Means of Social Influence (2nd ed.). Englewood Cliffs, N.J.: Prentice-Hall, Inc., 1976.

BRYANT, DONALD C., and KARL R. WALLACE, Fundamentals of Public Speaking (4th ed.). New York: Appleton-Century-Crofts, 1969.

CARSON, HERBERT L., Steps in Successful Speaking. Princeton, N.J.: D. Van Nostrand Company, 1967.

CRONKHITE, GARY, Persuasion: Speech and Behavioral Change. Indianapolis: The Bobbs-Merrill Co., Inc., 1969.

NADEAU, RAY E., A Basic Rhetoric of Speech-Communication. Reading, Mass.: Addison-Wesley Publishing Co., Inc., 1969.

CHAPTER CHART

Choosing a Topic

> *Key idea:* Know what change you are seeking in the audience and why you want it

Choose a topic you are committed to

Choose a topic that is manageable

Choose a topic that matches your audience's interests

Choose a topic that supports your intent

Choosing a Method

> *Key idea:* All messages are informative, persuasive, and entertaining to a degree

Instructional method—"show and tell"

Demonstration method—simulating the problem

Informational method—telling a story

Subjective method—personally embodying the topic

Persuasive method—making a "swap"

Choosing a Message Pattern

> *Key idea:* Recognizable patterns and contours help message transference

Main parts

> beginning, middle, and end
>
> thesis statements and subparts
>
> specific "for instances"

Forms of patterning

> cause and effect
>
> problem and solution
>
> time
>
> space
>
> comparison
>
> journalistic questions
>
> human equation
>
> numbers
>
> acronym/acrostic/alphabet forms
>
> catchphrases and quotations

> *Key idea:* Forms should fit the topic, speaker's method and aim, and audience's experience

Beginnings

> say and do the unexpected
>
> self-disclose
>
> use a shocking statement
>
> ask a rhetorical question
>
> ask a direct question
>
> use a crisp quote
>
> announce the point
>
> tell a joke
>
> use a prop
>
> make eye contact

Closings
Key idea: Messages should contain several "beginnings" and "closings"
Key idea: The clinching close is your last chance to emphasize the essence of
your message and your professionalism
use proverbs, aphorisms, and morals
use punch lines
use dares
use forecasts

Making Transitions
Sum up and infer
Change the time
Compare and indicate your position
Shift to doubt or to certainty
Use phrases that carry expectation

Supportive Materials
Expert opinion
Basic reference books
Local businesses and media agencies
Personal experience

Persuasion
Key idea: Persuasion is receiving in the guise of giving
Key idea: Establishing the need for audience change
Status quo has deteriorated, is deteriorating, or is going to deteriorate
Status quo is satisfactory but could be better
Changes are required to maintain status quo
Status quo is satisfactory but out of control
Comparing alternative plans for change
unworkable
too expensive
don't meet long- or short-term requirements
merely "more of the same with a new name"
connected with cultural taboos
Show superiority of your plan, based upon
questions of taste
questions of cause
questions of policy
questions of justice/fairness
questions of value
questions of fact

Humor in the Message
Key idea: Humor is an attitude toward life
Key idea: Humor prepares an audience for sympathetic reception of the
message
Types of humor
ridicule
exaggeration
incongruity

Guidelines for humor in professional communication
    talking funny and talking about something funny are different
    laughter is not the only test of success in humor
    anyone can tell jokes
    humor can be an icebreaker
    avoid subjects that may not be humorous

PART 3

OTHER FORMS OF BUSINESS AND PROFESSIONAL SPEECH COMMUNICATION

chapter 8

OTHER FORMS
OF BUSINESS
PROFESSIONAL
SPEECH
COMMUNICATION

chapter challenge

Contribute to the resonance of small group encounters
Recognize the principle of plurality and the "happy mistake"
Describe leadership characteristics
Distinguish between leading and leashing
Explain why businesspeople meet
Encourage self-disclosure

SMALL GROUP COMMUNICATION

confer-BEAR TOGETHER   confer-BEAR TOGETHER
confer-BEAR TOGETHER

A small group may consist of a handful of people who wonder why they have come together. A small group of professionals tends to be a handful of purposeful communicators who exchange viewpoints, examine pathways, and perhaps arrive at a course of action that everyone can "live with." This chapter considers the role of the professional communicator in small group encounters and examines the critical behaviors of ask–answer, send–receive, and give–take.

During many of your experiences—good and bad—with group encounters, you may have wondered whether several heads are really better than one. Committee work is, however, an ancient mode of letting people say, listen to, and respond to whatever idiocies members of a group indulge in. Group communication is, to a large extent, the business of business. The best discussions harness many energies; they dramatize the workings of interface and what can be called business communications axioms: the "laws" of *plurality*, of *resonance*, and of the *happy mistake*.

A group might be defined as a working collective of differing personalities who agree to meet for set periods of time in order to face a shared problem, question, and/or task. The most common types of professional small groups you are likely to be involved in include:

action committees   brainstorming groups
advisory boards and councils   caucuses
ad hoc committees   delegations

executive councils and boards	research and development teams
exploratory committees	subcommittees
fact-finding committees	search committees
negotiating committees	symposiums
panel discussions	task force groups
planning groups	think-tanks
quad-squads (rapping in the quad)	use committees

Of all the suggestions and advice given to small group participants, the most valuable ones come from their own experience. Test this statement in Enactment 18.

enactment 18   RESONATE

See what you can find out about from your encounter in...

enactment 18: RESONATE

group dynamics

participants

Group A, five students; Group L, five students; Group W, five students; Group Z, five students.

problem

Each group meets for a specified period of time; its task is to find answers to two questions: (1) Why are we named Group_____, and (2) why were we grouped together the way we were?

critique 18   TROUBLESHOOTING

1. How did the very first *decision* come about?
2. Did everyone share in the task? How do you know?
3. How did a "leader" or spokesperson emerge?
4. What steps were followed to solve the problem of the two questions?
5. Was the group "closer" at the end of the meeting than at the beginning? Why? How do you know?
6. What occurred or was said accidentally that helped the group answer its questions?

7. What evidence was there of professionalism?
8. Describe the ways the group arranged itself.
9. What indications were there that the group wanted to spend more time together?
10. What was said that did not seem to have anything to do with the questions at hand?
11. Who uttered the most words? Who said the least? Why do you feel this was so?
12. Who seemed to listen the best? How could you tell?
13. What pressure tended to make everyone "go along with the group"?
14. How did the fact that everyone was "different" help or hurt arriving at answers to the questions?

HOW WOULD YOU IMPROVE IT?

task 1   SHAKING OR RESONATING?

Figure 8–1 depicts five people interacting. Both Square A and Square B show business meetings with plural or different types of participants. Which of the following characteristics would you assign to each business meeting:

1. A unified group identity can be seen in Square ___, because _____

   _____.

2. The "interference" of each message builds up in Square ___, because _____

   _____.

3. Messages are "exposed to dangers of distortion," since they have a greater

   distance to travel in Square ___, because _____.

4. Differences of opinion get "welded together" in Square ___, because _____

   _____.

5. Each person appears to be isolated and the group fragmented in Square ___,

   because _____

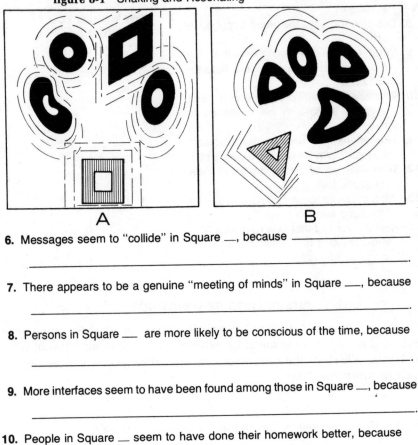

figure 8-1 Shaking and Resonating

A   B

6. Messages seem to "collide" in Square ___, because _____
_____.

7. There appears to be a genuine "meeting of minds" in Square ___, because
_____

8. Persons in Square ___ are more likely to be conscious of the time, because
_____
_____.

9. More interfaces seem to have been found among those in Square ___, because
_____.

10. People in Square ___ seem to have done their homework better, because
_____
_____.

GROUP DYNAMICS

group size

The size of the group dictates the number of possible (and necessary) relationships between members. A larger group has more people to talk and listen to. You have to wait longer for your turn to speak; you must listen harder and longer; you may have to note things down to remember them until your turn comes. The larger the group, the easier it is for members to hide or become lost in the crowd. You may have witnessed some of these obvious traits in Enactment 18.

Groups with an odd number of members seem to benefit from certain tensions. An odd numbered group is asymmetrical and unbalanced, a condition that frequently leads to a "happy mistake." It is harder for participants to pair off when the number is odd; confusion about how to divide tends to last longer than in even-numbered groups. An odd-numbered committee has the advantage of an enforced "extra" role-player—a leader, a gadfly, a devil's advocate, or a ready-made majority.

The group's purpose is another determiner of size. One general guide is that simple tasks require small sizes; tasks with multiple stages occurring over a longer period benefit from a group of six to eleven members, with five, seven, or nine people being the usual membership.[1] To attain a professional outlook toward communicating, however, you should modify the pragmatic or "efficiency" rule at times to consider all who might benefit from membership; many employees have a "please use me" need, and your invitations to them to do committee work signal your esteem as well as your grasp of full-channel communicating.

What did you find out about group size as it affected Enactment 18? You probably felt the advantage of prior acquaintance, and the five-member group may have seemed "right" for the task. Had the class been evenly divided and given the same task, size factors might have been much more apparent.

group leadership

Actual business conferences and committee proceedings frequently have designated leaders. The boss is chairperson, the ranking staff member "presents" the agenda, or an appointed leader structures the event. How did your group's leader emerge in Enactment 18:

1. Did the loudest, fastest-talking, "biggest" person take over?
2. Did a person's reputation in or out of class make the group choose that person?
3. Did the role just gravitate to somebody by default—nobody else cared, but your "leader" didn't care as little as the other four?
4. Was the leader selected because he/she was older or was a speech major or had taken a speech class before?
5. Was your leader the person with *the* solution to your problem?
6. Was there an unstated, perhaps unconscious, agreement that one individual should be leader, because he/she *needed* to be?

[1] Clovis R. Shepherd, *Small Groups* (San Francisco: Chandler Publishing Company, 1964), pp. 129–39.

Leadership/Headship.   Cecil Gibb[2] notes that "headship" is very different from leadership: heads are dominant, autocratic, and socially removed from the rest of the group. Heads are authority figures, possessing power beyond the immediate tasks of a group. The head in Figure 8–1, Square A, is psychologically "distanced" as well as spatially distanced from the other participants.

Leadership Tasks.   Here are some of the major responsibilities of the leader:

1. Small group leaders *set the tone* and adopt one of several roles. They serve as models for the tempo and rhythm of interaction.
2. Leaders *facilitate* posturing or role-playing in others, by helping them find where they stand and how they can best relate to the group and its task.
3. Leaders *order* the flow of business; they "keep the gate open, half-open, closed, or locked," by directing message traffic. They are sensitive to questions and topics that have been exhausted or are heading in the wrong direction.
4. Small group leaders *lead;* they point to ways by deftly injecting timely questions and summaries.
5. Leaders help groups *define* their own identities, their personal signatures and characters.
6. Leaders provide exchanges that *create cohesion* or "oneness" among members, by extending invitations to speak and by actually giving up some of the traditional leader's authority, thereby gaining, paradoxically, more authority, respect, and esteem.
7. Leaders *listen*. The good professional communicator operates with all languages and modes resonating. Resonating groups alternate the give-and-take reciprocal aspect of exchange, and listening is at least half of easing and coaxing fruitful exchange.
8. Small group leaders *assert a "whole picture"* viewpoint. They keep the reason for being in front, while they refer to things outside the immediate group. They are able to use both ends of the telescope—to see the specific and the general. They help the other participants to be conscious of this holistic outlook, while tracing problems, testing definitions, watching the clock and the calendar.
9. Leaders *recognize plurality* as the state of things. They find ways to encourage diversity of opinion, motive, and image-making. As in Figure 8–1, each diverse participant adds special character and texture to the group, which shapes itself to accommodate pluralities. "It takes all kinds . . ." is the view taken. This consolidates group efforts and, indeed, is one of the basic assumptions of trade and competition.

---

[2]Cecil A. Gibb, "The Principles and Traits of Leadership," in *Small Group Discussion: A Reader*, ed. Robert S. Cathcart and Larry A. Samovar (Dubuque: William C. Brown Company, Publishers, 1970), p. 373.

10. Small group leaders are able to *locate interfaces* easily. A shared belief that differences exist is, in itself, an interface basic to business. As you may recall, the interface model in Figure 1–5 depicted the single viewpoint made possible by an interlocking of surfaces directed at a given task. Experience, perception, coding, intent, set, feedback, invitation, and need were shown as "vectors of alikeness," which hook up collective energies or different talents. Looking now at Figure 8–1, you may be able to see the links in Square B; each member does not "mate" entirely but achieves some interface. Some part of each is in phase and is complementing part of some other. Leaders may suggest areas of interface, even when group members seem to exclude the possibility of links.

11. Leaders *recognize happy mistakes*. Such helpful errors continually occur, although they mystify communicators in business. Sensitive group leaders try to keep their eyes and ears peeled for errors, false leads, or fortuitous misdirections that contain real breakthroughs in creative thinking and problem-solving.

Leadership Strategies. Various approaches to leading committee work are based on the exercise of *restraint*. The restrained leader does not feel a loss when sharing the tasks of leading a group. The spectrum of leadership control follows an arc from this *laissez-faire* (noninterference) group process to rigid rubber-stamping group operations that merely give an obligatory "okay" to whatever the leader wants.

One middle-ground strategy is for the leader to launch meetings in a methodical, well-planned, autocratic way to establish his or her leadership credentials and then gradually to release authority and direction to individuals within the group. Other methods reflect variations in the type of businessperson who is the leader—such as hustler, manipulator, or exploiter. These strategies seek to gain leverage or to isolate weaknesses, vulnerabilities, and frailties. The autocrat selectively hears and sees messages. As supreme arbiter of procedure, the martinet-leader plots and directs the thinking of the group, exercising the absolute power of a Louis XIV.

Another strategy somewhere between the extremes uses degrees of restraint as necessitated by time or money. Such constraints may compel a more heavily structured or controlled ruling approach at times. The professional with leadership responsibilities takes pains to communicate the practical needs requiring tighter control and seeks a tacit acceptance of the structure from his or her colleagues.

task 2 LEADING OR LEASHING?

Think back to experiences you have had with small group leadership—in classes, jobs, your family, etc. Which combination of leadership tasks, traits, and strategies were used? Which would have been better? Were you led or leashed?

1. When I was thirteen, I should have been led/leashed more by my parents, using

   the following tasks, traits, and strategies: _____

   _____ .

2. My senior year in high school was marked by the seniors being led/leashed.

   What we needed was leadership that _____

   _____ .

3. In the largest college class I ever had, we were led/leashed, but we really could

   have used _____

   _____ .

4. The sales staffs of most big stores I've been in seem to be led/leashed. Maybe

   they would like their work more and serve customers better, if they received

   _____ .

5. An organization I belong to is led/leashed, and members can expect the following

   leadership traits: _____

   _____

   _____ .

group interaction

The overriding motive of persons in group communication is to "bear together," to carry the burden of decision or action. In a business context, groups carry two main responsibilities: to assist the group in accomplishing its agreed purpose, and to represent each larger parent organization—the firm, the department, the bureau. Several large American firms—General Electric, Caterpillar Tractor, and Bausch and Lomb among others—use small groups at their highest management levels. This is called the *office-of-the-president* concept. A half-dozen or so executives "carry the load" of top executive action.[3]

Interaction within the small group that *confers* follows a

[3]Reported in *Democrat and Chronicle* (Rochester, N.Y.), November 14, 1971, sec. C, p. 1. Copyright 1971, Newsday, Inc. Reprinted by permission.

pattern of thinking out loud. Group members carry several ways, as indicated by these phrases frequently heard in business transactions:

how he/she carries himself/herself   having to carry somebody
carrying news   carry the load/burden
carrying the goods   carry the weight
getting carried away   carrying the ball

If we approach thinking as a kind of weighing of alternatives, then one main function of the group is to weigh or carry alternatives out loud.

The original question in a group, "Why are we here?" is carried by everyone and is usually the first question to be dealt with. Some groups carry every answer to every possible question from the outset. Each member knows beforehand who is in charge, what the problem is, how it is to be solved, what the group's identity is and will be, and what time it will adjourn. Such a gathering, of course, is not a meeting, it is a form letter, a rite. Other groups have meetings for various reasons, however, including:

1. meeting to have a meeting; this may serve the function of acquainting (or reacquainting) members, breaking the ice, or allowing preliminary sizing up among coworkers, before discussions begins
2. meeting to inform, advise, or brief; this features one person telling the group something descriptive
3. the show-and-tell meeting where a proposal is offered for review
4. advisory meetings; these attempt to get members to advise out loud
5. report meetings; these serve to carry research findings back to be shared with the group;
6. exploratory meetings; each member's task here is to string together quantities of information in the hope that patterns will emerge—something will turn up.

House Rules. Member interaction—thinking out loud—is subject to rules; some are stated, some implied or hinted at, some generally accepted or proprietary, some unconsciously applied from previous encounters and wide-ranging experience. Stated rules include designation of the chairperson or leader or speaker, calendar and duration limits, limits on topics or a prescribed agenda. Implied rules are communicated in a wide variety of ways. Reading between the lines of an agenda, how each item is stated or asked, the title of the group—these all imply limitations on procedure. Generally accepted rules are those common to our culture, prescribed by the setting, the occasion, and the standards of professionalism being exercised. Such rules usually pertain to dress and language codes.

Phases of Interaction.   Communicating, we said, is a process that occurs in alternating bits. Communicators who are transacting "in phase" are *resonating;* those "out of whack" perform in a jerky, *shaking* manner. Figure 8–1 sketches the circular, pulsing, in-phase motion of the resonating group that is communicating well in Square B. The members' energies join, and they amplify each other's ideas and self-images. Square A shows the shaking group. Its motion is linear, tentative, halting, stop-and-start; this group wobbles rather than resonates. Its phases often overlap and occur simultaneously. For purposes of study, let us examine four circular *phases* that occur in group work.

The first phase *establishes behavioral norms.* Group members adapt to the sizes and distances of things—chairs, ashtrays—and the number and kinds of fellow members are quickly assessed. They try to "get comfortable" with their environment. Discussion specialist John Brilhart sees norms as those behaviors that are "repeatedly enacted or avoided," and he notes that "some sort of punishment or sanction [is] taken against a member who deviates from the norm."[4]

How far group members can go in any direction is part of the setting of behavioral norms; it is a testing of territory, potential alliances, possible "routes of escape" (clamming up, playing dumb, obfuscating, etc.). Obviously, the process may incorporate on-the-spot changes; things happen, points get made, and surprising revelations occur that may affect behavioral norms.

A second phase of small group interaction is *self-disclosure:* how much of your real self can you risk showing? How much *must* you risk showing? How much must you risk in order to get others to show their real selves? A device for examining self-disclosure that is popularly used in many study areas is a model designed by Joe Luft and Harry Ingham called the Johari Window.[5] The four window "panes" in Figure 8–2 depict four areas of your professional character and self-image. Area 1 is the open part that is known to yourself and to others. Area 2 represents parts that are also known to others, but that you blind yourself to. Areas 3 and 4 are both unknown to others, but Area 3 represents things you *keep* hidden.

The dynamic aspect of the Johari Window is that it can help you visualize what happens to these categories of disclosure when any

---

[4]John R. Brilhart, *Effective Group Discussion,* 2nd ed. (Dubuque: William C. Brown Company, Publishers, 1974), p. 27.

[5]Reprinted from *Group Processes: An Introduction to Group Dynamics* by Joseph Luft by permission of Mayfield Publishing Company, formerly National Press Books, Copyright 1970. See also the companion volume by Luft, *Of Human Interaction.*

figure 8-2   Johari Window. Reprinted from *Group Processes:*
An Introduction to Group Dynamics by Joseph Luft
by permission of Mayfield Publishing Company,
formerly National Press Books, Copyright 1970. See
also Luft, *Of Human Intervention.*

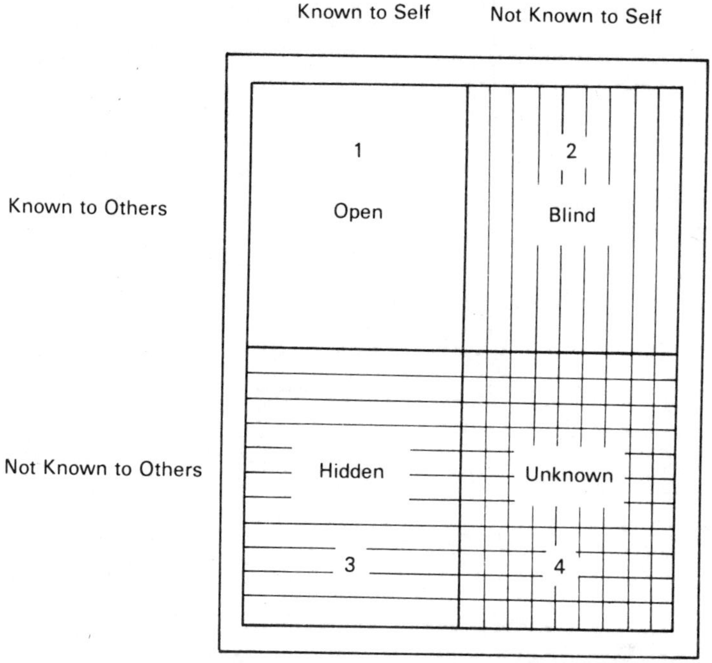

one or a combination of areas changes in size through transactions with others. If, for example, you move the window frame to expose more of your real self, as shown in Figure 8–3, the protected regions *shrink*.

Applying this dynamic to a group's awareness of itself and awareness of a group by others, Luft explains that Area 1 might stand for characteristics that are obvious to everyone in all groups. Area 2 represents traits of a group that are not seen by that group but are apparent to other groups. Area 3 might indicate things the group knows about itself but hides; while Area 4 is the unknown characteristics—motives and unconscious factors that nobody realizes the group has.

Luft suggests several group dynamics that occur when members change the size of their self-disclosure windows:

1. Changing any pane of the window changes the other three.
2. Hiding, denying, or blinding yourself during a transaction requires work.

figure 8-3 Openness Increased

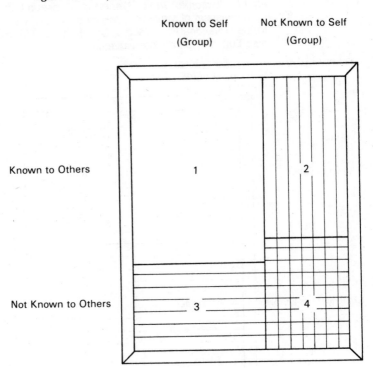

Known to Self
(Group)

Not Known to Self
(Group)

Known to Others

1

2

Not Known to Others

3

4

3. Mutual trust tends to increase your willingness to self-disclose. Perceived threats tend to make you unwilling to self-disclose.
4. Obvious or forced disclosure does not convince anyone.
5. Interpersonal learning signals a change to a larger space in Area 1 and to smaller spaces in the other three areas.
6. A large Area 1 helps you devote more energy to focusing on the task at hand.
7. A small Area 1 indicates poor communication.
8. Everyone wonders about the unknown area but usually avoids probing.
9. Sensitive people respect the hidden areas.
10. Practice in group communication tends to enlarge your awareness of everyone's Area 1 and to enlarge everyone's Area 1.

task 3   HIDE AND SEEK

Figure 8–4 is an enlarged version of the Johari Window and lists several group-to-group relationships that can be brought closer through self-disclosure. Suggest one characteristic that each group might add to its open area and note one possible change that might occur in its other three areas.

figure 8-4 Group Disclosure

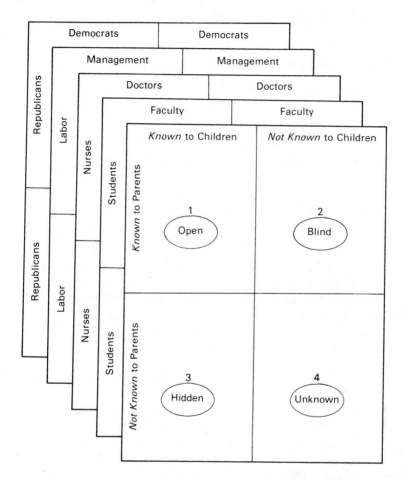

Example: Research and Development Group/Retailing Group: If the R & D group members revealed *what their spouses' real preferences of camping equipment were,* and the retailing group members revealed *their lack of training in the basic technology of manufacturing the product,* their hidden areas of job specialization, narrow perspective, and bias against plural viewpoints might be reduced.

1. Students/Faculty: If the student group would disclose _____

_____, and the faculty would disclose _____

_____, their hidden, blind, and unknown areas

might decrease _____.

2. Nurses/Doctors: If the nurses disclosed _____ in

Area 1, and the doctors disclosed _____, their

hidden areas could be decreased _____.

3. Labor Union/Management: If the labor group revealed _____

_____, and management revealed _____

_____, their hidden areas could be decreased

_____.

4. Republicans/Democrats: If each party would seek to add _____

_____ to its open area, perhaps their

respective hidden areas could be decreased _____

_____.

The third phase of small group interaction is the *formulation of roles* and the assertion of professionalism. Self-disclosure is partly a decision to show yourself in a particular way, "packaged" to give the effect you want. You become proficient in detecting how others expect you to perform, there is always the underlying hope that you will become what you act—at least in the eyes of others.

In business encounters you may see that certain individuals feel comfortable with a wide range of roles that match what they believe is expected of them. The six stereotypes cited in Chapter 5 can be divided and subdivided many times to include: tension-breakers—the clown or wit; the resident genius, with solutions and answers to everything; the sexist of either gender, sending and receiving messages and perceiving the world not in terms of figure and background, but of female and male. Others are politicized, coopted, kept, for sale, for hire, and so on ad infinitum. A professional attitude will, however, continue to be appealing and compelling. Members of the resonating group in Square B of Figure 8–1 are not conforming to each other in anything except perhaps their professionalism.

The fourth phase of group interaction consists of *forming bonds* with patterns of thought. Through free discussion of opinions and possibilities, a cerebral chain is formed. You locate members' positions on issues that educate you about views and positions *outside* the group. In this way the world is brought into the group and gets represented within its small universe.

The total effect of each phase of interaction is to solidify membership. Cohesiveness or identification with the group, high expectation of completing the task, mutual trust and respect are products of good small group work. Group dynamics facilitate the completion of group tasks.

group tasks

What are the specific jobs people perform in a group that contribute to completion of the overall task? Some of the most important ones include the following:

1. An essential activity performed individually and collectively is the notation of what is done and said. *Minutes* or digests of key statements are recorded to facilitate memory and help pass along the committee's work to other people. Accurate recording gives concrete evidence of what the group is doing, gives it a helpful base for future meetings, and gives other groups a record of its work that might help them.
2. A second necessary task is *division of labor.* Your group of five in Enactment 18 had ten eyes, ten ears, ten hands, five mouths, etc. This did not make it "better," but it may have provided many perspectives, sidelights, and insights. Dividing tasks means you do not have to repeat steps or say what someone else has said.
3. A nonprofessional communicator may tend to derail the trains of message flow; an exploiter may divert the overall group task, so that the leader must work—with everyone's help—to control digressions and personal excesses. This *gate-keeping* task helps focus energy toward an efficient interface attitude.
4. Group members, as we noted, "carry" ideas. Through exchanges of views, building on each other's thoughts, finding and making patterns of support, members establish a picture of *what is known* about their overall task.
5. The group must *assemble likely sources* where assistance in doing its task might be found. "Who do we see?" "Who can tell us?" "Who knows . . . ?" "Where can we find . . . ?" "Who has faced this problem before?" "What would happen if . . . ?" "What is the likelihood of . . . ?" are the questions put forward, considered, and refined.
6. Ultimately, groups must *decide* whether they are ready to end their business. Summaries are made, alternatives are weighed, and collective judgments are made by the group to act, recommend, legislate, restructure, regroup, or put itself out of business.

There is a special skill in all types of direct, face-to-face communication that needs examination—listening creatively. Listening, like all modes of communicating, requires work—expenditure of energy. Listening, too, is a total act involving your total self; you might inventory how you and your colleagues listen during Enactment 19.

enactment 19   FORECAST

This enactment is an exercise in group dynamics—leadership, task-sharing, self-disclosure, and decision-making.

Be alert to these concepts in...........................

enactment 19: FORECAST

plurality
resonance
the happy mistake
conformity to procedure
individuality of person and idea
leadership tasks
four phases of group interaction
self-disclosure principles
your competence factor/
  professionalism

participants

The class is divided into small groups of students with an interest in some function of university operation, such as purchasing, personnel, maintenance, public relations, athletics, or student services. Each small group can evolve its own identity and name; each should be composed of five to eleven members.

problem

Each group is assigned the following task: Report to the class your forecast of the conditions you believe will exist in your sector of college operation 100 years from now. Try to follow the leadership, recording, and phase development we have outlined above in the time allotted to you. Discover ways to divide the burden of the task and yet be efficient while asserting a high standard of professionalism. Design a good way to pass along your projection of future conditions to the class.

critique 19   TROUBLESHOOTING

1. What statements, actions, behaviors, silences, etc., *blocked* performance of the overall task?
2. Which of the four phases got the least attention? Did it need any?
3. Which role "types" did you see being played? Were there any changeovers?

212

If so, why did the participants try a different role? Did the switches help communication? Did they help those participants' self-esteem?

4. To what degree did the small group resonate? How was individuality maintained even while members conformed?

5. List the group members in order of *leadership contribution* (the member who led most frequently first).

HOW WOULD YOU IMPROVE IT?

6. Which languages were used most effectively in this group encounter—digital or analogic? Why?

7. One assumption made by professionals is that the job can be done. What evidence did you detect in the manner of communicating that members never considered the possibility that they could not complete the task?

8. Cite any examples you saw/heard of *hustling, exploiting,* or *manipulating.* What motives would you ascribe for each example? How were these attempts managed by the group? What would you have done to offset unprofessional behavior?

afterthought GROUPS: LEADERS AND FOLLOWERS

The exercise of professional communication makes it difficult for leader–follower polarities to take hold. Group work is an old tradition in the United States, going back to the town hall concept— government by public forum. From the early Greek assemblies and lyceums, the phenomenon of the meeting has been used as a device for giving and receiving opinions. It has given the problems of coexisting—among business, government, and the individual—a place for open disclosure. Meetings have provided a republican form of representation, where leaders are spokesmen and listeners substituting for their constituencies.

Good meetings are occasions of free exchange with a minimum of control by leadership. In them, a member is neither leader nor a follower only, but a person and a professional.

READ FOR YOURSELF

BORMANN, ERNEST G., and NANCY C. BORMANN, *Effective Small Group Communication*. Minneapolis: Burgess Publishing Company, 1972.

BRILHART, JOHN K., *Effective Group Discussion* (2nd ed.). Dubuque: William C. Brown Company, Publishers, 1974.

CATHCART, ROBERT S., and LARRY A. SAMOVAR, *Small Group Communication: A Reader* (2nd ed.) Dubuque: William C. Brown Company, Publishers, 1974.

ZELKO, HAROLD P., *The Business Conference: Leadership and Participation*. New York: McGraw-Hill Book Company, 1969.

CHAPTER CHART

Business Communications Axioms
    Law of plurality
    Law of resonance
    Law of the happy mistake
    Key idea: Group purpose determines group size

Leadership Tasks
    Set the tone, tempo, and rhythm of exchange
    Help members find comfortable roles
    Order the flow and direction of business
    Help the group to find its own identity
    Encourage cohesion
    Listen
    Maintain a total viewpoint
    Recognize plurality and encourage differences of opinion
    Locate interfaces among group members

Leadership Strategies
    Restraint—laissez-faire
    Planning and anticipation of needs
    Timely summations and key questioning

Types of Meetings
    Get-acquainted
    Briefings—advise and inform
    Demonstration
    Exploratory
    Key idea: Member interaction means "talking out loud"

Phases of Interaction
    Establishing behavioral norms—adapting to the environment
    Self-disclosure
    Formulating roles and asserting professionalism
    Emergence of patterns of thinking

Group Tasks
    Notation of proceedings
    Division of labor
    Gate-keeping—sticking to the group purpose
    Defining what is known about the group problem
    Locating sources of help
    Decision-making—ending the group's business

chapter 9

chapter challenge

Recognize how physical relationships affect the dyad

Identify leverage-seeking words

Compare the differences and similarities between dyads and speeches

List the purposes of interviewing

Follow preparatory guidelines for interviewing

Practice formulating and answering the questions and answers you want to exchange

Sharpen your awareness of the real message in communication encounters

THE AUDIENCE
OF ONE

DYAD-face-to-face   DYAD-face-to-face   DYAD-face-to-face

A *dyad* is a two-person relationship. It may be a friendship, a marriage, a business partnership; it may be a brief or a long-term basis for exchange—buying a newspaper, acknowledging the courtesy of a door held open, momentary contact between two pairs of eyes are examples of brief dyad transactions. The most common type of business dyad is probably the *interview:* two persons in a face-to-face exchange, each with an audience of one.

Much has been written about people's several selves. The tasks offered in this book have tried to encourage you to examine your sensitivity to personal motives and needs. The games people play and the stratagems and maneuvers they use to obtain "stroking" have been noted in previous chapters. "Vanity, vanity, all is vanity" has been a major theme of self-examination through the ages.

Historically, the dyad has been a focus of attention in life's great circus—the human comedy with its pushing and pulling, power struggles, leadership, and gamesmanship. Most of the great love matches, confrontations between mighty heads of state, heroic and climactic meetings of man and beast, man and the elements, man and God, were dyads—face-offs, showdowns, shoot-outs: two people facing each other, eyeball-to-eyeball.

In a sense, the dyad is what business is really about. It represents a test of your professionalism in a business setting with no witnesses. The dyadic encounter taxes your ability to adapt, to locate interfaces, to give, and to practice your competence factor; like all human exchange, the dyad also encourages your role-playing capability. Look at the following phrases and try to visualize a physical relationship of *dominance, superiority, deferring, sharing,* or *separate but equal status:*

1. "Look, I think I'm standing alone *in* this."
2. "Have you been able to get *to* the other people?"
3. "This problem is way *over* my head."
4. "What can I do *for* you?"
5. "The statement they made was something *like* that."
6. "Is your department *with* you?"
7. "Don't *under*sell yourself."
8. "*Between* you and me, I think you're right."
9. "There's total agreement *among* the supervisors over there."
10. "Why are you *against* the idea?"
11. "That's okay *by* me."
12. "I think I know what you're getting *at.*"

How you use words such as the twelve italicized prepositions indicates one possible effect of Benjamin Lee Whorf's idea that what you do and how you look at things are influenced by your language structure. Psychotherapists such as Sidney Jourard and Eric Berne might suggest that use of these prepositions reveals an intent to seek an *advantage* relationship. Task 1 is a check of your sensitivity to *leverage* phrases commonly heard in dyadic exchanges.

task 1   LEVERAGE-SEEKING WORDS

Each of these phrases implies an attempt by the speaker to gain leverage or an advantage in a dyadic encounter. On the basis of your previous exercises, complete the statement by giving a reasonable explanation of how each phrase could result in adaptive responses by the listener:

1. "Are you putting me *on?*" might gain the speaker leverage, because _____

_____.

2. "The company's *behind* you," might gain the speaker leverage, because

_____.

3. "Are they trying to get *out from under?*" might give the speaker leverage,

because _____

4. "Well, you really put one *over on* me," might gain leverage for the speaker,

because _____

5. "Get *with* it," might gain the speaker leverage, because _____

_____

6. "We're *between* a rock and a hard place," might gain a speaker leverage,

because _____.

7. "They'll fall *in* line," might gain the speaker leverage, because _____

_____.

8. "Is that *for* keeps?" might gain a speaker leverage, because _____

_____.

9. "Are you coming *in* or *out?"* might gain the speaker leverage, because ____

_____.

10. "It's just *like* them," might gain the speaker leverage, because _____

_____.

11. "Work *at* it," might gain the speaker leverage, because _____

_____.

12. "Maybe it's *beyond* our reach," might gain the speaker leverage, because

_____.

Each of these phrases and hundreds of similar variations convey at least three problem areas for professional communicators: (1) they *judge,* (2) they *burden* the listener, and (3) they *hint.* These are all legitimate messages, and everyone sends ones like them in some form at some time. They are all invitations to communicate, and each would have a context or frame of reference when used in a real situation. What reaction do you have when people judge you, burden you with barbed statements or questions, and hint at messages? You probably tend to feel that you are being pressured or "levered" into something. An invitation or "lure" might be any message that coaxes you to respond favorably; *leverage* challenges you to match the sender, who signals: "I'm one up; your turn."

INTERVIEWING AND PRESENTING

The interview is a conversation with a purpose, a visible or a hidden agenda, and a common goal. Presenting is a mode of transmitting messages commonly referred to as speech-making, the kind studied in

Chapters 6 and 7. Before you prepare for your first interview enactment, compare what you know about the dyad and the speech.

Interviewing:
An Audience of One

Greater spontaneity: The dyad allows and demands wider freedom to explore many bits and "tail ends" of issues and views. Both participants establish the rhythm of "talkus interruptus" and help each other arrive at commonalities by finishing phrases, supplying terms, "syn-storming" (see Enactment 8 in Chapter 4) in a free association of motive and need.

Greater reciprocity and feedback: Each participant, using his/her options, may fully "speak" the several languages mentioned in Chapter 2. Laughter, for example, is more pointed, its source is unmistakable, its meaning less ambiguous. The dyad allows for a greater quantity of feedback; participants take turns and therefore have more turns as listener and speaker. This provides a greater basis for "knowing" each other and for successfully locating interfaces.

Greater listening demands: Each participant must listen or he/she will jeopardize the chances of a genuine reciprocal exchange and self-disclosure. Monitors are finely tuned to only a single message source. Minimal attention is given to note-taking in dyads because it is an intrusion and splits the attention.

Greater range of topics: Two talker/ listeners multiply the potential for broad topic allusions or

Presenting:
An Audience of Many

Fewer departures from plan: A speech situation, though not strictly a one-way encounter, denies sender and receivers the freedom to explore. The message is programmed, fairly cut and dried. The speaker tends to operate on "speaking time" and the audience on "listening time"; this is more of a linear arrangement, whereas the dyad has mosaic potential.

More cluster feedback: Large groups may signal a generalized reaction; their options are limited by their membership in a group and its conditions for membership; their languages are limited. Members of speech audiences do have greater physical mobility, because they have greater anonymity. Feedback is largely a group-controlled or mass response. Audiences are more susceptible to distractions and more likely to "switch channels," start a dialogue with a neighbor, or fall asleep.

Limited listening demands: The speaker organizes listener thinking through the development of topics, making listening easier. Filtering is easier, and the speech occasion provides a greater preview of what to expect. Note-taking can be done less conspicuously.

Limited range of topics: Subject matter is generally restricted to fit the speech format and discussion. Since "total personalities" are communicated, many "unrelated" subjects can be included.

occasion. Audience needs are frequently the primary determiner of topic choice. The speaker's monitoring of audience reaction and question sessions may offer some topic flexibility.

Multiple structure: Dyads may incorporate short speeches, fragmentary comments, readings, telephone verifications; participants may switch roles, for example, by asking: "What would you do in my place?" Each member might speak in either first, second, or third person. All forms of reasoning, including on-the-spot empirical (experimental) research, might be used. Dyads may be enlarged by calling in witnesses for corroboration, consultants, passers-by, or guests. Participants may shift their physical relationships.

Single structure: Formal speech-making occasions have a more rigid structure. They may incorporate media languages—film, slide, tape, audience participation in a limited way. Spatial arrangements are usually set to focus directly on participants; occasionally the speaker may direct the audience's attention to an object, a person, or an image in another space or time frame. Enlargement of the presentation occurs, but this changes the proxemics and the format to a demonstration or perhaps an enactment.

Multiple role-playing: Each participant in the dyad has a greater opportunity to try out relationships, play games, send out trial signals. Members may shift ego states, behaving authoritatively, professionally, or immaturely; each may "kid," clown, adopt childish attitudes that partly reflect his/her real state of mind, or may be a "defense" against a felt threat to his/her esteem or well-being.

Fixed role-playing: The speaker has some flexibility within a narrow range—the range of the role of "speaker." Audiences play a collective role with a mass identity. If polarization occurs, it usually divides the large group into only a few different groups with differing personalities, leadership, and identities. Speakers may react to polarization by changing or softening their roles or following up the signals received from the audience.

Complex character: Dyads allow more opportunity for participants to convey their special mixtures of values, motives, needs, and sense of professionalism. It is much more difficult to hide or obfuscate trust, credibility, and "character" in an interview.

Simplistic character: Formal speech occasions are prepared, "staged" messages. Changes in how participants transmit their characters may result in *dysfunction*—creating more harm than good, hurting more than helping. Fewer interfaces make it easier for speakers and listeners to "put their best foot forward," but audience judgment of the speaker's character may be held in reserve, awaiting further confirmation.

Intimate distances: Varieties of closeness and perhaps touching are possible in the dyad. Changes in heights—sitting, standing, kneeling, stooping, leaning, etc.—are available and expected. Participants frequently exchange tactile objects—papers, friendship tokens, refreshments, etc. Sensory languages—taste, smell, sight, etc.—whether intended or not, are more influential and carry maximum impact. Dyads offer larger quantities of stimuli (information) to each participant.

Impersonal distances: Fewer varieties of distance and heights are available. Visibility and "frontal viewing" of the speaker are necessary to control participants' attention and concentration. Aloofness or remoteness underscores the form of public address—one person "having" the floor, greater space around the speaker than around audience members. The density of the audience helps create a mass reaction by impeding a sense of individuality. Use of tactile objects is more awkward, less personal. Greater distance between speaker and listeners reduces the impact of sensory communication exchanges.

Greater risk for both: Each participant "lays it on the line." Each is more vulnerable, if self-disclosure is mutual. Each faces a greater test of himself/herself, because there is closer scrutiny by the other. There are fewer masks each can hide behind and still communicate honestly. The faster tempo of the exchange makes misstatements more likely, forces a spontaneity that can "trip people up."

Greater risk for the speaker: Speaker/audience formats place the burden of truth, proof, and "goof" on the speaker. Planning may alleviate a great deal of risk, but surprises occur that force the speaker to deal with them, counter them, or incorporate them into his/her speech.

Fewer language difficulties: Dyads give participants the opportunity to restate, rephrase, explain, use analogies, etc., to make their meanings clearer. Visual

More language difficulties: Formal speaking formats demand clarity "the first time." The speaker may use repetition and extended comparisons, but,

languages—graphic formats or nonverbal symbols—are used more easily. Direct question and answer exchanges assist in clarifying confusions of language. Acoustical interference is greatly reduced in a private setting, and words do not have to travel as far.

because of its size and complexity, the audience tends to miss subtleties of language and thought. Difficult vocabulary and phrasing tend to strain the audience's capacity to listen creatively. Acoustics may interfere with understanding. Distortion may occur if the speaker fails to adapt his/her words per minute to the environmental factors.

Interviewer's home turf: The setting for interviews most often "belongs" to the interviewer. Dyads generally occur on neutral grounds—anywhere. Business exchanges take place in various kinds of locales, and the choice is sometimes left to the initiator or "inviter" of the dyad. Most interviews of a structured agenda/purpose type occur in the interviewer's stomping grounds—an office, a boardroom, a consulting room, etc. Whoever "owns" the locale assumes a role of host, thus thrusting the role of guest on the visitor.

Audience's home turf: Often the place for a speech is considered the audience's turf, since it makes the greater concession—"gives up" more communication "rights" by agreeing to listen. Sometimes the turf is a neutral meeting ground or a locale "owned" by a sponsor with whom the speaker is associated in the minds of the audience. If the audience is closely connected with the sponsoring authority, it assumes a host function and the speaker adopts the posture of a guest.

Greater flexibility in follow-up: Dyads allow for assessment and evaluation by either member. Confirmations can be made by phone, by letter, by an agent of either member, or in person by either member. Follow-ups of previous exchanges are frequently part of and may even be the major transaction made in dyads.

Reduced flexibility of follow-up: Assessment of the communication is difficult for speaker and audience, unless provision has been made for an immediate exchange. Size is a prohibitive factor. Some sort of "registration" of audience members is necessary for canvassing large audiences. Individuals may, however, decide that feedback channels are open and that either a tacit or an expressed "invitation" has been genuinely extended.

Flexible leadership: Dyads alternate leadership. Direction and control of the conversation may change at any time; "rules" may be introduced by either member, although one may use more leverage or may signal that he/she wishes to be deferred to for reasons of age, job-title, home-turf, etc.

Inflexible leadership: Generally, the speaker stays in control. Restraints are usually applied by the sponsor (if someone other than the speaker) and may be part of the rules of membership in the audience.

Some dyads are one-way exchanges. The message may be given in a speech-making way that offers no opportunity for questions or verbal response. The following lead-in phrases characterize these types of dyads: "Your orders for today are. . ."; "Let me tell you a little about our company's fringe benefits . . ."; "Our agenda will include . . ." Each of these opening phrases warns that a one-way speech, oration, harangue, exposition, or narrative is to follow. People, of course, make little speeches during interviews and conversations; the one-way message, however, signals "No answer expected" (or wanted).

enactment 20   ONE WAY

Enactment 20 is an exercise in one-way communication that might illustrate the difficulties of transmitting certain types of information while withholding other types.

Try to identify these characteristics in. . . . .

enactment 20: **ONE WAY**

dyadic traits

participants

The Four General Communicators, whose task is to plan a verbal method of explaining directions. *Map-Drawing Groups,* four groups of students, each group assigned to follow the directions of a General Communicator. *Communicator 1* prepares a message to Group 1 that describes how to draw several main routes for entering the state. *Communicator 2* plans a message to Group 2 that explains how to draw several main routes leading into the town. *Communicator 3* plans a message to Group 3 that explains how to draw several routes leading into the college campus. *Communicator 4* plans a message to Group 4 that explains how to draw several routes leading to the classroom.

problem

Each communicator wants each member of his/her group to accurately draw a map of the described routes on the chalkboard. Each of the four "sections" of the total route—from *state* borders to *town* to *campus* to *classroom*—should begin at the edge of each place. Group members should individually draw parts of their section in turn as best they can. They should mark an X at any point on the drawing where they do not fully understand the directions of their communicator. No questions may be asked by group members; they may not look at their communicator. Each group member should pick up the route at the point where a member of his or her own group stopped previously. Each group member should initial that portion of the total route he or she drew.

critique 20   TROUBLESHOOTING

1. Of the four sections, which one do you feel is the most accurate? Which one is least likely to get you lost? Why?
2. Collectively, which *section* was drawn the best? Why?
3. Count the number of Xs by section. Can you explain why one section had the most? Why did one have the fewest Xs?
4. At which juncture did more members write Xs?
5. Would it be easier for a stranger to find his/her way in or out, using one of these maps? Why?
6. What specific requirements does one-way communication have?
7. What are the strengths of one-way communication?
8. How did the necessary reliance on verbal language help and hinder the communicators?
9. What did each group and each communicator learn from watching the previous group?
10. In what ways did the *language* dictate the logic of the explanations, and how did language affect (restrict, shape, etc.) the drawings?

HOW WOULD YOU IMPROVE IT?

INTERVIEWING

An interview incorporates all the possibilities and combinations of modes of expression and exchange. It may contain a declaration of purpose; for example, a typical lead-in might be: "We want to create more jobs, but before we can go forward with the project . . ." Interviews may center on a dialectic or question–answer style, with lead-ins such as, "How did you make out on the sales chart last month?" The interview might also be mainly conversational—containing personal speculation, repartee, or banter.

The four main purposes of interviews are: (1) to get data, (2) to get decisions/choices, (3) to get solutions, and (4) to get action. These functions often overlap, but let us look at each one separately.

interviewing to get data

Information-gathering interviews, by telephone or face to face, require a delicate balance of self-assurance and professionalism, sensitivity, discretion, and objectivity (impartiality). *News reporting* involves interviews that gather information, usually by asking questions. Some television interviewing may take a more conversational tone after the initial questioning; this is particularly true where interviewer and interviewee are both of relatively equal status or have *parity* in their respective professions.

Data that are merely statistical or digital and disclosures that are nonthreatening or risk-free to the interviewee are generally easier to obtain; the interview for this type of news-gathering is fairly easy to complete. Like all data-gathering interviews, it follows eleven basic steps:

1. Know *what* you are trying to find out and *how* the data will be used. Gathering information from volunteers for a legitimate study is quite a different transaction from asking an expert for personal comments that will be made public. Find out the degree of anonymity you can guarantee the interviewee. As you probably know, data are used, reused, borrowed, loaned, and sold by certain organizations; sometimes these transfers are legitimate. In order to protect sources, you must try to offer an honest explanation—as you know it—of how the information will be used.
2. Think through your *professional image;* know where you stand; honestly assess your motives and your need to interview.
3. Check the communication *field*. Find out what you can about the locale of the interview, the audience group your interviewees might belong to. What are the biases, sets, language limitations of this group? What are its standards of decorum and propriety, its unique cultural codes and values? What might you

say or do that would offend or tend to threaten and alienate prospective interviewees?

4. Review the *kind of transaction* you want and what you are willing to settle for. Planning an efficient exchange saves everybody time; if formulating questions is part of your task, spend time planning which questions to ask and anticipating the responses you are likely to get. Review how you might reshape questions to suit your specific interviewee better.

5. Prepare an *attitude and role* that are in keeping with your task. Do not confuse the interviewee by sending false signals or shifting roles. Present yourself as a single, distinct person, not someone playing two or three roles. Say that you are a student or a reporter or a researcher—not all three.

6. Locate and *identify accessible sources* that are ready to provide the required information. Some sources want to do some data-gathering themselves before they are ready to respond to an interview. Find interviewees who are willing, who do not expect to be compensated for giving you help, and who do not place contractually binding conditions on the information, the recipient, or themselves. Identify sources who are able to provide data, whose emotional, mental, and physical conditions do not prohibit exchange.

7. *Identify yourself* and whom you represent. State your purpose and the necessity of gathering the specific data you are after. Identify your sponsor, and explain what the interviewee's role and task are to be.

8. Limit or *restrain digressions* and self-disclosure that might invalidate or influence either party. Try to direct responses to factual information, such as eyewitness testimony; guide the interviewee away from hearsay or conjecture unless that is specifically sought.

9. *Record responses* accurately. Assist the interviewee and give examples if forms are to be filled out. Tape-record verbalizations if desired and photograph the data and the source if necessary, but only if the use of such equipment is agreed on in writing and becomes part of the interview "contract."

10. *Read back* material such as direct quotes so that the interviewee can check what he/she has said. You may have noted it incorrectly, or the respondent may wish to change or add something.

11. *Complete the interview* on the affirmative side. Most people, even the busiest, like to be thanked and like to feel they have helped or contributed to a worthy enterprise. Everyone you interview for raw data is a valuable contact, and you may want to ask him/her again for similar help.

Several types of business and professional assignments require on-the-spot interviewing to get descriptions and impressions of activities. Accident reporting, construction progress reporting, legal procedures, credit checking, insurance reporting and data collection, property assessment, comparative shopping for materials, and many other situations require interviews to get data. Polling and market studies sometimes include personal interviewing, though most such surveys use telephonic dyads as a cheaper, swifter means of getting data.

interviewing to make choices and decisions

The remaining three goals of interviewing—to make choices and decisions, to find solutions, and to get action—are basically processes of *filtering* or selectively screening probable causes, contributing factors, expert opinions, and testimony. They entail the techniques discussed in both small and large group problem-solving (Chapter 6, 7, and 8).

A decision-making dyad may have the purpose of deciding who is the best candidate to fill a position, what is the best way to improve productivity, and so forth. The type of decision/choice dyad you may first encounter is the job interview. Individuals sometime "fall into," are born into, or marry into a job, but the great majority of hiring, firing, and promotion decisions require interviews early in the process.

No book can tell you how to succeed, but a few common-sense principles can help instruct both participants in a job interview. Examine the general guidelines offered here for job interviewer and interviewee.

For the Job Interviewer

Obtain statistical data in readable form: Foreknowledge is the most solid support for anticipating the filtering and interpreting problem of job interviewing. If you see vital statistics, test scores, professional references, and work records in advance you can allow more time to assess the applicant's behavior and communication skills. Valuable data show patterns of behavior on which more accurate predictions can be based. For example, growth patterns in salary, responsibility, or type of assignment, and temporal or geographic patterns can be obtained before the face-to-face encounter.

Assert professionalism: In many respects you will "be" the company to interviewees. Its total image is projected through your demeanor and speech.

For the Job Interviewee

Research prospective employers: Find out what you can about the specific job situation and how it fits in with the company's overall goals. Review what the interviewer knows about you and your background. What assets do you have that are not known to the interviewer and that match the employer's needs? Find out if the interview is with a job interviewer or with the person responsible for budgeting your salary—your prospective supervisor or administrator. Locate patterns in your vital statistics and prepare to explain these patterns as they affect your job preparation.

Assert professionalism: You will apply as a trainee, apprentice, credential holder, journeyman, or experienced worker. Your statistical data will corroborate

Think through an attitude of receptivity. Whatever procedures the individual firm and situation may dictate, the job interviewer is interested in finding talented, responsible employees for positions at all levels. Be willing to *receive* graciously and professionally the candidacy and esteem requests of interviewees.

Encourage self-disclosure:
Self-disclosure provides data that never appear on an application. You know already that trust and creativity flourish in a communication climate of receptivity and respect. If you talk less, the applicant will talk more. Do not hesitate to provide invitations to communicate and contexts that show promise of enhancing the applicant's self-esteem, that make him/her feel comfortable and valued as a person, not merely an applicant for a job.

Avoid double-think: Take pains to make your messages very clear. If you suspect that something is not understood, clarify, restate, reinforce it. Use summaries that recapitulate important points. Applicants may demonstrate an ability to converse on several levels and in several languages. Allow them to set the pace and the tone by literally "giving up" that right; try to fit in with the interviewee's patterns of thought and speech rather than send signals that he/she has communicated in the "wrong" way. Mode of expression

your status. Assert either that position or a transitional, on-the-way-up attitude. Indicate that you know there are several good applicants for every opening and that you understand the problem of choice and decision.

Look for opportunities to self-disclose: Your personal philosophy, values, and ethics are transmitted when you reveal a little of your hidden self. A variety of admissions and opinions give texture and dimension to the bare facts on your application. Frequently, interview decisions are influenced—consciously or not—by intuitions obtained from cycles of exchange that begin with a "risky" comment. Instant friendship is rarely the purpose of an interview, but self-disclosure might lead to a stronger relationship.

Avoid double-think: Do not hesitate to ask for clarification. Interviewers also need to know whether they are being successful. Your credibility is one of many traits being tested; avoid confusing your interviewer by jumping from reference to reference, language to language. Linear thinking in digital codes is the safer mode of speech, unless your interviewer signals a wish that you express yourself in any way you choose. You know that invitations to communicate will be extended, and as you progress the rhythm reveals as much about the applicant as disclosure; encourage variety of expression.

Ask the questions you need: Most job interviews use a *dialectic* or question–answer mechanism for initiating conversations and for covering desired topics. Some interviews can be ordered so that few questions have to be asked.

of exchange and the level of thinking and perception will become apparent. So will the time allotted and the space and distance rules.

Give the answers you want: An important interviewing skill that is applicable in many kinds of transactions involves answering questions *the way you want to* answer them. Your preparation in a sense is based on your anticipation of how to get *your* points across.

task 2   FINDING QUESTIONS FOR YOUR ANSWERS

This task is a test of your dialectic skill. Using a job interview as the context, write two questions of each type described. Then write the answers in a way that conveys an attractive impression of your professionalism and qualifications for the job.

1. Write two questions that contain their own answers.

a. _____

Answer: _____

b. _____

Answer: _____

2. Write two questions that have only one possible answer.

a. _____

Answer: _____

b. _____

Answer: _____

3. Write two questions that do not "expect" an answer.

a. _____

Answer: _____

b. _____

Answer: _____

4. Write two questions that have several "right" answers.

    a. _____

    Answer: _____

    b. _____

    Answer: _____

5. Write two questions that are in the form of statements.

    a. _____

    Answer: _____

    b. _____

    Answer: _____

6. Write two questions that have answers that cut you either way.

    a. _____

    Answer: _____

    b. _____

    Answer: _____

7. Write two questions that reveal possible later questions.

    a. _____

    Answer: _____

    b. _____

    Answer: _____

For the Job Interviewer

Discussion of the questions and answers in Task 2 might have shown that you recognize what can be called the *real message* (RM) in a question. The RM relates to the response you expect to get. Asking "What time is it?" could have several RM goals: "Apologize to me for being late"; "Tell me not to worry"; "Can't you hurry it up?" Using your skill with paralinguistic cues, you should

For the Job Interviewee

As an interviewee, it behooves you to cultivate an ear and eye for "reading between the lines" and for listening to the RM during the interview dialectic. Review the material in Chapter 2 and check the critique sheets you received from Enactments 3 and 4 that might show how misunderstanding occurs. Your recognition of an RM is helped when you identify the type of question asked; conversely, examine the meanings you give to questions. Questions of Type 1 in Task 2, for example, can be used to assist and invite the respondent to enter an exchange that enhances his/her self-esteem—a reply that makes the applicant "look good." Type 1 may also provide a "free sample" of what to expect, the tenor of the interview, your role as an interviewer, etc. Type 2 is also a "safe" question, because such questions usually deal with basic assumptions underlying the job or the selection interview. It may cover facts you already know about the applicant: that he/she needs a job, believes the company wants to fill a position, wants to find out more about his/her future status with the firm, etc. Type 3 is an invitation and a "throwaway." It provides an opening by publicly announcing the range of "official" topics. It serves the same purpose as reading an agenda for a group meeting. Type 3 questions usually take the form of declarative sentences; they invite the listener to come back to them, if he/she wishes to. Type 4 questions—those with several "right" answers—are nonjudgmental. They ask for a philosophical reply, self-disclosure, or personal revelation. These are frequently called open-ended questions, because the range and scope of response are literally open—infinite. Type 5 is the question that makes an assumption, that takes for granted an attitude or position but still needs verification or

your experience with these seven basic types of questions will help you to avoid the guessing of double-think. You might be better able to reduce the number of possible answers by recognizing the kind of response expected of you. The rhythm of dialectic often begins with "icebreakers." These are "free" questions that take care of amenities—getting you comfortable, offering refreshment, checking and regulating proxemic codes. Everything said by an interviewer is a question in a sense; your nodding, leaning, eye/mouth/brow signals, posture, hands, and use of all the language modes will be received as answers to the interviewer's descriptive or explanatory narrative. Your nonverbal responses during the interviewer's story-telling assists the transaction and helps the interviewer do a good job. This kind of feedback represents proof of successful communication; it verifies the interviewer's professionalism. Do not hesitate to show perplexity, to show that the message is not clear, or to show that you have an impulse to interrupt. In answering open-ended questions intended to get you to reveal your real self, include messages that show you are not afraid to admit to human frailty and sentiment. Admit to ignorance or inexperience, but avoid making these admissions major points—balance them with well-chosen qualified statements that temper their critical application to your

qualification by the respondent. Type 5 questions are similar to the major premises shown in Figures 4–5, 4–6, 4–7, and 4–8. Type 6 is any kind of question that traps the interviewee into a response that causes loss of face. These are the double-bind questions that hurt no matter how he/she answers them. "Why did you quit your past jobs without staying long enough to give them a fair chance?" can be answered several ways—each of which may cause a loss of face. Type 7 is the kind of question that hints at what is to come later. The RM may be to warn the interviewee to get ready for your most important question or set of questions. An example might be: "I'd like to hear more about your family —you know, how they feel about your traveling, how they like our community . . . things like that." Some businesses are keenly aware of family life, even to the point of hiring families, in effect, rather than just a single candidate. A question such as this may alert an interviewee what to expect from (and how to answer) later questions.

potential job performance. These risky admissions can, as you know from group work, be happy accidents that work in your favor, because they may be received as clues to your honesty and professionalism. In answering questions in any type of interview it is important to defuse unintentional boasting, name-dropping, or fact-dropping by freely calling attention to it. Convey to your interviewer that you know and choose what you say. Try to distinguish between questions that expect you to answer in the first person ("I believe . . . ," "We felt . . ."), the second person ("You indicated . . ."), or the third person ("She found . . . ," "They stated . . ."). Attempt to pick up the tense (past, present, future) of the question asked and use it in your answer. Seek opportunities to "turn the tables"—ask questions, ask for opinions and judgments, allow the interviewer to discuss his/her pet theories and forecasts, favorite people, aspirations, complaints, or grievances. Look around for artifacts that suggest a topic of common interest—magazines, photographs, smoking paraphernalia. Read award plaques and citations—if they are displayed, they usually are very important to the owner; ask about them and listen to the stories behind them.

Make a contract: Interviewers should always be prepared to offer something, and to agree on a "contract." The offer may be to inform the applicant of the

Obtain a contract: Your "contract" is a pact or agreement. Try to obtain a commitment of some sort, strike some type of bargain, or promise to fulfill your half of an

decision on or by a certain date, using a specific channel. The contract may be almost anything that promises a concession to the applicant. Examples are: "I promise to call/write/visit/send a visitor to you," "I promise to let you know of other openings," "I'll see if our competitors need somebody with your background," "I promise to find out . . . for you."

offer. If both you and the interviewer agree on a telephone call, promise to "be available"; if you agree to meet again, promise to be there; if the agreement is for you to "call us again," promise to do so; if a common ground has been found, promise to follow up by loaning an artifact, mentioning the interviewer's name to a common acquaintance, or acting to continue some shared experience.

enactment 21   A JOB INTERVIEW

This enactment of a job interview dyad is a trial run of your ability to transact in a professional situation.

Try to reflect these concepts in.............................

enactment 21: A JOB INTERVIEW

invitations to communicate
interface
seven types of questions
self-disclosure
professionalism
RM
contract

participants

The interviewer should prepare a range of job positions, requirements, and other qualification criteria. His/her task is not to evaluate a preestablished list of statistical qualifications but rather to assess the *communication skills* of the applicant; *the interviewee* should agree with the interviewer on an application procedure—time and place of the appointment, preliminary application, and so on.

problem

Each has the task of communicating in the highest standard of professionalism possible.

need to talk

Each needs to have the vacancy filled.

time/locale

To be determined in advance by the participants.

critique 21 TROUBLESHOOTING

1. Did you feel the interviewer asked the questions that the applicant wanted to answer?
2. Were one or more contracts made?
3. Who initiated each contract, and how was each concluded?
4. Would you hire the job interviewer for your firm? Why?
5. How did you know that either was really listening?
6. How would you score each for use of invitations to communicate?
7. Did you feel the interviewer received the kinds of answers he/she needed to make a choice or decision? Why?

HOW WOULD YOU IMPROVE IT?

8. How would you describe the role the applicant played?
9. Did self-disclosure help or hurt a harmonious relationship?
10. How did either participant use leverage during the interview?
11. Describe how the leadership changed hands, if it ever did.
12. What are the advantages and disadvantages to each participant of interviewing in his/her home turf? Would a neutral site be better?

interviewing to find solutions

An interview whose purpose is to "get a solution" to a problem copies the tasks examined in small group and large group problem-solving. Interviews themselves are "problems" in communication that require balancing, but a professional exchange aims at solving the myriad problems encountered in business. The goal of this dyad is a contract or bargain that may correct an imbalance—a bottleneck, personnel friction, or some other dysfunction in the total operation of an enterprise.

This type of interview may, of course, force an action; the interview contract may contain an agreement to do something or to behave a certain way or to follow a given pattern of performance. The solution dyad differs from the action interview in three ways, however: (1) the solution interview is fact-finding and exploratory; (2) the solution interview does not attempt to effect an action during the interview or as part of the final contract, and (3) proposals for action are introduced, if at all, at the conclusion. A solution interview is *diagnostic*; an action interview is *surgical*. This important distinction is made to counteract the human tendency to jump to conclusions and "go off half-cocked." Objectivity and thoroughness are the key attitudes in determining problems and their causes. Speed may be essential in a crisis, but it has little virtue in locating the boundaries of a problem that may affect large numbers of people or the identity of an entire organization.

The checklist of interview techniques that follows repeats several basic communication principles, but a number of the suggestions apply directly to solution-seeking business exchanges and may be useful in that context.

Determine the Initiator.   Who first recognized that a problem or problems existed? Who initiated the interview? Who is senior in authority or job title? Who is more directly involved with the problems? Who will have jurisdiction over the action to be taken? As much as possible, these and related questions should be answered by participants before the interview occurs. Anticipate personal involvements, such as ego threats and diminished esteem possibilities. Attempt to identify biases and individual perceptive sets—tunnel vision, personal priorities and values that may affect objectivity and thoroughness.

Review Policies.   Organizational or house rules for contingencies—promotion, selection, decision-making, fact-finding, etc. —should be reviewed and clarified. A problem of below-standard behavior, for example, might be compared to the published company standards for employees. Personal conduct should be made part of the original hiring contract, just as duties and responsibilities, safety requirements, health conditions, company benefits, and other aspects of professional conduct may be tacit in a work agreement.

Policies that are not codified should be checked with the appropriate manager or work station supervisor. If many company rules and policies are unwritten, or if specific departments communicate policy only indirectly, this itself becomes an important factor in many personnel problems.

Review Role Expectations.   The brief section earlier in this chapter dealing with leverage suggested that poor communication relationships are spawned by "one-upmanship." Each participant should avoid maneuvering the other into roles of judge, cause, defendant, victim, etc. Rather both should freely share responsibility for accumulating data on the nature of the imbalance. "We need help" is a better approach than "I need your help" or "You need my help." An assisting or sharing attitude might be strengthened by taking the posture "It needs help," because this places blame, cause, responsibility in some impersonal context that needs fixing instead of in a person's behavior.

Placing the blame within the problem is a way of helping participants to remain objective and to explore the deficiency rather than use their energy planning face-saving messages. Similarly, each member of a solution dyad can assist by remaining aloof from topics and cycles of dialectic that open the way to confrontation or that entrap the other into a showdown.

An individual known to be deficient can still assist in problem-solving and is much more likely to contribute to the solution if the causal patterns and context are discussed as "being out there," "on the paper," "in the figures." Responsibility, if it can be attributed to a single person, will undoubtedly emerge, and it is better for the individual at fault to realize this and admit it.

Review What You Know About the Problem.   It is particularly important to "do your homework" when you are expected to have documented proof of a condition. As always, your competence factor is visible, and your prepared contribution to a thankless task will aid in eliciting a reciprocal exchange. Avoid labeling persons as causes. A professional attitude is aloof, above the pettiness of hearsay and fabrication; do not pass along groundless rumors and surmises; avoid dredging up obvious scapegoats and preparing self-justifying narratives.

Try to provide testable evidence—phenomena you know to be true, things you have seen or heard and have tested. "Selective evidence" or card-stacking—covering up—will not help solve problems; these and strategies like them will succeed in muddying the water and may create awkward binds for everyone.

Work out a Contract.   Some people are action-oriented; they are doers. Some people do things in quantity, such as brainstorming for ideas in quantity, in the hope that some act will satisfy their particular need or solve their problem. The outcome or contract phase of the problem-solving interview should narrow attention to *sets* of possible solutions—sequences of action called *options*. A satisfactory option is one that shows promise of eliminating or reducing the total problem, not merely the symptoms of the problem. The task in the solution interview is not to adopt a course of action, but merely to delineate the options available and reach agreement on those that seem the best routes to take to correct the problem.

Plan to Implement a Solution.   "Where do we go from here?" is the final topic in the solution interview (and is the common question asked at the conclusion of all types of business encounters).

The implementation plan considers the transitional phases of dyadic communication; the discussion anticipates connecting the accomplishment of the contract with the next step. This is the plan for follow-up.

Implementation, itself, may be executed by people not involved in or aware of the problem; implementation may present a good opportunity to "go public" on the nature of a problem, on the rumor-mongering elements, on weaknesses in the organization's communication systems, and on all the attendant symptoms that interact to create the overall imbalance. The plan, therefore, should include a specific list of steps for publicizing the suggested implementation.

The plan to implement may include a proviso to seek further input, advice, or consultation as the first step. It may include plans to present options at action meetings or interviews, where the actual decision to activate a plan is made. Consultation may be prescribed in the plan because it is an established necessity; higher clearance may be required, legal rulings may have to be checked, or special interest groups—unions, municipal groups, political parties—may have to be informed.

The two parties could possibly agree to do nothing. A null plan is an agreement to "let the problem solve itself." It relies on the old remedy: Time cures all pain; if you do not "mess with it," it will go away or blow over. Deferred decisions are temporary null plans that divide the task into two or more interviews. This may be done when triadic or small group exchanges are considered necessary to explore the solutions thoroughly.

task 3   PART OF THE PROBLEM OR PART OF THE SOLUTION?

These sample phrases in solution interviews would add to the problem rather than the solution. Ask yourself: "How could these viewpoints be expressed so that they would help the task of locating causes and patterns of imbalance rather than compounding the difficulty?" Write an acceptable version. (The first one is done as a sample.)

1. "I heard that she said we'd have the results by tomorrow." Improved, helpful

   version: *I'll call her to verify when the results can be expected.*

2. "We both know what the real problem is; why wait?" ——————

   _____

3. "Nice to see you. I'm told you've got yourself a real nice problem." ——

   _____

4. "I'm not sure everybody looks at it that way." _____

_____.

5. "The last study indicated that information of that kind was worthless."

_____.

6. "I think they'll be able to put two and two together and figure out what we're

doing here." _____.

7. "People around here are either part of the problem or part of the solution."

_____.

8. "Well, whose fault is that?" _____.

9. "What would you have done in my place?" _____.

10. "How have they been getting away with it all these months?" _____

_____.

11. "Let people think what they want to think. They will, anyway." _____

_____.

12. "I've seen this coming for a long time, but my hands were tied." _____

_____.

interviewing to get action

In an action-seeking interview you want to persuade or exert influence on the other person sharing the dyad. The action is frequently described as "buying" an idea, a product, a plan. This exchange mechanism is at the heart of all transactions; you have seen contracts being "sold" in many of the enactments, particularly in the job interview. The contract emanating from this type of interview is a "go agreement"; a specific action or block of actions begins at the end of or perhaps during this kind of exchange. The action may be a change in behavior, a change of direction, an exchange of services, a legal compact or agreement; it may involve one or both members. Contract negotiations and high-level diplomatic discussions seek to be action interviews.

Chapter 7 examined the elements of persuasion used in business presentations, and you may want to check back to it for a more complete treatment of persuasive techniques. Included here, however, are more suggestions for dyadic encounters that require the use of your persuasive skill.

Know Your Audience of One. It bears reiteration that foreknowledge of your opposite number in the dyad helps both members. Knowing your partner's personal needs, values, priorities, and professional commitments will help you find an area of sympathy for yourself and the thing you wish to sell.

Know Your Product.   You must have a full understanding of the specific details of your product. In addition you will be helped by projecting potential—not yet realized—uses and applications of it. You should also be prepared to show how many people and things will relate to your product significantly. Your inventory of product knowledge should include the standard six broad categories of appeal: cultural or social, commercial, educational, aesthetic or artistic, political, and religious or moral/ethical.

Another large area of awareness—perhaps the most important—is your knowledge of the psychology of the product and the market that will use it, apply it, or believe it. The interview is not with the public, but these and many other demonstrable evaluations may be part of your partner's concern.

Know Your Competition.   "What alternatives are there?" is a question basic to all solution and action exchanges. It implies the need to support the excellence or pragmatic appeal of your proposal or product. Your proposal's weakness is a "competitor" you should anticipate and be ready to discuss, as well as learning the limitations and strengths of its alternatives. One of the most competitive factors in any proposal is *change*. It is much easier to keep things the way they are, following the path of least resistance. An action interview must somehow carry the impetus or momentum of the proposal to break through this tendency of inertia.

Assert Your Professionalism.   The roles you play are exterior ways of showing a state of mind, but not necessarily your real self. Professionals in business use techniques and strategies of selling that suit individual circumstances. In this sense their roles change to fit a given need and context. Businesses adapt to their markets and to the people with whom they associate.

One strength of any proposal is its author and/or sponsor. It is difficult, as you saw in Chapter 6, to be sure what ultimately sells an idea, the source (speaker) or message (idea). The competence factor as used here means that you behave *as if* your ability were actual; your competence becomes a fixed part of you as you practice believing and asserting the 16 characteristics of the professional manager, discussed in Chapter 5.

Fairness to competitors, objectivity, self-effacement, under statement, a global and plural viewpoint, your individual signature trademark, and your willingness to compromise are traits that will aid you as a persuader. Communicated well, these characteristics are read by others as belonging to a person who desires—most of all—to help others assume competence. This is the professional viewpoint that others see and hear for themselves.

enactment 22   "I KNOW WHAT YOUR PLAN WILL DO *FOR* ME, BUT WHAT WILL IT DO *TO* ME?"

This enactment examines the problems of the action interview. Review your critique sheets from previous enactments, especially the job interview; if you participated as a member of a critique team, review the troubleshooting you did and think about which problems occurred most frequently.

As you plan this interview, carefully go over the suggestions in each of the interview types; commit yourself to an idea or plan that you strongly believe in; your doubts will be communicated to your partner. Choose a topic problem you know a lot about.

Convey these concepts in. . . . .

professionalism
helpful dialectic
contract of agreement
objectivity

enactment 22: "I KNOW WHAT YOUR PLAN WILL DO *FOR* ME, BUT WHAT WILL IT DO *TO* ME?"

participants

A *persuader* who prepares a plan or concept for presentation to an *administrator* in some field or enterprise who is empowered to accept, reject, or defer judgment on (table) the proposal.

problem

Each participant in a given interview needs what the other has the power to contract for. The persuader wishes to "sell" (lease, exchange, swap, etc.) the proposal for something of value to him/her (real property, cash, stock, a job, etc.). The *administrator* needs the idea, project, system, property, or other item offered for any combination of professional reasons.

time/locale

Locale and time are at the discretion of the initiator—the administrator.

critique 22 TROUBLESHOOTING

1. Score each participant for his/her use of invitations to communicate.
2. Explain what you feel would be the benefits and disadvantages of the proposal. What would it do *to* each member of the dyad?
3. Were there any language problems? How were they solved?
4. What problems were apparent from the exchange that might have resulted from inadequate or misplaced leadership?
5. How were both egos "stroked"; how were both self-images enhanced?
6. Which member would you personally *trust* with an important decision involving billions of dollars and thousands of people? Why?
7. How did the seating/standing arrangement affect each member's listening performance?
8. Explain how this interview might have been helped by scheduling a series of solution interviews before this meeting.
9. How was it made clear that this plan was preferable to its competitors?
10. Faced with the same needs and situation, describe a way of communicating to get action other than interviewing that would be better.

HOW WOULD YOU IMPROVE IT?

THE COUNSELING INTERVIEW

The counseling dyad is concerned with all the vagaries of the human spirit that intrude on and affect business communication. You have no doubt already experienced personal behaviors in many transactions that ask for help and guidance. You have encountered adults thinking and behaving like six-year-olds, adolescents experimenting with adult behavior, people enveloped in several binding impulses, and individuals who seem forever in the process of making transitions in their lives.

Counseling in its many forms is itself a big business. You might readily notice the abundance of aid that is available from camp counselors, recreation counselors, family counselors, pet counselors, decorating counselors, marriage counselors, employment counselors, educational counselors, investment counselors, and many others who have advice for sale.

To *counsel* means to consult, but in another sense it also means to *defend*. In some situations counseling might mean meeting to discuss options, choices, strategies, or plans as in the decision/solution/ action interviews. In other types of encounters counseling might imply the defense of something that is felt to be threatened or in danger of loss. In its most subtle and complex form, counseling requires great skill and experience, because it entails the defense and "handling" of sensitive areas of the psyche. A high degree of training is required of counselors who expect people to entrust them with the most fragile and least revealed regions of their personalities.

It is not within the purview of this text to consider the intricacies of this very specialized field of dyadic communication. A few steps worth following and some that should not be followed are offered, however, to introduce you to some of the problems in the counseling interview.

directive counseling

Directive counseling means giving directions. This method usually entails listening to a problem and telling the client what to do about it. Some individuals rely on the authoritarian, all-knowing sage as an oracle and source of direction. In this category are "financial experts" who will, for a fee, unscramble your personal money problems and direct how you can stay out of financial trouble.

Directive counseling is an efficient and often satisfactory method of offering people expert service and training in the management of some area of technical complexity. Telling a person what to do about a problem over the phone, by letter, or by newspaper column involves little risk; the counselor's Johari Window would scarcely open in this type of communication.

Risk is perhaps the most crucial factor in communication; it is particularly at issue in a counseling interview where the problem is an emotional one or is manifested through emotional display. Even the simplest transaction places the initiator in the position of risking rejection, embarrassment, humiliation, loss of anonymity, misunderstanding, and finally entanglement.

People in the professions maintain codes of acceptable behavior. This is another way of saying that they keep basic personal problem displays at a distance; people who repeatedly violate the code may be referred to specialists (counselors) for expert advice. Many businesspeople are not prepared to cope with the emotional problems of others, especially within their professional environments. They sense the risks demanded by the role of counselor. Their contribution might be to direct the needy person to a more qualified professional.

nondirective counseling

Nondirective counseling uses what can be called the *mirror approach*. The counselor "reflects" the messages sent by the client. The child who whines, "I want friends my own age," and the person who pleads, "You've gone through it—I've got to talk to you," are expressing their belief that transacting with someone like themselves will somehow mirror their own condition and help them.

The effect of this nondirective approach is that the person with the problem sees himself or herself—runs the risk of confronting himself or herself as if in a mirror. When you confront yourself, it is you who must assess, decide, and act. The counselor functions to repeat the client's statements or rephrase them.

The following suggestions apply to directive and nondirective techniques and are intended as general guides for high risk counseling interviews.

For the Counselor

Sympathetic neutrality:
The counselor's role as "emotional drain"—the shoulder to cry on—is a difficult balancing act. The professional attitude is one of sympathy and receptivity without personal commitment or involvement.

Tasks:
The counselor's overall task is to assist the client to verbalize and test set ways of thinking and behaving. By feeding back the client's narrative descriptions of relationships and expectations, the counselor may remain a kind of umpire of clear thinking and honest self-assessment.

For the Client

Objective self-appraisal:
Self-knowledge is the overall goal in counseling. Analytically, the troubled person attempts to sort out personal facts from fictions and delusions.

Tasks:
The client's overall task is to "think out loud" and to try to follow the direction (with the counselor's help) of his/her thought.

Dialectic patterns:
Open-ended questions encourage
    self-disclosure by the client.
    Questions and answers should
    avoid judgments on values,
    behavior, and decisions. The
    counselor's response should
    avoid reinforcing irrationality.
    The dialectic should tend to
    discourage theorizing and quick
    conclusions by either
    participant. The counselor
    should be prepared to accept
    and follow the client's pattern of
    dialectic. For example, if a
    minimal response, such as a
    nod of the head or a smile,
    answers a question and
    encourages further elaboration,
    this pattern of response may be
    more conducive to the client's
    self-appraisal and eventual
    remedy. It might convey the idea
    that you do not want to butt in,
    but that you are listening to and
    assisting the exchange.

Dialectic patterns:
"Why?" is probably the key question
    for a client. Why questions
    directed toward the counselor
    are usually "thrown back" to the
    client as an indication that
    answers must come from the
    source of the problem. The
    dialectic also serves to release
    tension. Sometimes the client
    puts a round of questions and
    discussion in a distanced
    context as a kind of preliminary
    warm-up for talking about
    himself/herself. The client may
    use the impersonal "one" rather
    than "I" or discuss a problem
    that a "friend" has experienced;
    perhaps the topic will be set in
    the past or future, until the client
    is ready to confront his/her
    immediate self. Clients should
    try to "surprise" themselves by
    the questions and answers they
    think up; they should try to cover
    new ground by seeking out
    novel juxtapositions of factors in
    their experiences.

Follow-up:
Each participant shares the desire to
    "see things through to the
    end." Perhaps the end is never
    fully reached, but the counselor
    should remain available for
    further consultation as long as
    the client wishes. Counselors
    may take great pains to check on
    the progress of a client by
    visitation or inquiry.
    Postinterview checking should
    be explained to the client and
    made part of the interview
    contract.

Follow-up:
Ideally, a client will conclude an
    interview with the feeling that
    he/she has made progress and
    that further assistance is always
    open to him/her. The client
    should not expect a prescription
    as part of the contract. Often,
    this notion of an instant cure or a
    simplistic answer to a problem is
    the greatest obstacle the client
    has to face. The knowledge that
    the client has someone to talk to
    is a self-prescribed "medicine"
    and tangible proof that he/she is
    capable of self-help.

enactment 23 YOUR WITNESS

Enactment 23 is a test of your ability to direct and respond to the questioning in a professional dyad. How well do you field questions? How well do you give the answers you want to give? How well do you follow the train of the dialectic? Are you able to anticipate questions and answers? Can you adapt to surprise topics and contexts?

Use these tests during the questions and answers of . . . .

enactment 23: YOUR WITNESS

can you see connections between early and later
questions?

can you see what is assumed
in each question?

can you see all the connections in two- or three-part
questions?

can you see that a value, bias,
or prejudice is being
tested?

can you see if you are being
forced into a test of re-
call, analysis, or pro-
jected problem-solving?

can you see inaccurate re-
phrasings or summaries
of statements?

participants

Witness 1 begins the story of an event—any occurrence, actual or fictional; Interviewer 1 begins the questioning sequence. At a certain point witness and interviewer switch roles. Any number of subsequent witnesses and interviewers in turn assume the positions of the first dyad and continue the story and questioning.

problem

The participants want to develop a description of an event, with each witness contributing a little bit more than the predecessors. As each interviewer and witness switch roles, they should ask questions and give answers consistent with the previous testimony. Each witness may be tested for his/her recall of earlier information and should try to answer so that the event makes sense. Time limits may be set so that each class member gets practice in both roles.

critique 23   TROUBLESHOOTING

1. Why were summaries helpful? How did they confuse?
2. What did people do in the enactment when they could not recall information?
3. What were the most commonly used leverage-seeking words? Why do you think this was so?
4. Explain how this method of dialectic might be used in a business context.
5. Would all these participants come up with the same story if they met as a large group? How might the story differ had they met in small groups?
6. How did your listening attitude change after you had participated?
7. What influences did the listening audience have on the testimony and on the witnesses?

HOW WOULD YOU IMPROVE IT?

afterthought   THE AUDIENCE OF ONE

The ongoing interviews that are so much a part of business management often develop into close friendships. The audience of one provides communicators with the uncomplicated axis of a balanced relationship. The dyad is bipolar no matter who dominates, no matter who is superior.

There is a tendency, it seems, for a bond to develop even between enemies or incompatibles. When you experience such dyads over a period of time, you can hardly call them friendships, but they often produce an "understanding" and sometimes a tolerance for people and things different from yourself and what you know and believe. The dyad is a near-perfect testing ground for your professionalism and for encouraging your growth.

READ FOR YOURSELF

GORDEN, RAYMOND L., *Interviewing: Strategy, Techniques, and Tactics.* Homewood, Ill.: Dorsey Press, 1969.

Lerbinger, Otto, *Designs for Persuasive Communication.* Englewood Cliffs, N.J.: Prentice-Hall, Inc., 1972.

Stewart, Charles J., and William B. Cash, *Interviewing: Principles and Practices* (2nd ed.). Dubuque: William C. Brown Company, Publishers, 1978.

Wilmot, William W., *Dyadic Communication: A Transactional Perspective.* Reading, Mass.: Addision-Wesley Publishing Co., Inc., 1975.

CHAPTER CHART

Key definition: Dyad, a two-person, face-to-face encounter
Key idea: Dyad relationships are shown in prepositions—*in, to, over, for, like, with, under, between, among, against, by, at*
Key idea: You use certain words to gain leverage or advantage in the dyad

Leverage-Seeking Words and Phrases
Tend to judge
Tend to hint
Tend to place a burden on the listener

Interviewing and Presenting
Interviewing
    greater spontaneity
    greater reciprocity and feedback
    greater listening demands
    greater range of topics
    multiple structure—greater variety of relationships
    multiple role-playing
    complex character
    intimate distances
    greater risk for both members
    fewer language difficulties
    interviewer's home turf
    greater flexibility in follow-up
    flexible leadership
Presenting
    fewer departures from plan
    more cluster feedback
    limited listening demands
    limited range of topics
    single structure
    fixed role-playing—speaker and audience
    simplistic character
    impersonal distances
    greater risk for speaker
    more language difficulties
    reduced flexibility of follow-up
    inflexible leadership

Purposes of Interviewing
To get data
To get decisions/choices
To get solutions
To get action

Data Interview
Know how data will be used
Think through your professional attitude

Check the communication field
Review the type of transaction wanted
Adopt the attitude and role that match the task
Locate interview sources
Identify yourself to respondents
Limit self-disclosure
Record responses
Read back responses
Complete the interview affirmatively

Decision/Choice Interview—Job Interview

Interviewer
> get statistical data on candidates
> assert your professionalism
> encourage self-disclosure
> avoid double-think
> plan your questions
> make a contract

Interviewee
> research prospective employers
> assert your professionalism
> look for opportunities to self-disclose
> avoid double-think
> give the answers *you* want
> obtain a contract

Questions in the Interview

Questions that contain their own answer
Questions that have only one possible answer
Questions that do not expect an answer
Questions that have several "right" answers
Questions in the form of a statement
Questions that cut you either way
Questions that reveal possible later questions
Key idea: RM is an abbreviation for *real message*—what is the
> questioner really saying or asking?

Interviewing to Find Solutions

Fact-finding and exploratory purpose
No action is taken during interview
Proposals for action may be introduced
Interview is diagnostic
Preparation
> determine the initiator of the interview
> review house rules and policies
> review what other members will expect your role to be
> review what you *know* about the problem
> work out a contract for action
> plan to implement or carry out the solution

Interviewing to Get Action—Selling/Persuading
    Know your audience of one
    Know your product or plan
    Know your competition
    Assert your professionalism

Counseling Interview
    Directive counseling: gives directions
    Nondirective counseling: the mirror approach
    Counselor suggestions
        seek a sympathetic neutrality
        assist clients to verbalize and test their thinking
        avoid judgmental questions
        use minimal responses
        follow up
    Client suggestions
        try to appraise yourself objectively
        think out loud
        try to surprise yourself
        follow up with self-help

chapter 10

chapter challenge

Describe the characteristics of organizations

Recognize the principle of interdependence in organizations

Trace the flow of messages in an organization

Identify people in an organization who control message flow

Assemble lists of suggestions that professional communicators
might use to aid the flow of verbal messages

Explain how rumor, gossip, and the grapevine help and hinder
overall communication within an organization

Describe the opposite of rumor

List the types of channels that link organizations

ORGANIZATIONAL COMMUNICATION

FLOW-circulate FLOW-circulate FLOW-circulate FLOW-circulate

Business transactions are at the heart of human exchange, but our emphasis in this book has been that careers in the professional world are built on professional communication attitudes. The concept that the professional communicator helps people coexist on an individual basis can be applied to larger group endeavors—it can be part of the character of a business or a profession, and it can be the quality that makes the enterprise professional. This chapter examines professionalism as it affects organizational communication and amplifies the discussion of the prerequisites for basic business and professional speaking.

ORGANIZING

Organizing might be described as the task of locating matches. When you organize you try to put ideas, people, and things into categories that are knowable, predictable, manageable. From your critiques, however, you have found that plurality is the norm; many things just will not fit into neat classifications.

Despite these human differences, you know from the exercises that people tend to organize experience as best they can, regardless of how things fit. They work to sequence the flow of stimuli that comes to them from their internal and external environments. They want to see and hear patterns where there may be only fragments.

The organization of a message event was the system you

253

used—to control transactions, explore and reinforce similarities, and locate the languages that matched your receiver's awareness. The enactment critiques may have aided everyone's appreciation of systematic planning by citing communication breakdowns. Did you ever say things you did not mean or fail to give the type of feedback your partner needed to confirm the message cycle? As you watched and listened, perhaps you had the feeling that an exchange was slipping—getting out of sync with the intended direction of conversation.

As you read the following pages, try to visualize the three sample organizations and their respective parts and characteristics. Ask yourself how a professional communication approach in organizations might eliminate a few of the causes of misunderstanding that hinder business and human transactions.

THREE ORGANIZATIONS

The three organizational "models" presented here all deal with human systems, subject to human control. In a way they are specimens of organizations that you probably are most familiar with—your body/mind, your home, and your school. The models progress from compact and centralized membership to sprawling and segmented membership over a large area.

body/mind

The first example is an organization of highly condensed pluralities. Your body/mind is coordinated in some ways and out of touch in others. Its organs and systems are not always compatible, they do not always work together or follow directions.

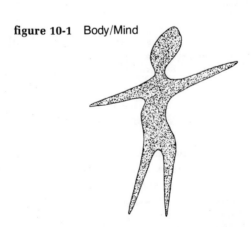

figure 10-1   Body/Mind

task 1 GETTING THE PARTS TO WORK

Explain why you can or cannot get your body/mind to perform these physical acts:

1. I can/cannot get myself to hiccough, because _____
_____.

2. I can/cannot get myself to sweat, because _____
_____.

3. I can/cannot say words backwards, because _____
_____.

4. I can/cannot get myself to cry, because _____
_____.

5. I can/cannot clap with one hand, because _____
_____.

6. I can/cannot get my pupils to dilate, because _____
_____.

7. I can/cannot make myself get gooseflesh, because _____
_____.

8. I can/cannot get myself to itch, because _____
_____.

Each of these physical acts depends upon a system of organization. Sometimes you might have been able to make the system work by applying certain excitements or stimuli. You might have used tools to get the system to function; maybe you enlisted help of an agent—some other friendly "organization"—to assist with ice cubes, a flashlight, a feather, or whatever it took to get the system to itch, shiver, or dilate.

The principle here is that even the body/mind with its efficient assemblage of interacting systems and organs requires sometimes two or more people to make it work the way you want it to. It may need a larger organization. From your experiment, you might conclude: *An organization is a group of two or more persons whose differences are outweighed by a shared desire for a similar result.*

apartment building

The next organizational model is larger and less centralized than the body/mind. One of its components is your family, with its collective desire for nurturing and shelter, its systems of communication and support that are more spread out and independent. Perhaps your family is part of the larger organization of a clan or a tribe. Is your family a member of a city block of families, a residential tract, or an apartment building of families as in Figure 10–2? Complete Task 2, and see if you can plot a few of the major concepts of communicating within the family organization that help explain its nature.

task 2   KEEP IN TOUCH

Discuss how your answers to these questions suggest communication links within your family:

1. How do age and gender groups dictate communication channels?
2. How is wealth accumulated, stored, and shared?
3. How is collective family wisdom, knowledge, and experience accumulated, stored, and shared?
4. How do family rituals help members to "keep in touch"?
5. How is leadership determined, and how is it shared?
6. How do new ideas circulate and flow?
7. What system does your family have for communicating with other families?

Your answers may have centered around the shared needs of the family organization and its reliance on each member to support the entire project of living together. With this in mind, you might further describe an organization as: *A group of people who associate and communicate for as long as the need exists.*

Figure 10–2 depicts an apartment building as a type of or-

figure 10-2   The Apartment Building

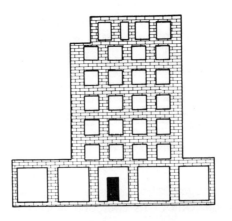

ganization. The two dimensions of the drawing might suggest that communication moves upward, downward, side-to-side, and around corners—similar to chessboard movements. Why does each family need the others? Try to collect a few more answers about what to expect in professional organizations by discussing Task 3.

task 3   ROOM AT THE TOP

1. In what ways do families at the top need the families at the bottom?
2. Which channels of communication are controlled by the architecture of the building?
3. How does each household depend on those adjacent to it?
4. How do upper, lower, and horizontally aligned families meet and exchange?
5. Can the "bottom dwellers" exist in the same way without the upper-floor families?
6. Why would some families want to switch levels?
7. What *product* does this organization produce?
8. What does the apartment organization consider *profit*?
9. How does an organization of this type interact with others of the same kind?
10. How does each member of each suborganization (family) share in profit and productivity?
11. How is organizational *work* divided among members?
12. Who in the apartment organization "owns" the organization?

Gerald Goldhaber, defines an organization as a "network of interdependent relationships."[1] In the instance of the apartment building, each family needed the others, each hoped that enough rent or sales money would be brought in by tenants to save it from forced eviction. Physically each apartment space depends on the others to hold the structure together, to keep water, heat, and energy flowing through the organization.

Because of these and many other interdepencies you thought of, an organization possesses a collective identity. The apartment dwellers have the same address and perhaps building name. They share a statistical trademark in the eyes of the many agencies that count, assess, tax, deliver mail to and think of the apartment as a single entity. And like your body, it has a name.

school

The third organizational drawing, Figure 10–3, shows a linear series of school buildings. The school complex presents multiples of two previous examples—the body/mind and the family. Messages in this

---

[1]Gerald M. Goldhaber, *Organizational Communication* (Dubuque: William C. Brown Company, Publishers, 1974), p. 24.

figure 10-3 The School

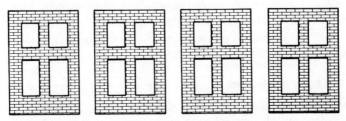

organization circulate in all directions; numbers, spaces, distances, and members are vastly more complex.

Each of the three organizational models stands for something; their names tell you generally what that something is. We have said that the real business of business is communicating, doing what you can to help people coexist. The essential quality of an organization and its business lie in the work it performs and the style of communication it encourages or discourages.

You have heard expressions such as "that's a private school," "he's a private person," "talking in private." Your experiences with Enactment 20 demonstrated that privacy in one sense means *no feedback.* An organization such as a school may be either private or public—encouraging one-way or reciprocal exchange—but does it work by itself and for itself or with and for others? Does it work by itself for others; does it work with others for itself? In Task 4 keep these questions in mind as you put together your description of "school work."

task 4   SCHOOL WORK

1. What subjects would most likely be taught in the ground-floor classrooms of the sketch in Figure 10–3?
2. Where do you think the faculty offices would be located?
3. Where would the administrative offices be located?
4. What is the product of this organization?
5. Who "owns" this organization?
6. Are there schedules and deadlines for the product?
7. Who decides what the work and the product will be?
8. Is membership turnover desirable in this organization?
9. Describe the organizations that exist within your speech class organization.
10. Whom does the school work with? Whom does the school work for?

CHARACTERISTICS OF ORGANIZATIONS

Each of these examples and exercises should have contributed a little toward your understanding of communication problems in business organizations. The eight characteristics offered below attempt to focus on basic areas of communication whose essential ingredients determine the organization's identity and style of communicating. As you read these descriptions, try to compare the traits with those of an organization you know well.

organizations assert power

An organization's assertion of power means that it exercises a sovereignty over the volition or will of its members. Sometimes power is vested in written documents or laws; it may be highly centralized—located in one place, such as a person, an office, a group. In the body/mind example, power is highly centralized, although direct control is not always possible, as you demonstrated.

If you had trouble willing your body to hiccough or sweat, it meant that control was delegated to a reflexive or involuntary subsystem. These subsystems were not organized to listen to your message, because channels were not open. You might have asserted *indirect* control, however, by locking yourself into a sauna. Using that channel, your sweat glands would have heard the message, and you would have controlled the organizational effect.

Power is exercised in the apartment organization on the basis of tenancy. The right of access, domicile, and territoriality is given or loaned to families by a lease. The legal owner of the building may delegate power to various subagents—a bank, law firm, managerial service, holding company, building engineer or supervisor, or protection agency—and to each tenant. The organization may or may not provide direct channels that link each member, but a kind of collective will is exhibited in the individual supervision of safety, behavioral codes, and activities that could jeopardize the overall functioning of the building and the collective well-being of its tenants.

Power is usually delegated to professional managers in a school organization. Responsibility may be divided and distributed many times, as in the apartment example. Like most businesses, the school may confer leadership on any member who develops a professional attitude and does his or her job well.

organizations create work

Organizations transform one kind of energy into some other kind; this constitutes one definition of *work*. The transformations of energy may be very specialized—accomplishing relatively few tasks; bodily organs usually have only a few tasks to perform. Each task, however, creates work for other organs, and the entire process requires scheduling or sequencing, so that work is carried forward in stages.

Family units in an apartment complex assume many tasks in

contributing to the well-being of their organization. Individuals work cooperatively to plan and sequence movement and traffic, cartage and storage of goods, the use of building facilities, and supportive maintenance of building regulations affecting everyone.

Various types of work using many skills and types of communication are characteristic of school organizations. Work is created in the sense that the organization's aim and distribution of power is transformed into activities and projects. These in turn create the necessity of monitoring and evaluating progress and direction. A certain amount of housekeeping work or maintenance is also basic to an organization and may come under the heading *cybernetics*.

organizations are cybernetic

Most organizations devote part of their workload to serving and perpetuating themselves. The servomechanisms of the body, for example, monitor every cell in each phase of its work. Collectively, the body works to become self-sufficient by balancing and allocating its energy, but it shows favoritism toward the "vital" organs and systems, sometimes at the expense of its extremities.

The apartment dwellers organize their work with an eye toward keeping the building filled and its support systems operating properly. Families must try to perpetuate the coalition of tenants, since few could afford to rent or buy the entire building, and the division of expenses among them makes the whole thing possible.

Servomechanisms of a school may extend far beyond the four modules drawn in Figure 10–3. This type of organization may employ a variety of groups—boards, student associations, faculty committees, alumni associations—to check on how everything is working.

A college operation or work schedule, for example, may be monitored by political, religious, commercial, academic, or financial agencies. Its work is subject to public and media criticism. As one of many subsystems, the speech class uses critique and discussion methods as a type of servomechanism that helps you keep tabs on how your work is going.

organizations determine membership

Membership in an organization may be determined by right of birth, inheritance, marriage, selection/election, or perhaps accident. The school organization contains a hierarchy of members ranging from those eagerly sought as members to people who just "show up" in libraries, seminars, or at the movies.

Varieties of member categories exist in apartment complexes; in addition to apartment owners and rent-paying tenants, there may be visiting relatives or friends who are "temporary" members. With the body/mind example, however, membership is strictly a matter of birth, unless you are an alien impostor or a grafted intruder. Task 5 is a review of what you know about membership rules in organizations.

task 5   HOW DO I JOIN?

Write a brief description of the qualifications needed for these organizations:

1. This class: _____ .

2. A varsity sport: _____ .

3. A labor union: _____ .

4. The National Association of Manufacturers: _____ .

organizations seek efficiency

The idea of efficiency deals with maximum return for the minimum investment of time, capital, energy, or whatever commodity is used. Your body organization requires efficient use of food; you try to keep your intake of calories about equal to the number you burn up.

Most organizations seek a "steady state," a condition of negative *entropy* where income/outgo, turnover, overhaul/replacement, or restocking tends to either grow or remain constant. A business enterprise usually strives to bring in more energy, tenants, students, or money than it loses, sends out, graduates, spends, or transforms into marketable goods.

A family, among other things, may seek to increase its membership through natural issue or through intermarriage, and like any organization it may suffer negative entropy by decline in membership. Reduced sales or income and cutbacks in personnel, student admissions, faculty, or services because of higher costs may all be signs of inefficiency.

organizations tolerate redundancy

Redundancy means duplication. Many sizable organizations repeat messages, tasks, and operational routines. Provisions are made to recheck or update activities involving new ideas and information.

The body/mind routinely checks its environment to get its bearings; you may often retrace your steps and duplicate much of what you say and do. Evidence of redundancy in the behavior of apartment dwellers is abundant; you only count the milk bottles, newspapers, and cars to assess this basic characteristic.

Cheap or efficient redundancy is, of course, one key to profit-making. Assembly-line techniques and inventory methods rely on redundancy to make them work, be predictable, and therefore be controllable. Sometimes an organization will also accommodate differing points of view and approach, if only to add freshness.

organizations tolerate plurality

The "freshness" of allowing people to do things their own way repeats what has been said about plurality in communication. Rigidity does not accommodate plurality. In a highly centralized and ultraefficient organization, such as your body, there is only one way to do things. Body systems are self-contained but narrowly dependent; they cannot, for example, detach themselves, leave, and continue to function. You cannot leave parts of yourself behind to "keep an eye on things" for you.

Less centralized organizations—the apartment and school—employ what might be called *plural means to an end*. This is the axiom that there are lots of ways to skin a cat. Plural means are visible, for example, in the diversity of projects people undertake and are encouraged to pursue in school organizations.

Sometimes rigidity exists side-by-side with plurality. Forms for application, permission, payment, etc., may be carefully prescribed, while at the same time regulations may be waived or modified to accommodate individual situations. Thus, an organization is not always rational.

organizations are sometimes irrational

An important characteristic affecting the flow of messages is that an organization is never totally *sane*. Your encounters with eccentricities and unexpected reversals in the enactments may have suggested that people are clever and very creative when it comes to making exceptions to a rule.

Organizations and their members sometimes do things that are rational to only a few of them. Important decisions are made because somebody proves that apartments contain 2.65 persons. A tax-supported school may have students who pay (tuition) to work (assignments), but some students in work-study programs may be paid with the provision that they work and pay back to themselves, the taxpayers whose tax money pays for the whole thing.

To summarize, these eight organizational traits—power, work, cybernetics, membership, efficiency, redundancy, plurality, and irrationality—have been culled from the many factors in organizational study, because they influence communication. While other characteristics are based upon organizational size and complexity, tasks performed, ownership, goals, and interorganizational relations, the eight aspects listed here seem to reemphasize the professional's need to communicate well.

TYPES OF ORGANIZATIONS

A similar emphasis is present in the Blau-Scott[2] classification of organizations, which is based on the question "Who benefits from membership?" This classification scheme is shown below. Try to apply what you know of the eight selected traits to these categories.

Mutual Benefit Type . . . Members Benefit Most

county medical associations
county political parties
farm cooperatives and federations
labor unions
private country clubs
religious/fraternal organizations
trade associations

Business Type . . . Owners Benefit Most

banks
hotels/motels
manufacturing plants
marketing organizations
newspapers
private TV/radio stations
transit companies
public utilities
railroads
restaurants
retail stores
trucking firms

Service Type . . . Clients Benefit Most

civil rights organizations
reformatories
insurance companies
parochial and other private schools

[2]Peter M. Blau and W. Richard Scott, *Formal Organizations* (San Francisco: Chandler Publishing Co., 1962), pp. 40–58.

private hospitals
public schools and colleges
religious service organizations
mental health centers

Commercial Type . . . Public Benefits Most

city recreation services
educational TV station
fund-raising agencies
government regulatory agencies
law enforcement agencies
municipal airports and harbors
post offices
municipal street/public works/garbage services
state hospitals/penal institutions

enactment 24   PASS THE WORD

This is a "review enactment" to allow you to recheck the dos and donts of dyadic exchange by preparing an interview with a guest. Your general topic is: "Passing the Word in an Organization."

Try to include these basic areas of organizational communication in your conversation during. . . . .

enactment 24: PASS THE WORD

why people need organiza-
      tions
why organizations die
who owns organizations
passing the word in organiza-
      tions
the weakest and strongest
      links in organizations

participants

The *interviewer* is a student from class; the *guest conversationalist* a friend, not in the class, asked by the interviewer to come as a guest speaker.

problem

The interviewer's problem is to conduct a public conversation/interview in such a way as to put the guest at ease, while structuring a conversation that centers on how an organization passes the word to its membership and how the membership passes the word to the organization.

need to talk

Locate a friend who feels strongly about some aspect of communication, an organizational experience, or just organizations in general. Explain (privately and publicly) that the purpose of the conversation/interview is to examine experiences from the standpoint of the eight characteristics you have studied.

critique 24   TROUBLESHOOTING

1. Score each participant for invitations to communicate.
2. Describe five communication bottlenecks that change your perception of an organization.
3. Explain why there was/was not some reference to one-way communication.
4. How can you get an organization to self-disclose?
5. How do organizations obtain feedback?
6. Did either participant do most of the talking? Why?

**HOW WOULD YOU
IMPROVE IT?**

FLOW AND CIRCULATION OF MESSAGES

Organizations use an incredible quantity of diverse messages. Enactment 24 may have shown that reencoding and multiple channeling of messages are difficult to chart. You will recall that it is difficult for two or more messsges to exist in the same space and retain their original character; they will invariably *interact*, much like the strands of musical parts played simultaneously, creating a blend. The enactments about group work and especially about auctioneering, with the simultaneous buzzing of several messages, tended to illustrate this point.

In a similar way, messages that are directed up or down, making stops for interpretation and reencoding, face the perils of blending, reading between the lines, and double-think. Message *flow* means the movement of an utterance from one person and place elsewhere over a period of time. To think of a message as a bucket that passes in a direct line from hand to hand is erroneous. Some messages are supposed to follow a linear route, but the closest approximation of this ideal might be village-to-village transmission of a simple digital message by drumbeat. Instead, organizational messages seem to spread more like a stain; they flow in all directions. Figure 10–4 shows four types of flow. Flow by bunching spreads in a network emanating from a single source and reaching several listeners who in turn spread the message to further

figure 10-4   Communication Flow (BLAB)

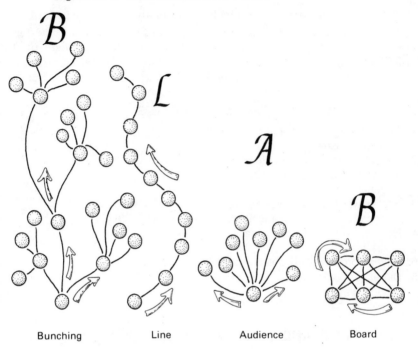

| Bunching | Line | Audience | Board |

bunches. The *line* method shows the flow proceeding from and to a single source and receiver in a sequence. The *audience* method is illustrated as a small presentation of the message (from one source to many receivers at one time), and the *boardroom* indicates the message being assembled by several people who all contribute to the word before it is released. The four flow patterns are symbolized by the acronym BLAB.

The business manager as a communicator may be seen as someone who decides which messages are most needed and when and where they are needed. Managers also induce flow and circulation by determining how often a message will be sent or re-sent. The communicator/manager may decide how many messages the available channels can hold and whether messages should be stored until needed. The student who is told, "That's a good question; ask it in about a week," has encountered this *queuing* or standby channeling of an idea whose time has not come yet.

Jay W. Forrester of M.I.T., dealing with these vagaries in business situations, helped pioneer the *systems approach* as a managerial control over such procedures as message flow. The systems idea views a company's separate departments as an integrated structure of varying rates and flows and takes into account varying rates of queuing.

The approach is applicable to the flow networks in the organizations listed by Blau and Scott or any other business where you need to trace people, money, materials, orders, capital equipment, or other components that circulate—except vocalized messages in their living form. Trying to pin down who said what and when is as difficult as passing the word in a linear method without it leaking or straying to either side.

Perhaps because of the tendency for messages to stray (and become modified) en route, certain organizations rely heavily on *preparatory channels,* such as the telephone and the memorandum, as means of controlling messages. Even these "closed" paths are sometimes vulnerable to leakage, however. Among the many insights offered in Max Weber's work in organizational theory is that bureaucracies prefer written messages to vocalized ones, which may make it easier for a piece of paper to see the boss than for an employee.

Using the eight selected organizational characteristics as guidelines, you might be able to arrive at a kind of beginning systems approach to the circulation of live vocalized messages in Task 6.

task 6 HEARD THE LATEST?

After checking the brief "starter" phrases, list your suggestions for a professional communicator/manager to try to manage the circulation of messages in an organization.

1. *Power:* Influence resides in the person who decides to initiate, relay, store, or lose vocalized messages. The receptionist may not own the clinic, but he/she has the power to help make it run smoothly or disastrously. The professional communicator might try to _____.

2. *Work:* The work or responsibility of company employees is largely the task of communicating well. A professional communicator/manager might try to

_____.

3. *Cybernetics:* The ability to find clogs or stoppages and to sift input sources is a managerial skill. The professional communicator might try to _____

_____.

4. *Membership:* Hiring may be an important juncture in message control, and the professional communicator might try to _____.

5. *Efficiency:* The efficient enterprise may expect a continual broadening of personal contacts, with new channels cross-connecting among its personnel. This might be achieved by _____.

6. *Redundancy:* Companies use bulletins, periodicals, posters, and suggestion boxes as redundant paths for message flow. The professional manager might try to _____.

7. *Plurality:* Tracing message flow by managers requires an understanding and tolerance of plural ways to communicate the same thing. Cultural, linguistic, or idiomatic differences in expression are equally deserving of respect. To ensure that individual differences will not lead to message bottlenecks, a manager might _____.

8. *Irrationality:* Temporary insanity in an organization is difficult to map or chart. Organizations can be literal and digital to a fault, for example. They may be overdefensive or may confuse the corporate world with the real world outside. A professional communicator might try to _____ _____.

enactment 25   THE TROUBLESHOOTER

This enactment is the last "public speaking" experience offered in this book. Using the lists you made in Task 6, prepare a brief description of your plan for systematically controlling word-of-mouth messages in a large business organization. Your classmates will be your audience; tell them who you want them to be, and address them as you think you might in the actual circumstances you have constructed.

Try to stimulate these thoughts in the minds of your audience in

enactment 25: THE TROUBLE-SHOOTER

"The speaker is a professional."
"The speaker's easy to listen to."
"I know why I need to listen."

participants

Each student prepares a brief descriptive plan for controlling word-of-mouth messages in a large business organization.

audience

Speakers will choose an identity such as "company stock-holders" for their classmates and will address them with this identity in mind.

problem

Your organization is plagued with late-arriving messages and inaccurate and misleading memos and is completely out-of-step with organizations of similar characteristics.

need to speak

Your future and that of your organization are at stake. Try to convey your professionalism, while telling them what you feel they truly *need* to hear. Provide some way of getting feedback from them.

critique 25   TROUBLESHOOTING

1. How did the troubleshooter get and hold your attention?
2. Why would a mimeo handout or tape recording have/not have served just as well as the live speaker?
3. What was said and done that made the presentation easy *and* hard to listen to?
4. Did the troubleshooter create any bottlenecks in talking about what to do about them?
5. What was said that made you want to interrupt and talk back?
6. In what sense is every employee a manager?

HOW WOULD YOU IMPROVE IT?

MESSAGES IN BUSINESSES

Small businesses of one, two, or three employees need and usually have a centralized pattern of power and coordination. Decision-making is done by the owner/proprietor and message flow is unrestricted by time lags and distances, because of the simplicity of the operation.

Organizations larger than this, however, may use a number of charts to show how people are spaced by responsibility and by physical distance. These charts will often reveal some of the major difficulties in the message flow

One typical plan for arranging an organization's activities has four steps: (1) determine the activities, (2) evaluate activities, (3) group related activities, and (4) assign activities. The fourth step, the assignment of activities, creates a system or plan for vertical or in-line channels from the chief administrator "down" to the lowest trainee. Figure 10–5 is an example of a chart for a single division of a large company. In addition this vertical chart might have an accompanying horizontal diagram showing sales, production, finance, research and development, marketing, foreign sales, investment, and legal office divisions. These various "families" within a business transact in much the same way as the body/mind, apartment, and school organizations. Each separate family reaches out and up and groups itself with a collective departmental identity; the families of families communicate with a divisional identity that is its own organizational signature.

rumor/gossip/grapevine

The flow of messages occurs through channels and in groups that usually do not appear on anyone's charts. Some people receive messages through systems that are beyond the BLAB example of dispersal. You might be one of the people who are more attuned to things; you may "get feelings" about things before they are announced; you may intuit or "smell" a situation before it actually occurs or you may develop a "nose" for business.

The usual mode of message flow in school is being told, lectured, coached, tutored, and counseled. If you were absent or late for class, however, you probably found your own channels by asking somebody, "What happened?" or "What did I miss?" You got the message by the grapevine. The company grapevine is a network not on the organizational chart that acts as a kind of collective string of worry beads. It serves as an outlet for employees to express the wildest fantasies and direst prophecies imaginable. This informal, unofficial network exists in between the message terminals shown in Figure 10–5 and, of course, bends the messages a little as they get passed along.

Gossip and rumor deal with all the things that could happen in a business. They frequently manifest the insecurities and ill feelings people have but don't seem able to make others in positions of authority feel too. Some studies[3] indicate that the grapevine is quick, heavily used, and relatively accurate. The extraorganizational channels in the follow-

---

[3]You may wish to compare the following articles on the grapevine and "extraorganizational channels": Keith Davis, "Management Communication and the Grapevine," *Harvard Business Review,* 31 (September-October 1953), 43–49; Eugene Walton, "How Efficient Is the Grapevine?" *Personnel,* 28, no. 5 (September-October 1961), 45–49.

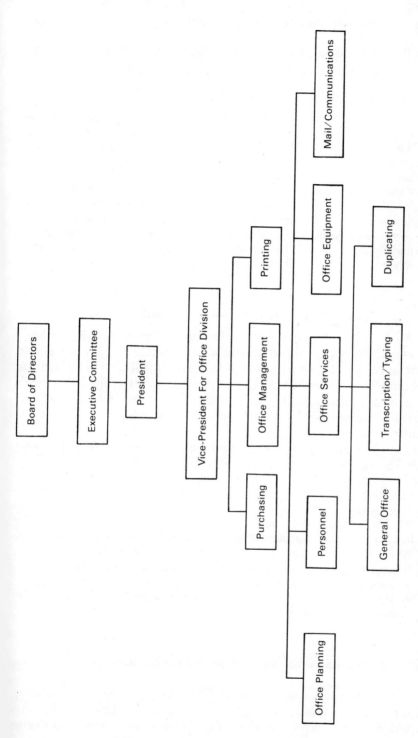

figure 10-5   Single Division Organization Chart

ing list offer company members from all strata and divisions occasions to meet to talk shop and plug into the company grapevine.

Unofficial Channels

the coffee break
the engagement party
the retirement party
the company picnic
the company tour
the waiting-room
  encounter
the luncheon date
the company bridge club
the parking lot
  conference

the water cooler
  get-together
the Christmas party
the promotion party
the company foreign
  tour
the restroom encounter
the elevator meeting
the cafeteria group
the car pool
the season-ticket club

the wedding/baby shower
the vacation send-off party
the moving-to-a-new-job
  party
the award dinner
the bowling league
the golf date
the softball team
the stairwell meeting
the punch-the-time-card
  line

task 7   THE WHOLE BALL OF WAX

The not-quite-coherent "ball of wax" drawing in Figure 10−6 shows a little of the confusion with which unofficial channels operate. Efficient as it is, the grapevine adds to the irrationality of some business organizations. Some managers intentionally exploit unofficial channels as a means of sharpening competition, canceling the influence of troublesome personnel and work sectors, and carrying out a host of other management strategies.

In completing Task 7, try to use what you know about effective business and professional communication.

1. Explain how the redundant channels in Figure 10–6 help *and* hinder a company's efficiency.
2. What is the opposite of *rumor?*
3. In what way does delegation of responsibility create more responsibility?
4. Why might "personality conflict" be a good thing for a company?
5. In business is there something *between* winning and losing contracts, sales, or promotions that is good for a company?
6. What are some of the advantages and disadvantages of rotating company personnel from top to bottom?

MESSAGES BETWEEN BUSINESSES

Businesses spend a great deal of energy directing their attention to other businesses and kindred organizations. Occasionally, this interdependence takes the form of an interschool rivalry. Businesses

figure 10-6   The Whole Ball of Wax

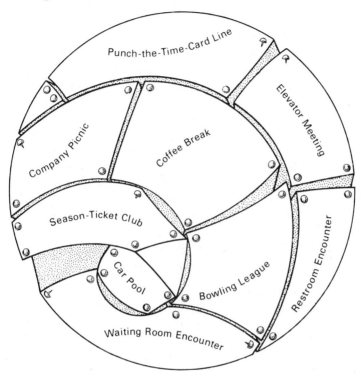

may adopt the attitude, "What have you got that we haven't got? What have you got that we can get?" And, too rarely, they may ask, "What do we both have that we can share?"

Most businesses practice the advice of their public relations experts and seek to open new channels between themselves and "out there." For example, companies fund and support numerous service projects and contribute skills and a cooperative attitude to community efforts. They give huge sums to public as well as commercial television programming. They donate their resources to schools, libraries, the arts, research, and scholarship.

In towns and cities professional people are also community people, church people, better business bureau and merchants' association people. They serve on committees, school boards, and a wide variety of other enterprises—all of which create and cement diversified channels for transorganizational communication.

Beyond their immediate communities, professional organizations find channels and share in the flow of messages at state, regional, and national conventions. They exchange viewpoints and biases through relay agencies such as lobbyists, advertising agencies, government councils and subcommittees, and sometimes regulatory and investigative commissions.

Television screens are today the most common meeting ground for businesses and the public. As they extend the signature of companies, they deliver a one-way message that confirms or casts doubt on what the companies have accomplished through use of all the other channels mentioned.

The face-to-face dyad is still a very important format in communication between businesses. At seminars and symposiums, "Who are you with?" is one of the first questions to be asked by colleagues, associates, and motel/hotel registrars. Most of these exchanges provide an opportunity for businesspeople to relate to plural ideas and attitudes and to assert their individual communication skills as a deterrent to organizational excess. The organization is its membership.

enactment 26   TASTEE DELIGHT 30

Demonstrate your professional communication skills in...

invitations to communicate
establishment of common
    ground (interface)
willingness to "risk"
ability to listen

enactment 26: TASTEE DELIGHT 30

participants

Isabel Durazo, 27 years old, married to Mike Durazo, four children, co-owner of Tastee Delight 30; Miguel Durazo, 27 years old, married to Isabel Durazo, co-owner of Tastee Delight 30; Cindy Waller, 27 years old, married to Al Waller, four children, housewife; Albert Waller, 27 years old, married to Cindy Waller, systems analyst for American Dairy, Inc. The Wallers, college graduates and urban, are accustomed to moving among medium-level management people in a large food subsidiary. The Durazos are educated through community college night school, and they have successfully managed a small, fast-food outlet in a small town on Highway 30.

relationship

The Durazos and the Wallers have been paired off at a state convention of dairy producers, manufacturers, and retailers. The intention of the matchmaking is to mix differing viewpoints and to thus enrich the number of cross-connections in the industry.

need to talk

The Wallers yearn for a small town life with an outlet of their own. The Durazos want to use their experience and knowledge of retailing to get positions with a big company—like the Wallers' present status. Both couples believe they would work better, make a more significant contribution, and be happier if their jobs and lives were switched.

time/locale

By prearrangment the Wallers are meeting the Durazos in the Durazos' hotel suite for a before-dinner, get-acquainted visit.

critique 26   TROUBLESHOOTING

1. Was most of the conversation shared by the four participants, or was it gender-to-gender or some other split?
2. Did a superior–inferior relationship develop?
3. Whose membership in the total dairy organization was the most firm, most secure, and strongest?
4. Score each participant for use of invitations to communicate.
5. Who worked hardest to locate interface?
6. Who was the best listener? How could you tell?
7. Was a two-way, a three-way, or a four-way contract made?
8. Describe the professionalism of each wife.
9. Which was the stronger organization affiliation—family (marriage) or job?

HOW WOULD YOU IMPROVE IT?

afterthought   SELF-FULFILLING PROPHECIES

This section of study has given you a basic overview of the professional communicator's role in organizational activity. In a sense we are prophesying a series of conditions that you will encounter early in your career. In another way, the communication experiences you have had to this point dealt with human variables you have known about for a long time. How you have communicated those unique qualities is a prediction of your future communication behavior.

A recurring axiom in these pages has been: Practice professionalism and the responses you get will confirm your professionalism, whether it was *real* or not. This approach strongly influences your actual behavior, because you in turn will react to those reactions, thereby fulfilling everyone's expectation. As we have described it, communication is intrinsic and unavoidable. We hold the belief that effective reciprocity is synonymous with effective organization. And effective exchange fulfills its own prediction.

READ FOR YOURSELF

BAIRD, JOHN E., JR., *The Dynamics of Organizational Communication.* New York: Harper & Row, Publishers, Inc., 1977.

BORMAN, ERNEST S., and others, *Interpersonal Communication in the Modern Organization.* Englewood Cliffs, N.J.: Prentice-Hall, Inc., 1969.

ETZIONI, AMITAI, *Modern Organization.* Englewood Cliffs, N.J.: Prentice-Hall, Inc., 1964.

GOLDHABER, GERALD M., *Organizational Communication.* Dubuque: William C. Brown Company, Publishers, 1974.

HALL, RICHARD H., *Organizations: Structure and Process.* Englewood Cliffs, N.J.: Prentice-Hall, Inc., 1972.

MAILICK, SIDNEY, and EDWARD H. VAN NESS, eds. *Concepts and Issues in Administrative Behavior.* Englewood Cliffs, N.J.: Prentice-Hall, Inc., 1962.

REDDING, W. CHARLES, and GEORGE A. SANBORN, *Business and Industrial Communication: A Source Book.* New York: Harper & Row, Publishers, Inc., 1964.

CHAPTER CHART

Key idea: Organizing is a system of finding matches
Key idea: An organization is a group of two or more persons whose differences are outweighed by their shared desire for a similar effect and who associate for as long as the need lasts
Key idea: Organizations exist within organizations

Characteristics of Organizations
Assert power
Service themselves
Determine membership
Seek efficiency
Tolerate redundancy
Tolerate plurality
Are sometimes irrational

Flow of Messages—the BLAB System
Flow means the circulation of an utterance from one person and place elsewhere over a period of time
Bunching flow means simultaneous reception of a message by a number of people
Line flow means a message is sent from and received by one person at a time
Audience flow means a message from a single source goes to a fairly large audience at once
Boardroom flow means the message is put together by several persons before it is officially "released"

Gossip, Rumor, and Grapevine
Key idea: The company grapevine is an outlet for frustrated messages
Grapevines are heavily used, relatively accurate, and rapid carriers of unofficial messages
Grapevines may be used and exploited by all employees

Messages Between Organizations
Company support of service projects
Company participation through loaning of skills and a cooperative attitude
Employee membership in community organizations
Media presentations and public relations projects

appendix

CASE STUDIES

Offered here are skeleton structures of real occurrences. A great deal of the missing information can be supplied by tracking down the factors that might lead to the descriptions provided. You will, of course, find a rich area for questions and discussion by speculating about what might follow these situations. Consider other variables such as : (1) "the time it takes," (2) invitations to communicate, (3) interface, and (4) how each bit of data in the study can multiply a small problem into a big one.

If names of persons or companies in these case studies bear any similarity to those of actual persons or companies, the similarity is purely accidental.

CASE STUDY A: A PROBLEM IN REPLICATIVE FEEDBACK

Ken Smith is an inside salesman for a southern regional industrial supply firm. Most of his workday is spent either receiving sales orders or soliciting sales orders by telephone. Ken has been working as an inside salesman for five years and is considered a highly motivated worker, sold on his company, and exhibiting above-average product knowledge. He needs a great deal of product knowledge because of the enormous variety and highly technical aspects of many of the products sold by his firm.

The company, over the past several years, has written off as losses numerous instances in which errors were made in ordering specific custom-made items (for nonstandard lengths, designs, etc.). These losses run to thousands of dollars annually. An analysis indicated that most of the errors occurred in orders taken by telephone. The analysis pinpointed Ken as one of the salespeople having a high error ratio. To correct the problem, a communication consultant was retained by the company to examine the communication behavior of the inside salespeople.

The consultant noted that Ken used the following telephone technique:

1. Answered the telephone in a most pleasing and affable manner
2. Asked directly what he could do for the caller
3. Appeared to listen carefully
4. Wrote down the items ordered
5. Figured the cost, less shipping and handling charges, and reported the amount to the caller
6. Indicated how soon the item could be expected to be received
7. Asked if there were any additional items the caller needed
8. Closed cordially

Questions for Analysis

1. The initial assumption was that a communication problem caused the errors. Do you agree?
2. Examine Ken's telephone technique by applying several communication models that you are familiar with. Are any of the elements missing?
3. What recommendations would you make to help control the errors due to communication breakdown?
4. What special problems might telephone communications pose?
5. How does "I know what I mean; you should know what I mean" apply to the case?
6. Do people often assume too much as senders and receivers? Explain.

CASE STUDY B: SEMANTIC CHANGE

Father: That Charles is really a square fellow.

Son: Gee, Dad, I thought you liked Charles.

Father: But I do!

Son: Then why did you call him a square?

Father: I'm afraid I don't know what you mean!

Questions for Analysis

1. What miscommunication has taken place?
2. Why did it occur?
3. Is the father on the right track to achieve understanding?

4. *Square* at one time had a positive connotation. Can you think of other words that have changed meaning?

CASE STUDY C: A GROUP DECISION?

J.B. is the president of Beefo, Inc., a nationwide fast-food chain that has more than tripled in size in the past seven years. J.B.'s personal assets are in the millions and his current salary from Beefo is $150,000 per year plus numerous fringe benefits. Beefo, Inc., has four vice-presidents who are currently salaried at $30,000 per year plus fringe benefits.

J.B. has called a board meeting with his vice-presidents to discuss last year's profits and the possibility of adding a new item to Beefo's menu.

J.B.: Fellows, it is good to have you here today. I want to discuss some very important business. As you are aware, our last year's rate of growth and our increase in profits were down somewhat compared to the previous year. In an effort to increase our profits this year I think we should add a basic item to our menu—the "Beefo-Taco." Now, what do you fellows think?

Vice-President A: I agree.

Vice-President B: J.B., you've done it again.

Vice-President C: Absolutely!

Vice-President D: You're right.

J.B.: Thanks for your advice, fellows. I knew you'd agree.

Questions for Analysis

1. Was a group decision made?
2. What style of leadership did J.B. exhibit in this incident?
3. Do you think he got an honest answer from anyone?
4. How can a group leader discover the opinions and attitudes of others in a group? Describe the technique.

CASE STUDY D: NONVERBAL PROBLEMS

Wharf Imports sells $5 million worth of foreign, mass-produced household goods a year and has retailing outlets in six cities. In one medium-sized, coastal city, Wharf runs a small shop in a shopping mall that was built with the assistance of municipal land grants but is managed by the bank-controlled Mall Association.

The Wharf shop has a payroll work force of eight employees—a store manager, a bookkeeper, two stockpersons, and four salespersons. Many of the shipments received must be assembled and displayed using instructions translated from a non-English original. Many items appear damaged but are actually only in a state of disarray due to improper packing and cartage, though they leave the impression that they are shoddy and cheaply made. Certain international clients who come to the shop have complained about this reflection on their home countries and have suggested other ways to display such goods. The manager has also received criticism about displays that are too close to objectionable merchandise such as lurid pulp magazines and graphic materials, and employees have had lengthy discussions about the sequencing and mixing of display items, so that cultural improprieties may be avoided.

The shop next door sells children's shoes and has complained to the Mall Association that the "incense and sitar music at Wharf Imports attract a clientele that drives away mothers with small children." The manager of the Wharf shop would like the Mall Association to realign the shops and form an international cluster that would combine the travel and sight-seeing agency, the Schnitzel House, and an ethnic clothing store in one wing of the concourse with the import shop.

The storefront on the other side of the Wharf shop is unoccupied, but three tenants have applied for a lease: a smoke shop, a book store, and a record store. Smoking is prohibited in all the shops except the restaurants and movie theatre, although smoking supplies and artifacts are sold at the import shop. As a member of the Mall Association, the manager of Wharf Imports may cast one vote on the selection of new tenants.

Questions for Analysis

1. What influence and input should the sales staff have on the nonverbal misunderstandings such as static displays and their solution?
2. Discuss the topic of interdependence in the business sector—how the actions of one affect all.
3. How will "happy mistakes" probably occur in this situation?

CASE STUDY E: THE EMPLOYMENT INTERVIEW

Ms. Smith is an executive vice-president for personnel of a major industrial manufacturing company located in the Midwest. The company is national in scope and has regional offices in several strategic locations throughout the United States. It has been the practice of the company for several years to interview prospective college graduates for managerial training positions. Ultimately it is hoped that these prospective employees will attain top-level managerial positions after only a few years of in-service training to develop skills and acquire information specific to the company.

Bob Butler, age 22, is a candidate for graduation in the spring from a large southern urban university. Bob is a comprehensive general business major with an emphasis in management. His goal is to obtain a management position with a major United States company. Bob considers himself ambitious and has studied hard for his degree. His grades, work, and extracurricular activities indicate that he has taken his college studies seriously and is highly motivated.

Ms. Smith has arranged with the Placement Service of Bob's university for a week-long series of interviews to screen applicants for several positions now open in her company's executive development program. Bob has registered with his Placement Service and is scheduled to meet with Ms. Smith for the screening interview at 9:45 A.M. on Tuesday morning.

Bob is on time for his interview and walks confidently to the interview space assigned to Ms. Smith. Ms. Smith is occupied with some paperwork and hardly notices that Bob is now standing in the door. Ms. Smith glances at Bob and then returns to her paperwork. Bob is at a loss for words, but politely asks if he might come in. Smith hesitates a moment then without looking up says in a harsh tone: "After looking through your vita, I'm really not sure why you would bother to take up my time and yours for an interview. I've had your type in for interviews before. They demanded a short week and a big salary. No doubt you're just like them." Bob is still standing in the doorway.

Questions for Analysis

1. As an interviewer, did Ms. Smith act in a professional manner?
2. What reasons might Ms. Smith have for developing the screening interview in such a way? What was her purpose?
3. Can such a beginning for a screening interview ever prove beneficial from the interviewer's point of view? From the interviewee's point of view? Why?
4. Who stands to gain the most from this encounter? Why?
5. What options does Bob now have?
6. What would you personally do in Bob's situation?

CASE STUDY F: THE PERSUASIVE ENCOUNTER

John and his wife Margie live in a comfortable, newly built apartment complex. John has recently completed his masters degree in personnel management and is currently employed as an assistant to the director of personnel. He and Margie have recently discussed buying additional furniture and appliances for their apartment, including the possible purchase of a freezer. Margie agreed that a freezer would certainly be practical, to cut down on food costs, but she insisted that she would consider buying one only if it matched the avocado color of the other appliances in their attractive kitchen. John agreed that the freezer would be a wise investment, but that, due to their limited space and the choice of color, a careful selection would have to be made.

 The next evening Margie asked John to accompany her to a local department store while she shopped for fabrics. John consented, thinking this might give him an opportunity to browse in the appliance department. As John approached the freezers in the store, he was met by a salesman.

Salesman: Certainly glad to have you shopping with us this evening. As you probably know, we're running a special on freezers this month. You've definitely chosen the right time to buy—the price will never be lower. What did you have in mind?

John: Well, uh . . .

Salesman: Let me show you our top seller. Everybody's buying it. Come right over here. This is it. It's got to be the best freezer on the market today. This is our biggest freezer for the money. It has a ____-pound capacity. Never has to be defrosted, has adjustable racks, and this white baked-on-enamel finish goes with every decor. Of course, all our appliances carry a two year warranty on all parts and labor. You simply can't get a better one anywhere. What do you say? Let me send one out to you in the morning.

John: Thanks, but I'll have to talk to my wife.

Questions for Analysis

1. What decisions had John and Margie made?
2. What is happening in the communication encounter between John and the salesman?
3. Has the salesman followed acceptable persuasive techniques in the encounter? Why or why not?
4. What important step(s) did the salesman omit?
5. How could you reconstruct the sales presentation to meet the goals of both seller and consumer more appropriately?

CASE STUDY G: THE VISUAL AID SPEECH

 Jane, a 20-year-old student at a large western university, was assigned to make an informative speech using visual aids. The instructor allowed the students to choose their topics. The length of the presentation was set at six to eight minutes.

The classroom audience was composed of students ranging in age from 18 to 50 with a variety of majors. After careful consideration of her audience, Jane decided to speak on "The Art of Raising Chinchillas." Jane and her family had been raising chinchillas for several years, and she was very knowledgeable about the subject.

Jane chose the following items for her visual aid presentation: handouts on the basic economics of the industry, a drawing of the fundamental structure needed to house the animals, a profit and loss sheet, a list of rules on how to get started, ten eight-by-ten color photographs of models wearing chinchilla fur garments, three chinchilla pelts showing various colors, and finally two cages, one of which contained a live chinchilla.

On the day of the speech Jane was eager and excited about sharing her information with the classroom audience and asked the instructor if she could make her presentation first. Permission was granted, and Jane immediately went to the room to "set up" for her presentation.

After the class was assembled, roll taken, and instructions given to the listeners, who were to give written critiques, Jane was announced as the first speaker. She walked energetically to the speaker's stand and began her speech by saying, "Today I want to share with you my experiences on the art of raising chinchillas." She then proceeded to pass out all the handouts to the class, including the photographs and the pelts. Jane then returned to the speaker's stand and continued her introduction. As she spoke, whispers could be heard from the audience. It was evident that most of the listeners were focusing on the handouts, passing materials, watching others, and otherwise conversing about the pretty models and soft pelts of luxurious fur. Jane, seemingly undaunted by the audience's escapades, was now ready to reveal the last of her visual aids—the live chinchilla. She removed the cover from its two adjoining cages with a flourish. The audience's attention was quickly directed to the chinchilla, which jumped onto the exercise wheel and began to make up for the time it had lost while the cages had been covered. Jane continued to speak, even though the sound of the unoiled revolving exercise wheel made much of her presentation unintelligible. The chinchilla then jumped from the wheel and ran through a tube joining the two cages. The second cage was filled with a fine silicon dust used to remove oil from the animal's fur. The chinchilla began to scratch the silicon with its legs, producing a cloud of fine tiny particles; after a few moments this began to engulf the speaker and the first row of listeners. Jane continued her remarks.

Questions for Analysis

1. What did Jane do right?
2. What problems developed that made the presentation ineffective? Describe the effect of interference on focus.
3. What could the speaker have done with the visual aids to enhance the message and produce effective communication?

INDEX